Buddhism

A SHORT INTRODUCTION

OTHER BOOKS IN THIS SERIES:

Islam: A Short Introduction, Abdulkader Tayob, ISBN 1–85168–192–2
Islam: A Short History, William Montgomery Watt, ISBN 1–85168–205–8
Jesus: A Short Biography, Martin Forward, ISBN 1–85168–172–8
Judaism: A Short Introduction, Lavinia and Dan Cohn-Sherbok, ISBN 1–85168–207–4
Judaism: A Short History, Lavinia and Dan Cohn-Sherbok, ISBN 1–85168–206–6
Muhammad: A Short Biography, Martin Forward, ISBN 1–85168–131–0
A Short History of Buddhism, Edward Conze, ISBN 1–85168–066–7
A Short Introduction to Hinduism, Klaus K. Klostermaier, ISBN 1–85168–163–9
A Short Introduction to Islamic Philosophy, Theology and Mysticism, Majid Fakhry, ISBN 1–85168–134–5
A Short Introduction to the Old Testament Prophets, E. W. Heaton, ISBN 1–85168–114–0
A Short Reader in Judaism, Lavinia and Dan Cohn-Sherbok, ISBN 1–85168–112–4
The Bahá'í Faith: A Short History, Peter Smith, ISBN 1–85168–208–2
The Bahá'í Faith: A Short Introduction, Moojan Momen, ISBN 1–85168–209–0

RELATED TITLES PUBLISHED BY ONEWORLD:

Buddhism and the Mythology of Evil, Trevor Ling, ISBN 1–85168–132–9
Buddhist Texts through the Ages, trans. and ed. Edward Conze, I. B. Horner, David Snellgrove and Arthur Waley, ISBN 1–85168–107–8
The Gospel of Buddha, Paul Carus, ISBN 1–85168–026–8
A Short History of Buddhism, Edward Conze, ISBN 1–85168–066–7
What Buddhists Believe, Elizabeth J. Harris, ISBN 1–85168–168–X
What the Buddha Taught, Walpola Sri Rahula, ISBN 1–85168–142–6

Buddhism

A SHORT INTRODUCTION

Klaus K. Klostermaier

ONEWORLD
OXFORD

BUDDHISM: A SHORT INTRODUCTION

Oneworld Publications
(Sales and Editorial)
185 Banbury Road
Oxon OX2 7AR
England
http://www.oneworld-publications.com

Oneworld Publications
(US Marketing Office)
160 N. Washington St.
4th floor, Boston
MA 02114
USA

A CIP record for this title is available
from the British Library

ISBN 1-85168-186-8

Cover design by Design Deluxe
Typeset by LaserScript Limited, Mitcham, Surrey
Printed and bound in England by Clays, St Ives plc

CONTENTS

FIGURES AND TABLES

FIGURES

TABLES

PREFACE

An introduction to Buddhism, however short, is always a major undertaking. Buddhism is a vast and varied phenomenon: its history goes back over two and a half millennia and its geography spans a large part of the globe. It has found expression in a score of languages and has stimulated a great variety of art styles. It has deeply shaped a great part of humanity past and present.

Works on Buddhism have been written from many angles: there are numerous expert historical, sociological, philosophical, anthropological, comparative and psychological studies that provide important information and insight. Since texts have always been very important to Buddhists, I have chosen a textual approach for this introduction. My aim has been to present Buddhism as a living wisdom-tradition, with a rational basis and a coherent worldview; a tradition that has proved its strength during its long history and that is capable of critically reflecting on itself, without thereby destroying itself.

Recognizing the immensity of the task and my linguistic limitations, I am restricting the scope of this work to Indian Buddhism, that is to those branches and schools which arose in India and whose sources are written in Indian languages. Since Buddhism began in India and experienced its blossoming into a great tradition during the next fifteen hundred years in India, such a narrowing down of the study may be acceptable. I am aware, of course, that the historical developments of Buddhism in Tibet, in Mongolia, in China, in Japan, and more recently also in the West, are important and often unique and that they deserve great attention.

This introduction is intended for the non-specialist reader. It does not presuppose anything except interest in the subject. While necessarily far from being exhaustive, it aims at giving a fair picture of the origins and the foundations of Buddhism, as well as of some of its more sophisticated theories and practices, as they were developed by some later schools. There is no shortage of material to continue and expand the study of Buddhism from here. Texts and translations, general and special studies of Buddhism abound and are easily accessible today. If this book arouses the reader's curiosity and desire to learn more about Buddhism, the author's expectations have been amply fulfilled.

It goes without saying that this book is no more than a short summary of original texts and the works of a large number of scholars past and present, on whose writings it depends even when not explicitly acknowledging their contributions in specific references and I express my indebtedness to all of them. For detailed personal advice and numerous suggestions for improvement I wish to give special thanks to Rupert Gethin, co-director of the Centre for Buddhist Studies at the University of Bristol. For all the shortcomings, of which I am only too aware, I have to take responsibility.

I dedicate this book to my students at the University of Manitoba, whom it has been my privilege to introduce to the religions of India during the past three decades and for whom most of the materials of this book were originally prepared.

Winnipeg, February 1999 K. K. K.

INTRODUCTION

Buddhism in all its great variety traces its origin to the teachings of the historical figure of Gotama (S: Gautama) the Buddha. The many different branches of Buddhism developed various scriptural traditions, a large commentarial literature and an untold number of scholarly treatises attempting to summarize, synthesize and further develop words and ideas attributed to the Buddha.

Early on Buddhism branched out into a great diversity of orders, schools of thought, ordination and teaching lineages. Some have developed mutually incompatible positions on matters of discipline and doctrine; others have retained a large number of common teachings and practices.

A teacher or practitioner of Buddhism will always follow one particular tradition that has been legitimized by authentic exponents of that interpretation of Buddhism; nobody can teach or practice 'Buddhism' as such. Some of these traditions have a lineage that goes back to ancient Indian origins; others are based on more recent regional developments outside India. Buddhists early on showed a great eagerness to communicate their teaching to the whole world: they not only carried the Buddha-word in their memories and their manuscripts to countries like China, Tibet, Mongolia, Korea, Japan, Thailand and Indonesia and translated it into the languages of these peoples, they also adapted it to local needs and circumstances in the belief that its universality was best expressed in a variety of local idioms.

The discovery and adoption of Buddhism by Europeans and Americans from the mid-nineteenth century onwards created new expressions of Buddhism. Differences in climate and upbringing do not allow a wholesale transplantation of existing Asian Buddhist traditions. Apart from the few Westerners who joined Buddhist monasteries in Sri Lanka, Burma (Myanmar)and Thailand, the majority of those who find Buddhism attractive attempt to practise it in their Western homelands under very different circumstances. To belittle these attempts and the resulting Western expressions of Buddhism would not be right. The Buddha himself was convinced of the universal validity of the truth and the Way that he had discovered and he was very flexible with regard to lifestyle and the circumstances in which his teaching would be practised.

A large amount of scholarship has been devoted to attempts to uncover the original teachings of the Buddha. Philological and historical evidence has been marshalled to distinguish various layers in the sources, and much has been found out about the process through which the various canons of Buddhist scriptures came into existence. Buddhism is not necessarily identical with what the historical Buddha originally taught; it consists of interpretations, adaptations and additions to the original teachings, made in an attempt to arrive at logically coherent and workable systems of ideas and practices.

In this work no effort has been made to isolate what might have been the original teaching of the Buddha: even that 'original teaching' underwent a development over the forty-five years of the Buddha's public ministry. It is intended to represent Buddhism as understood by traditional Buddhist schools, relying on text and ordination traditions. The presentation is based on the assumption that there has been a continuous tradition leading from the historical Buddha to the present, that this tradition has preserved in its written sources the substance of the Buddha's teachings and that even if it did not always uphold the ideal, it always knew about it. Juxtaposed, the very many different 'Buddhisms' would cancel each other out by their often mutually contradictory interpretation of texts and doctrines; individually, they usually make sense and have been found helpful by many over the centuries.

THE MAKING OF A BUDDHIST

The first Buddhists became Buddhists because they recognized in the Buddha's teaching the fulfilment of their own endeavours, truth coming from enlightenment. Later on, during the lifetime of the Buddha, as the ancient sources tell us, people became Buddhists because they admired the poise and inner peace of the early Buddhists. Some also became Buddhists because they thought they would find material security, a relatively easy life and a great deal of social prestige. Throughout, however, the proper motive for becoming a Buddhist was the overriding concern for reaching a state of complete inner freedom and emancipation. It was always the content of the Buddha's teaching that attracted serious people to Buddhism.

When the first Westerners learned something substantial about Buddhism in the nineteenth century[1] they found it attractive as a religion that had a lofty ethic and was not rooted in a belief in a personal creator or redeemer God. It appeared to nineteenth-century Western philosophers as a better alternative to Christianity.[2] It was especially the emphasis on non-violence that Europeans, who had seen the horrors and devastations of the First World War, welcomed. Disgusted with their Christian leaders who had been preaching chauvinism and who justified the atrocities of the war as necessary for the defence of faith and civilization, many eagerly embraced a religion that prided itself on never having used force and violence to propagate or to defend itself. Some European converts to Buddhism in the early twentieth century became prominent figures in contemporary Buddhism,[3] helping through translations of classical texts and expositions of Buddhist teachings to spread Buddhism in the West.

Becoming a Buddhist is one of the easiest and also one of the most difficult things to achieve. First, there is a great variety of 'Buddhisms' and Buddhist communities, each with its own specific notions of membership. One cannot become 'Buddhist' in a general sense; one has to choose a specific form of it.

If one chooses to join Theravāda,[4] prominent today in Sri Lanka, Burma (Myanmar) and Thailand, one has just to recite three times the 'three refuges': *Buddham saraṇam gacchāmi – Dhammam saraṇam gacchāmi – Saṅgham saraṇam gacchāmi* (I take refuge in the Buddha, in the Dhamma, in the Saṅgha). In addition one has verbally to express faith in the Enlightened One and accept the Four Noble Truths and the Eightfold Path. Every neophyte Buddhist also promises to observe five basic ethical rules. The highest ideal of Theravāda Buddhism is the state of the monk or nun,[5] taking solemn vows: not only have the members of the monastic community to promise to keep, in addition to the five general rules mentioned above, five more specific monastic regulations, they also have to submit to periodic public examinations of conscience in which they must check their past behaviour against several hundred regulations. The whole life of a Buddhist monk or nun is governed by rules; nothing is left to whim or chance.

And that is only the outward aspect of 'professional' Buddhists: their motive for joining was enlightenment, which could only be reached through arduous work on themselves. The more they progress, the more subtle and complex that work becomes.

Someone who joins a Mahāyāna Buddhist community is expected to take the *bodhisattva* vow and practise a number of virtues to a truly heroic degree. While it is fairly simple to learn the names of these 'Six Perfections' – the perfection of giving, of morality, of forbearance, of steadfastness, of meditation and of wisdom – it is infinitely more difficult to practise them.

INSIDER AND OUTSIDER WRITING ABOUT BUDDHISM

Buddhism as a historical phenomenon is of enormous importance. As a religion and a way of life it spread over the whole of Asia and in its long history it has exercised a profound effect on Asian culture as a whole, in all its aspects. It has produced a huge literature in virtually all Asian languages, sublime art and ideals of life that have pervaded Asian mentality. Buddhism addresses perennial human concerns and articulates profound insights into human nature. Nobody interested in human values and ideals can ignore Buddhism, a vast experiment in elevating humanity to its noblest. Wisdom and compassion are the proverbial hallmarks of the Buddha, and humankind today is certainly in dire need of these. Buddhism not only talks about wisdom and compassion, it also teaches how to acquire these.

Writing about Buddhism initially appears easy: Buddhists themselves have developed well-organized schemata in presenting their tradition: the Four Noble Truths, the Eightfold Path, the twelve Links of the Chain of Dependent Co-origination, the three steps of morality, concentration and wisdom. Besides these simple formulae there are dozens of others, and sophisticated intellectual edifices with an incredibly intricate architecture. There is, of course, by now a huge literature on Buddhism, written by knowledgable insiders and outsiders, a literature covering all aspects of historical and present-day Buddhism from many different angles.

Only a small part of the immense phenomenon of Buddhism can be presented here. Even this fraction can be approached from many different angles. There is traditional, 'insider' presentation of Buddhism and there is critical, 'outsider' historical scholarship. To begin with, Buddhists have shown much greater interest in their own history than Hindus. The canonical writings themselves provide information about rulers who were contemporaries of the Buddha, about the sequence of events in the Buddha's life and the time immediately after his death. Sinhalese Buddhists wrote chronicles that faithfully record the history of Buddhism in Sri Lanka from the third century BCE to the early eighteenth century. Tibetan Buddhist scholars[6] wrote histories of Buddhism in India and Tibet which preserve ancient traditions.

Traditional Buddhist accounts mix legend and history. While the historicity of Gotama and the Indian rulers mentioned in the Pāli Canon is beyond question, the dates assigned to them are not.[7] Thus various chronologies have been developed on the basis of comparisons with Western dynastic lists. Until recently[8] Western scholars were in agreement that the life of the Buddha spanned the period of c. 540–480 BCE. The Buddhist world, however, celebrated the 2,500th anniversary of the Buddha's *parinibbāna* in 1956, assuming the Buddha to have lived from 624 to 544 BCE.

The Buddhist dating relies on the ancient, and on the whole reliable, chronicles of Sri Lanka. Those chronicles[9] give precise dates for the events recorded, based on which the traditional chronology has been established.

Similarly, there is disagreement between traditional Buddhist and modern Western scholars regarding the facts and dates of the creation of the Buddhist canon and the Buddhist councils. While Buddhists in general tend to accept the accuracy of the reports in the ancient chronicles, Western scholars, drawing on text-critical methodologies, tell a more complex and complicated story.[10]

Without wishing to disparage scholarly efforts towards solving questions of chronology and literary criticism, in the Buddha's – and Buddhists' – opinion these concern marginal matters: they do not touch the core of the Buddha's teaching and contribute nothing to 'progress in virtue' or to enlightenment. The mass of ancient Buddhist literature and the general agreement found in it on important matters of practice and doctrine are sufficient for those who want to follow the Buddha path, accepting the trustworthiness of the Buddhist tradition as a whole. Different opinions regarding the dates of the Buddha's birth and death do not change the insight provided in the Four Noble Truths, nor do text-critical investigations of the Pāli Canon affect the central requirements for finding enlightenment as taught throughout the centuries by Buddhist teachers.

BUDDHIST TEXTS AND BUDDHIST PRACTICE

The practice of those who call themselves Buddhists does not always agree with the ideals expressed in Buddhist writings. This is a universal feature of all traditions that demand a more-than-average refinement of mores. The Pāli Canon itself records all kinds of misuses and misunderstandings of the teaching of the Buddha by contemporary followers of his way.

An introduction to Buddhism for non-Buddhists is expected to offer a presentation of the ideals of Buddhism rather than a description of possibly less-than-ideal Buddhists. There are sufficient books available today, written by anthropologists and sociologists, by journalists and travellers, describing in great detail the actual life of contemporary Buddhists. This discussion will be based on the texts that outline the Buddhist ideal and that serious Buddhists consider as guidelines for their practice – texts that have been preserved intact notwithstanding the frequent degeneration of Buddhist practice, texts that have been the basis of every Buddhist reform over the centuries.

Texts have always played a great role in Buddhism. The Buddha's immediate disciples memorized his sermons and his rulings on matters of discipline. The Pāli Canon must have been one of the earliest collection of texts to be fixed in writing, and memorizing texts, copying texts and translating texts were some of the chief activities of Buddhist monks throughout the centuries. These texts have transmitted the precise wording of Buddhist doctrine and are the basis for orthodox Buddhist practice.

While many local exceptions were made to the rules laid down in the Canon, the text itself was not changed to accommodate the exceptions. Thus, while it is not possible to derive from a knowledge of the texts the actual practices of an individual Buddhist monastic community, the community preserves the textual tradition and recites it ritually.

ABOUT THIS BOOK

This short introduction to Indian Buddhism wishes to provide a general overview as well as some in-depth treatment of issues central to Indian

Buddhism. It is text based, introducing the reader to some of the most important textual sources of Buddhism. It is divided into three parts which are subdivided into a varying number of chapters.

Part I deals with the basics of Buddhism, the proverbial 'Three Jewels': the Buddha, the Dharma and the Saṅgha. In that context the Indian background to the Buddha's teaching will also be mentioned, as well as the development of Buddhism. A summary and discussion of the content of two classics of early Buddhism – the canonical *Dhammapada* and the post-canonical *Milindapañha* – will present Buddhist teachings on specific issues in traditional Buddhist expressions.

Part II offers a systematic study of Buddhist teachings: a comprehensive account of the path to liberation according to the Pāli Canon; a detailed study of meditation, the most typical Buddhist practice; and a summary of the *bodhisattva* path as presented in the Buddhist classic, the *Bodhicaryāvatāra* by Śāntideva.

Part III introduces more technical philosophical expressions of Buddhism and the teachings of distinctive schools that emerged in the course of time. Chapter 8 deals with the theoretical framework of Theravāda Buddhism in the *Abhidamma* and with the controversies between Buddhists and (primarily) Hindus; chapter 9 discusses Madhyamaka and Yogācāra, two important (Mahāyāna) philosophical systems, and Vajrayāna, a late development of Indian Buddhism, its Tantric expression.

Given the nature of the subject matter, a certain overlap between some chapters is unavoidable. There is considerable overlap already in the sources of Buddhism, such as the Pāli Canon, in which the Buddha himself is represented as explaining his teaching in a variety of mutually complementary and overlapping ways. Even the best modern texts on Buddhism cannot avoid overlap in one form or another. The story of Buddhism is not linear; it progresses in a spiral fashion, returning time and again to the central points, but from different perspectives. In order to familiarize the uninitiated reader with the basic teachings, certain terms (such as *dharma*/*dhamma*) will have to be used, but will receive a more detailed treatment in a later chapter. Similarly, in order to provide a broad outline of the development of Buddhism, names of persons and schools will be introduced and explained in greater detail in another section. Again, there is no linear historic development from an original 'primitive' to a fully developed 'modern' Buddhism. What we consider to be the Buddha's own teaching gave rise to a great variety of interpretations. These, again, were not developed under the aegis of a central authority but by individuals, groups and schools of thought that operated fairly independently.

As the large number of books about Buddhism proves, there is no single, best way of writing an introduction to Buddhism. While not aiming to be exhaustive, this presentation endeavours at integrity, hoping to offer a genuine, if selective, picture of Buddhism. Each of the issues mentioned has received extensive treatment at the hand of experts, as the bibliography proves. References to sources and to secondary literature are far from exhaustive – this is meant to be an introductory text for beginners, not a synthesis of the whole of Buddhism for the expert.

The Buddhist sources and their English translations have not been incorporated into the general bibliography, but have been listed separately in Appendix 1 and 2 respectively. Most of the English translations of Buddhist works are found in the three series: Sacred Books of the East, Sacred Books of the Buddhists and the Pali Text Society Translation Series.

One last remark concerns the use of technical terms from Pāli and Sanskrit, the two languages in which the sources upon which this book draws are written. I shall be using Pāli words (with Sanskrit equivalents in brackets) when referring to the Pāli Canon, and Sanskrit when referring to sources in Sanskrit.[11] In the glossary all Indian words are identified as either Pāli (P) or Sanskrit (S). The standard transliteration of both Sanskrit and Pāli has been followed, except in those cases where the Indian word has become part of English vocabulary. Most of the vowels in both Sanskrit and Pāli (in transliteration) are pronounced like Italian vowels. Most of the consonants resemble the English consonants. A dash on top of a vowel indicates length(ā = aa); an accent on top (ś) or a dot (ṣ) underneath an *s* means it is pronounced *sh*.

NOTES

1. Some vague notions about Buddha and Buddhism were current in the West since pre-Christian times. There are references to Buddha in some of the early Church Fathers and reminiscences of late Buddhist teachings are found in some forms of Gnosticism. Medieval travellers encountered Buddha figures all over Asia and learned about certain beliefs associated with these. However, it was only in the mid-nineteenth century that Westerners became familiar with major textual sources and began to study Buddhism in earnest.
2. Nietzsche, in a well-known paragraph in *Wille zur Macht*, maintained: 'Buddhism is a hundred times more realistic than Christianity – it has inherited the cool and objective attitude of looking at problems, it arises

after centuries of philosophical movement, the concept "God" was already done away with, when it arose' (my translation).
3. The first modern Westerner known to have become an ordained Buddhist *bhikkhu* was Ananda Metteya (Allan Bennet, 1872–1923) who also founded the Buddhist Society of Great Britain and Ireland in 1907. The famous *bhikkhu* Ñyāṇatiloka was German-born Anton Walter Florus Güth (1878–1957). Among his German disciples was Bhikkhu Ñyāṇaponika, German-born Siegmund Feniger (born 1901), author of important books and translator of many Pāli works, whose English-born disciple Bhikkhu Ñyāṇamoli (Osbert Moore, 1905–60) continued his activities.
4. Theravāda, 'The School of the Elders', claims to represent 'original' Buddhism, the teaching and practice of the Buddha, preserved through 2,500 years.
5. Only by making Buddhism one's profession can one expect to reach emancipation from rebirth. 'Lay Buddhists' expect to be rewarded for their good behaviour and their good deeds by being reborn into a life in which they become monks or nuns.
6. Especially Tāranātha and Bu-ston.
7. Bechert, *The Dating of the Historical Buddha*.
8. See Dissanayake, 'Notes on Revising the Historical Date of the Buddha', responding to R. Gombrich's suggestion of placing the Buddha in the fifth century BCE and, more recently, Cousins, 'The Dating of the Historical Buddha'.
9. The first of these is the *Dīpavaṃsa*, 'The Chronicle of the Island', which tells the history of Buddhism in Sri Lanka from the time of the Buddha's legendary three visits to the island to the end of the reign of Mahāsena in the late fourth century CE. It is continued in the *Mahāvaṃsa*, whose last portion, the *Cullavaṃsa*, brings the report of events up to 1815, the time when the British took control of the island. The great fifth-century Buddhist commentator Buddhaghosa in his *Bahiranidāna*, the introductory chapter to his commentary on the *Vinaya Piṭaka*, also offers a short conspectus of the history of Buddhism up to his time, using the traditional dates for the councils and the rulers.
10. See chapter 3, pp. 49ff.
11. Often these are written in what has been called 'Buddhist hybrid Sanskrit', i.e. a language which uses many Prakrit (Middle Indian) words, while overall following Sanskrit vocabulary and grammar.

Part I

THE THREE JEWELS OF BUDDHISM

Each and every religious act of Buddhists begins with 'taking refuge' in the Three Jewels (*triratna*): the Enlightened One (the Buddha), the Teaching (the Dhamma), and the Community (the Saṅgha). Thus each and every book about Buddhism has to begin with explaining the Three Jewels as the basis of Buddhism.

While the faithful Buddhist accepts the story of Buddha's life as described in the ancient sources, modern scholarship has scrutinized these reports and attempted to establish the 'facts' by means of scientific historiography. Similarly, practising Buddhists consider the teaching of their community the word of the Buddha, while Western scholars study the various traditions in a comparative manner, trying to find historical reasons for the development of particular forms of Buddhism. The Buddhist community as a whole, and specifically its ordained members, are the custodians not only of the teachings but also of the practices that make Buddhism a living religion. Here too, the approach of a modern Western scholar and that of an active member of the Buddhist community will differ.

In the following pages attention will primarily be given to traditional Buddhist views and to texts from within the Buddhist tradition to describe what the Three Jewels mean for the followers of Buddhism. In order to do this, a fairly extensive summary of two important Buddhist works, the *Dhammapada* and the *Milindapañha* has been added to the systematic presentation, as well as an explanation of the traditional representation of the *bhāvacakra* (Wheel of Becoming).

1 THE BUDDHA

THE HISTORICAL BUDDHA

Hardly anyone today doubts that Gotama the Buddha, the founder of Buddhism, was a historical figure.[1] However, there are no documents to describe his life and work other than the canonical Buddhist writings which are clearly biased in favour of Buddhist tradition. The traditional Buddhist texts have an interest in reinforcing Buddhist teaching through the telling of the biography of the Buddha and in harmonizing the events in his life with what was believed to be his teaching.[2]

While the exact dates of his life are still disputed among scholars,[3] his existence and the major events in his life are commonly accepted as historical.[4] They have been the subject of artistic representation for almost two thousand years and provide the key topics in Buddhist sermons even today. The ancient sources characteristically mingle factual report with religiously meaningful interpretation. The canonical writings were not established to provide raw materials for future historians but to give support and guidance to the community of Buddhists, who saw in the Buddha's life the exemplification of their own ideals.

Tradition reports that Māyā, the mother of Gotama Siddhattha (S: Gautama Siddhārtha) desiring a son, had a dream in which a white elephant appeared and entered her side. Consulting an astrologer, she learned that the meaning of her dream was that her future son would either be a world-ruler or a world-renouncer.[5] Delivered from his mother's right side in the Lumbinī Park, where Māyā had stopped on her way to her paternal home,[6] the newborn announced with a clear voice his high standing and walked seven steps. Learning about his son's birth, his father, the ruler of Kapilavatthu (S: Kapilavastu), a petty kingdom belonging to the Sākya (S: Śākya) clan in what is today Nepal, rushed to greet him.

Māyā died a week after she had given birth, and Gotama was brought up by his father's second wife, his mother's sister. At the age of 16 he was married to Yaśodharā, a princess from a neighbouring realm. Growing up in luxury and surrounded by an attentive family, Gotama was shielded from everything that could disturb his mind and make him think of renouncing the world. At the age of 29 Gotama became the father of a little boy, who was called Rāhula.

Gotama's father had ordered that everything unpleasant must be removed when his son took an outing, but it happened that as Prince Gotama was driven through town in his chariot, he encountered on successive days an old man who could barely walk, a leper whose extremities had been eaten away by his disease, and a procession with a corpse on a bier on its way to the cremation grounds. Enquiring of his charioteer what kind of beings these were he was told that old age, disease and death were the lot of all humans, including himself. He also encountered a man who had renounced the world, radiating peace and contentment. Gotama began to reflect on his own life and its end.

The father, noticing his son's darkening mood, promised to give him everything he wanted, in order to make him happy. Meeting his father, Gotama laid these four requests before him: eternal youth, not followed by old age; unchanging beauty and health, unimpeded by sickness; and eternal life without death. When his father told him that it was impossible for him to grant him these wishes, he reduced his wish-list to just one item: to be assured that he would not be reborn after leaving this present body. The king could not grant him this wish, either.

Thus Prince Gotama left his father, his wife and his young son, and at the age of 29 'went from home into homelessness', becoming a wandering ascetic, like many of his contemporaries, seeking freedom from rebirth. In later Buddhist art the 'Great Departure' became a favourite topic. The most moving images show his servant returning with Kaṇṭhaka, Siddhatta's horse, the saddle empty.

Gotama at first joined the company of Āḷāra Kālāma (S: Ārāḍa Kālāma), a brahman sage who taught meditation, residing at Vesālī.

After Gotama had learned everything that Āḷāra Kālāma had to teach, his teacher offered him the leading role in his own community. Siddhatta declined, because he had not found what he was looking for. So he left him and joined Uddaka Rāmaputta (S: Udraka Rāmaputra), another teacher of meditation, who followed a different system. Siddhatta soon mastered the new technique and, again, was offered the position of leader in this community too. Siddhatta, however, striving for something higher, set out to find alone what he was seeking for.

He spent a long time in the loneliness of the woods around Uruvelā (S: Uruvilva) in Māgadha, close to a small band of five ascetics. He avoided all contact with people, neglected his body and went to extremes of self-mortification, intent on finding in this way the emancipation of the spirit from the bondage of nature. Later sculptures show him at this stage reduced to a skeleton, hollow-eyed, close to death, but far from being enlightened. He realized that this was *not* the way to find enlightenment. He began to eat nourishing food; the five companions, who previously had admired his asceticism, ready to become his disciples as soon as he had accomplished his aim, now departed, convinced that Siddhatta had given up the ideal of renunciation.

But Siddhatta, far from having given up the quest, was determined not to leave the place until he had reached enlightenment. Accepting a bundle of grass from a grasscutter, he spread it under an Aśvattha tree, later to be called the Bodhi tree, and sat down in meditation with the resolution: 'Skin, sinew and bone may wither away, my flesh and blood may dry up in my body, but without attaining complete enlightenment I shall not leave this seat.'

At this resolve, Māra, the god of life and lust as well as death, became alarmed. He undertook either to frighten Siddhatta out of his resolve or to seduce him into returning to a life of pleasure. He caused a violent storm to break out, casting a shower of sand and rocks, glowing embers and sharp pieces of metal upon Siddhatta. Māra's missiles turned into flowers when they reached his body. When he saw that violence would not accomplish his aim he instructed his three beautiful daughters, Taṅhā (Thirst), Rati (Desire), and Rāga (Passion), to seduce Siddhatta. Failing in their efforts, they wished him well in his endeavour towards enlightenment.

The great moment that transformed the seeker Gotama into the Buddha, the Enlightened One, came during the full-moon night of Vesākha (S: Vaiśākha) (May/June), while he was sitting under the Bodhi

THE BUDDHA'S SELF-PORTRAIT

Victorious over all, omniscient am I,
Among all things undefiled,
Leaving all, through death of craving freed,
By knowing for myself, whom should I follow?

For me there is no teacher
One like me does not exist,
In the world with its devas
No one equals me.

For I am perfected in the world,
The teacher supreme am I,
I alone am all-awakened,
Become cool am I, nirvāṇa-attained.

To turn the dhamma wheel
I go to Kāśi's city,
Beating the drum of deathlessness
In a world that's blind become.

Like me, they are victors indeed,
Who have won to destruction of the cankers;
Vanquished by me are evil things,
Therefore I am a victor.

(*Mahāvagga* I, 8, trans. I. B. Horner, SBB, vol. XIV, pp. 11–12)

tree, the tree of enlightenment. The enlightenment did not consist in achieving the kind of transcendental self-consciousness (*turīya*) that the Upaniṣads speak of, but in understanding the concatenation of causes and effects responsible for the fetters that keep a person in *saṃsāra*, thus enabling him to snap that bond and become free. Time and again in his later sermons the Buddha would emphasize that he had found his enlightenment alone, without the help or advice of a teacher.

The *Mahāvagga*, the first book of the Pāli Canon,[7] begins by recounting the events of the first night after the Buddha's enlightenment: 'Then the Lord sat cross-legged in one posture for seven days at the foot of the Tree of Awakening experiencing the bliss of freedom.' During each of these nights he contemplated the chain of causes and effects, the content of the enlightenment experience, forwards and backwards.

Free from all desire and ecstatically happy to have reached the end of the arduous journey and gained the ultimate insight into the nature of reality, the new Buddha was ready to leave this world behind for ever. Contrasting the fickleness and the sensual desire of the average human with the subtlety and peacefulness of what he had found, he thought it would be a waste of effort to teach his insights to other people. It required the intercession of Brahmā Sahampati to persuade the Buddha to teach the Dhamma (S: Dharma) for the benefit of humankind on the grounds that the world would be lost without it, and that there were people who needed just a little help to gain enlightenment as well. Compassion for his fellow beings who were still entangled in the world of birth and rebirth, and who did not know a way out of suffering, then moved the Buddha to continue life in the body and to teach humankind the Dhamma.

The first people to whom the new Buddha wished to communicate his message of enlightenment, were his former teachers, Āḷāra Kālāma and Uddaka Rāmaputta, for both of whom he had maintained great respect as wise, learned and intelligent men. Learning through his newly acquired mental insight that both had died a short time ago, he thought of his five ascetic companions in the Uruvelā forest. He traced them in his mind to a deer park called Isipatana, not far from Benares.

They had left Gotama, believing that he had fallen from the ideal of renunciation, and on seeing him from a distance they decided to snub him. However, when he came near, they instinctively understood that something transforming had happened to him and honoured him by washing his feet and offering him a meal. They were willing not only to listen but to become his companions.

In the famous Sermon in the Deer Park at Benares, as it later became known, the Buddha explained to the five for the first time the *ariya saccāni* (S: *ārya satyāni*), the 'Noble Truths' of the universality of suffering, its arising, its disappearing and the means to deliverance from it. The five, having prepared themselves through years of asceticism and meditation, instantly reached enlightenment on hearing the Buddha explain the Dhamma. They became the Buddha's first community 'free from the cankers, without grasping'. The *Mahāvagga* concludes its account by stating: 'At that time there were six *arahants* (S. *arhat*) [liberated ones] in the world.'

The beginning of the Buddha's teaching at Benares became known in Buddhism as 'the first turn of the wheel of Dhamma', the initiation of the victorious movement of Buddhism. Soon the community grew: a rich young man by the name of Yasa became friendly with the Buddha and felt attracted by his teaching. Not only did he join the order himself, but he brought his whole family, his relations and friends to the Buddha, increasing the number of *arahants* tenfold. More and more people joined; wives and mothers complained about being deprived of husbands and sons; but women also wanted to join and the Buddha eventually established an order for nuns, accepting his aunt and foster mother as the first member.

As the community grew, the complexity of religious community life became apparent and the Buddha had to issue a large number of precepts and prohibitions to regulate the life of an ever larger Saṅgha. The Buddha did not consider himself the leader of a new religion. While announcing that he had found the greatest truth and reached perfection and enlightenment without the help of a teacher, he did not for a moment demand worship and submission as most other gurus did. He taught the Dhamma, which when understood and accepted makes all people equal. Later on he insisted that the order as a whole act as highest authority, and that no individual arrogate the authority to make decisions independently that affected the community.

For over forty years Gotama the Buddha, also called Sākyamuni (S: Śākyamuni), the ascetic from the Sākya (S: Śākya) clan, wandered north-eastern India with an ever increasing number of followers, preaching to the masses and teaching his close followers how to live in order to reach enlightenment. The 'Middle Way', the avoidance of self-indulgence and extreme self-mortification, combined with an ethical life and a positive attitude towards all, attracted many who otherwise would perhaps not have sought renunciation: 'The followers of the Buddha eat well and take a good rest afterwards', people said, and the Buddha took care that all his monks and nuns had sufficient provisions and did not lack anything essential.

To ensure the maintenance of high ethical standards, the monks and nuns were enjoined to meet in groups every fortnight and to listen to a recitation of all the rules of the order, called the *Pātimokkha* (S: *Prātimokṣa*). The most senior among the group proclaimed the several hundred regulations that had been laid down by the Buddha,[8] mostly in answer to questions of discipline that had arisen. Those who felt guilty of breaches of any of the rules had to speak up and confess their

THE BUDDHA'S TESTAMENT

I have preached the truth without making any distinction between exoteric and esoteric doctrine: for in respect of the truths, the Tathāgata has no such thing as the close fist of a teacher, who keeps some things back.

Now the Tathāgata thinks not that it is he who should lead the brotherhood, or that the order is dependent on him. Why then should he leave instructions in any matter concerning the order? I am now grown old, and full of years, my journey is drawing to its close, I have reached my sum of days.

Therefore be you lamps unto yourselves. Be a refuge to yourselves. Betake yourself to no external refuge. Hold fast to the truth as lamp. Hold fast as a refuge to the truth. Look not for refuge to anyone besides yourselves. (From the *Mahāparinibbāna Suttanta*, trans. by W. Rhys Davids, SBE, vol. XI, pp. 36–8)

---

transgressions. Unless this was one of the serious breaches of the Buddhist rule, the offender would be given a penance to atone for the lapse. Monks and nuns were also encouraged to report breaches of the regulations observed in others if the offender did not speak up. The *Mahāvagga* and other writings are full of reports of either monks and nuns or laity denouncing to the Buddha or to senior members of the orders behaviour they disliked or found objectionable and unfitting for members of the Saṅgha.

When the number of members of the order grew into the thousands, the Buddha delegated much of the responsibility for the ordaining of new members and the refining of the regulations to groups of experienced senior monks and nuns.

The *Mahāparinibbāna Suttanta*, which describes events from the last year of the Buddha's life,[9] reports that Ānanda, who had served the Buddha for a long time, asked him about the leadership of the community after his death. Customarily, Indian gurus appointed a successor during their lifetime, who would then continue to teach and guide with the founder's authority. Not so the Buddha. The Dhamma alone should be the rule and guide of the community; a Dhamma fully and unreservedly communicated to the members. 'Be islands unto yourselves, be lamps unto yourselves', the Buddha told them. His teaching and the regulations of life of the monastic community as it had developed over the forty years of the Buddha's active life would guide them.

When asked what funeral arrangements he wanted to be made, the Buddha said that this was not to be the Saṅgha's concern but that of the laity. Nevertheless, he gave detailed instructions. His dead body should receive the honours of a *cakkavatti* (S: *cakravartin*), a world-ruler: it should be embalmed, put in a coffin and later be cremated. The remains should be deposited in a tumulus, later called a *thūpa* (S: *stūpa*), at a crossroads. He also promised blessings to those who would honour his memory by putting flowers on the *thūpa*, whitewash it or otherwise express devotion to him.

Everything was done according to the Buddha's wishes. The devotion to the Buddha's remains was so ardent, that a 'war of the relics' broke out between different communities who claimed a right to possess them. Eventually they were divided up, as tradition has it, and placed in eighty-four *thūpas*.

BUDDHAS OF THE PAST AND THE FUTURE

Gotama the Buddha did not claim to have invented 'Buddhism': he described his own enlightenment as the rediscovery of lost and forgotten wisdom, the clearing of an ancient jungle path from the brush that had overgrown and concealed it for generations. According to one utterance he thought that his own clearing would remain open only for five hundred years and that then another Buddha would have to appear to proclaim the true Dhamma for another generation. Similarly, he believed that he had been preceded by other Buddhas. One of the side-effects of his enlightenment was his ability to look back into his previous births and observe his growth as a *bodhisatta* (S: *bodhisattva*).[10]

The Pāli Canon, like other Buddhist canons, contains a section called *Jātakas*, 'birth-stories'. They report 547 earlier births of the future Gotama Buddha: fully fledged Buddhas like Vipaśyī (P: Vipassī), Viśvabhū (P: Vissabhū), Krakucchanda and Kanakamuni, whose life stories resemble in many details that of Gotama the Buddha, and humans and animals that made heroic exertions towards gaining enlightenment. One of the best known and most beloved of the earlier incarnations of Gotama Buddha is that of Prince Vessantara. As an exemplar of the practice of heroic altruism, the prince was willing not only to part with his material belongings when asked by needy fellow humans, but even to give away his wife and his children and to offer his own flesh.[11]

Among the stories told about the previous lives of Gotama the Buddha there are also some that describe evil acts committed by him, for which he was punished in hells. The incarnation, however, that took place immediately before that as the Sākyamuni was in the Tuṣita heavens and it is a sign of the Buddha's boundless compassion that he gave up this extremely pleasant form of existence for the sake of an earthly one in which he could become the benefactor of countless human beings.

The purpose of these fanciful and entertaining stories is to demonstrate that the Buddha's life experience encompasses everything possible, and that birth as a human is a unique opportunity to gain enlightenment and thereby freedom from the cycle of existence. In addition, these stories helped to inculcate in the listeners the inexorability of the law of *karma*, one of the cornerstones of Buddhist teaching. Even the future Buddha was not spared the consequences of his actions, and good deeds, done in lifetime after lifetime, eventually lead to a life in which enlightenment is reached.

If Gotama the Buddha's past reaches back over aeons to previous Buddhas whose teachings have been forgotten, his future is open as well. The Buddha himself was silent when asked whether he would continue to exist or cease to exist after his death, but his followers believed that in one form or other he would be with them and at some time in the future reappear. A large part of the Buddhist world expects Buddha Maitreya, the next Buddha, the embodiment of friendliness, to appear and to enlighten the world in the near future.

THE IMAGE OF THE BUDDHA

One could hazard a guess that the Buddha is the most frequently portrayed personality in history, and that Buddha images are more numerous than those of any other religious personality. According to tradition the first likeness of the Buddha was a sandalwood statue made during the Buddha's lifetime under the instructions of King Udāyana of Kosambī (S: Kauśambī). The king ordered it to be made in the likeness of the Buddha at a time when the Buddha himself dwelt for an extended period in the Trāyastriṃśa heaven, so that he could look at him during his absence.

The oldest preserved stone sculptures at the *stūpas* of Sāñchī and Bhārhut (c. 300 BCE) represent the Buddha symbolically in the form of the imprints of his feet, showing the thousand-petalled wheel on the soles, one of the signs of a great personality,[12] a tree (the Tree of Enlightenment), a wheel (the *dhammacakka* [S: *dharmacakra*], the wheel of Dhamma) or a column of fire. The oldest known figurative representations of the Buddha are linked to two centres: Gandhāra and Mathurā. Gandhāra was situated in the area of the Indo-Greek kingdoms founded by Alexander of Macedonia after his invasion of India around 324 BCE, and the Buddha figures of Gandhāra are visibly influenced by Greek Apollo figures. Mathurā was the capital of an ancient Indian kingdom; its sculptures are truly and purely Indian. Soon some standard images of the Buddha figure developed: a seated Buddha, a standing Buddha and a reclining Buddha. The latter was exclusively used to represent Buddha's *parinibbāna* (S: *parinirvāṇa*). The standing Buddha is usually represented in a regal pose; the sitting Buddha in a meditative or teaching position.

Among the most frequently encountered images is the Buddha in *bhūmi-spassa-* (S: *sparśa-*) *mudrā* (earth-touching pose): the Buddha is seated in the lotus position, his left hand resting in his lap, his right hand reaching down to the earth. It commemorates the Buddha's invocation of the earth as witness for the truth of his teaching. Another frequently found representation is the Buddha in a*bhaya-mudrā* (fearlessness pose); either standing or seated, the Buddha shows his elevated right palm to the onlooker in a gesture of reassurance.

The Gandhāra school followed the conventions of naturalistic Hellenistic sculpture and (mass-) produced representations of the Buddha with an often effeminate face, a halo encircling the head, with heavily draped clothing. The Mathurā school developed its own style: it did not aim at reproducing a physical likeness of the historic Buddha but rather at expressing the essence of the Buddha's enlightenment – a completely calmed mind and body, a supernatural radiance, ethereal garments.[13] Popular art, in evidence on thousands of reliefs and panels, kept recalling the miraculous events in the Buddha's life and the best-liked *Jātaka* stories.

In line with Indian traditions, the creation of images of the Buddha was soon regulated by a canon that exactly defined the proportions between the different limbs and required the establishment of a grid of vertical and horizontal lines before beginning the work. One such is shown in figure 2. Buddha images are still made today in Sri Lanka

Figure 1 Giant statue of the Buddha in Dhyānī mudra, *Polonnaruwa, Sri Lanka*

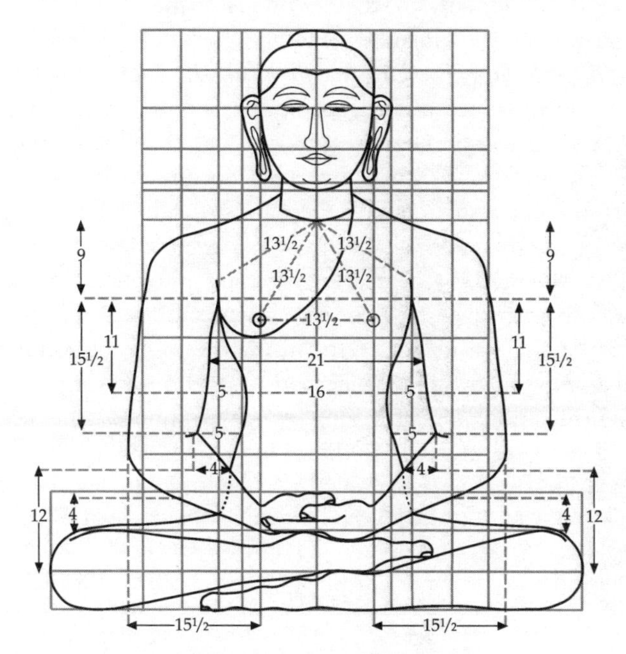

Figure 2 Construction schemata for the sitting Buddha image according to the Sāriputra, *a Sri Lankan text*

according to this schema. There is also formal and regular worship of Buddha images in Buddhist temples. A special festival is observed during which the Buddha statue is bathed and anointed and carried in procession.[14]

THE REMEMBRANCE OF THE BUDDHA

Remembering the Buddha and evoking his presence has been for long one of the most popular and highly recommended practices of Buddhism. As P. Williams says: 'A need for the Buddha to be present, to console, clarify, teach, and perhaps protect, was a significant factor in the development of Buddhism in the centuries after the death of the Master.'[15] The Pāli Canon contains in many places[16] a short formula that enumerates the salient features of the Buddha, which Buddhists dwell upon to express their devotion to him: 'He, the Lord, is *arhat*, Perfectly Enlightened, endowed with knowledge and exemplary conduct, the Happy One, knower of the worlds, the peerless guide of men to be tamed, teacher of gods and men, the Buddha, the Blessed One.'[17]

Each of these attributes of the Buddha is further developed according to traditional exegesis. Thus the meaning of *arhat* is expanded to include freedom from all vice, the cutting off of all the spokes of the wheel of existence, the worthiness to be worshipped as one who does no evil, not even in secret. The extended meaning of 'being endowed with knowledge' includes insight, psychic powers of the mind, the divine eye, the divine ear, the faculty of reading the minds of others and the ability to remember former existences. In this way the practice of 'remembering the Buddha' becomes a rehearsal of a great deal of Buddhist doctrine.

Paul Williams suggests that the visualization of the Buddha in meditation 'was a significant factor in the origin of the Mahāyāna and Mahāyāna *sūtra* literature'.[18] The *Rāṣṭra-pāla Sūtra* turns the remembrance of the Buddha into a glowing description of the beauty and attractiveness of the glorified Buddha:

> I praise you, who are of a golden hue, with distinct marks of eminence, and a face like the bright moon. I praise you, who are unequalled in wisdom; nobody is as pure as you in the whole universe. Your hair is soft, friendly, shiny; your *uṣṇīṣa* [19] is like a royal mountain and dazzling to look at. Between your eyebrows a circle of hair is shining. Your eyes are beautiful like jasmine, like an oystershell, like bright snow, like the blue lotus. You look with tenderness on this earth. Your tongue is long, thin

> and red [20] and you conceal it in your mouth, with which you teach the Law to the world. I praise you and your sweet and lovely speech. Your teeth are bright, firm like a diamond, forty in number, set close. You teach the world through your smile. I praise you and your sweet and truthful speech. Your beauty is unequalled and your glory illumines a large area. Your legs are finer than that of a deer; with the gait of an elephant, a peacock, a lion you walk. Your body is covered with auspicious signs, your skin is soft and golden. The world is never satisfied, looking at your beauty . . . Your mind is full of compassion for all creatures. You delight in generosity and virtue, in tranquillity and fortitude. Your voice is like that of a cuckoo. I praise you, the highest and best of men.[21]

THE WOMEN IN THE BUDDHA'S LIFE

All traditional accounts report the miraculous conception of the Bodhisatta and his extraordinary birth from Māyā, as well as Māyā's death within a week of the Buddha's birth and her sister's taking over motherly responsibilities for young Prince Gotama. There are many reliefs depicting these scenes, with Māyā being quite prominent. Similarly, all traditional accounts of the Buddha's life report the youthful Gotama's marriage to Yaśodharā,[22] a princess from a neighbouring country.

The Sanskrit work *Mahāvastu* has preserved a story about Gautama's wooing that adds some interesting features. King Śuddhodana, Gautama's father, invites a number of nubile high-born maidens to see to whom the prince will be attracted. Gautama's eyes fall on Yaśodharā, daughter of the Śākyan noble Mahānāma. When King Śuddhodana asks Mahānāma to give his daughter in marriage to Gautama he is rebuked: 'I cannot give Yaśodharā to the young prince. Because the lad has grown up among the women, he has not advanced at all in the arts, in archery, in elephant riding, in handling bow and sword, and in kingly accomplishments. In short, the prince has made no progress at all.'[23] King Súddhodana agrees: 'Out of too much affection I have not trained the lad in any art.'

Gautama, upon learning about the rejection and its reason, invites all the youths from the surrounding towns and provinces, who are known for their skills in the martial arts, to a competition. At this Gautama shows extraordinary strength and skills in all disciplines and easily wins all the sporting events. There no longer is any hindrance to his marrying 16-year-old Yaśodharā, who loves him as much as he loves her. Her love towards him, and her rejection of all who ask her to marry them, after the Buddha's departure, is a constant theme in these stories.

Yaśodharā appears in the *Jātakas* as Gautama's spouse in all kinds of circumstances. One *Jātaka* in particular is noteworthy. In this we learn that it was Yaśodharā, in the form of a tigress, who at one time appointed the Bodhisatta, in the shape of a lion, as king of the animal world.[24] We also learn that Yaśodharā, in former incarnations, had often saved the Bodhisatta's life.[25]

Quite generally, there is a tendency in the *Mahāvastu* to identify Yaśodharā with important mythical figures and to give her a fairly active role in the life of the Bodhisattva. She is described as resourceful and as a strong and an important person at the court of Kapilavastu: she is third in rank after the king, his father, and Mahāprajāpatī Gautami (P: Mahāpajāpatī Gotamī), his foster mother. Gautama's leaving her does not seem to have diminished her position: she is recounted as being at the head of a retinue of women to receive the Buddha on his first visit to his home town and to witness his first encounter with his son, whom he had left as a newborn in the arms of his mother.

Most traditional accounts have Yaśodharā encouraging Rāhula to ask the Buddha, when he comes to visit his home town, for his patrimony and the Buddha showing him his robes, his begging bowl and his followers as his inheritance.[26] The Pāli Canon tells of Rāhula's taking ordination and of Mahāpajāpatī's entreating the Buddha to allow women to join the Saṅgha. The *Mahāvastu* reports how Mahāprajāpatī had turned blind from weeping about Gautama's departure and how the Buddha miraculously restored her eyesight. Both she and Yaśodharā take monastic vows and become highly respected nuns.

The frequency with which Yaśodhara is mentioned, and the very positive role which she plays in the successive births of the Bodhisattva, indicates a loving relationship. Why then did he leave her without asking for her consent? It was certainly not a case of personal disaffection or mutual dislike, but rather the perception of a higher goal that required full engagement of the mind, and that he perceived as incompatible with life in a family. It was a 'calling' that demanded a total dedication – something all religions are familiar with, and that jars with ordinary perceptions of the good life.

NOTES

1. For a survey of existing scholarly (Western) Buddha biographies and extensive bibliography see Shaner, 'Biographies of the Buddha'.
2. There are several traditional biographies (or rather hagiographies) of the

Buddha, which are widely known in the Buddhist world. One of these, the *Buddhacarita*, served as the background to Edwin Arnold's famous *Light of Asia*, which did more than any other book to make Buddhism known in Europe in the late nineteenth century. Indian leaders like Mahatma Gandhi and Jawaharlal Nehru loved it and recommended it.

3. In 1956 the Buddhist world celebrated the 2,500th anniversary of the Buddha's *parinirvāṇa*. Assuming a life span of eighty years, that would give us 624–544 BCE as the dates of the Buddha's life. Most Western scholars prefer dates of c. 480–400 BCE.
4. See Bechert, *The Dating of the Historical Buddha* and Dissanayake, 'Notes on Revising the Historical Dates of the Buddha' which refers to Richard Gombrich's suggestion of dating the Buddha in the fifth century BCE.
5. The prognostication was made on the basis of the 'thirty-two signs' (*lakṣaṇa*) which the body of a world-ruler or world-teacher exhibits. They are mentioned in various texts (e.g. *Dīgha Nikāya* III, 142–79). Buddha, when challenged at some later time in his life, showed them to a doubter.
6. Traditional history emphasizes – and traditional Buddhist art shows – that she gave birth to her son standing upright, holding fast to two *sal* trees that were growing close together.
7. In the Chattasangani edition, followed by the Pāli Canon in Devanāgarī (1956ff).
8. It is a question of scholarly debate as to when exactly the present form of the *Pātimokkha* as found in the Pāli Canon was finalized. There is no doubt, however, that the institution of fortnightly meetings (*uposatha*) and the core of the regulations contained in the *Pātimokkha* go back to the Buddha's own mandate.
9. English translation by T. W. Rhys Davids in *Buddhist Suttas*, SBE, vol. XI, pp. 1–136.
10. The term *bodhisat(t)va* has not been satisfactorily explained according to its grammatical form. It is usually translated as a 'Buddha-to-be', a person on the way to enlightenment, and is used variously to describe previous births of Gautama Buddha as told in the *Jātakas* which form part of the Pāli Canon, or an aspirant towards Buddhahood who has made the vow to engage in heroic activities on behalf of humankind, or supernatural beings who aid humans in their struggle towards enlightenment.
11. See Gombrich and Cone, *The Perfect Generosity of Prince Vessantara*.
12. The thirty-two *lakṣaṇa* (great signs) are supplemented by eighty *anuvyañjana* (lesser signs). The former are enumerated in the *Lakkhana Sutta*, *Dīgha Nikāya* III, 142–79.
13. See Ray, 'The idea and image of "bodhi"', in *Idea and Image in Indian Art*, pp. 9–52.
14. de Silva, 'Worship of the Buddha Image' and Bhikku Punnaji, 'The Significance of Image Worship'. See also Harvey, 'Venerated Objects and Symbols of Early Buddhism'.
15. Williams, *Mahāyāna Buddhism*, p. 219.

16. E.g. *Dīgha Nikāya* I, 49.
17. A very detailed description of the 'Meditation on the Buddha' (*Buddhanussati bhāvanā*) is provided by Paravahera Vajiranana Mahathera in *Buddhist Meditation in Theory and Practice*, pp. 185–97.
18. Williams, *Mahāyāna Buddhism*, p. 219.
19. The *uṣṇīṣa* is a protuberance on the head, which appeared when the Buddha reached enlightenment. It is one of the distinguishing marks on all figures of the Buddha.
20. This was also one of the thirty-two distinguishing marks of a great personality. In a story concerning the demonstration of these to a king, Buddha is said to have shown his tongue capable of reaching both ears, when stretched out.
21. As quoted in Śāntideva's *Śikṣāsamuccaya*, chapter 18.
22. The Pāli Canon reports the marriage of Gotama to Yaśodharā, her receiving the Buddha in Kapilavatthu, her prompting their son Rāhula to ask for his patrimony, and her eventual joining the order. There are numerous references to her in the *suttas*, but she does not play a major role. By contrast, the *Mahāvastu*, which according to S. Bagchi, the editor of the Mithila edition text, 'occupies a position of supreme importance in the entire domain of Buddhist Sanskrit literature' *Buddhist Sanskrit Texts*, vol. XIV (Darbhanga: Mithila Institute, 1970), Introduction, p. 1, accords a fairly central role to her. She is mentioned in virtually all the *Jātakas* as a previous spouse of the Bodhisattva and plays an important role.
23. *Mahāvastu*, II, trans. J. J. Jones, SBB, vol. LIII, pp. 70ff.
24. The story is about the animals looking out for a king and agreeing that the one who first reached the Himālayas would be their king. A tigress arrives first and since 'nowhere are females kings, everywhere males are kings' the other animals persuade the tigress (in order not to break their agreement) to choose a king from among the male animals. She rejects the bull and the elephant, and chooses the lion. The tigress, Buddha tells his listeners, was Yaśodharā, the bull was Sundarānanda, the elephant Devadatta, and the lion the future Buddha.
25. E.g. in the *Śyāma Jātaka*.
26. There is a version in the *Mahāvastu* that makes Yaśodharā conceal the Buddha's fatherhood of Rāhula. Rāhula has to find out by questioning why he feels so comfortable in the 'recluse's shadow' (Vol. III, p. 247).

2 THE DHAMMA: BACKGROUND AND EXPRESSIONS

THE CONTEMPORARY INDIAN BACKGROUND

Karma (P: *kamma*) and *saṁsāra*

In spite of the uniqueness which the Buddha claimed for his insight and the originality of his teaching, he shared most of the culture and the world picture of his Indian contemporaries. He accepted the common belief in reincarnation: his father's inability to guarantee him exemption from this universal fate was the last confirmation for his resolve to leave the world and devote himself to the search for immortality. He likewise shared the common beliefs in gods and demons, in heavens and hells, in auspicious and inauspicious omens. What made his belief different from that of his contemporaries was that he did not consider any of these ultimately relevant.

Similarly, the Buddha believed that his present, last existence had been preceded by many other existences, and that the Buddha had not come just once into this world, but many times before. Unique as his teachings appeared, they were but a restatement of an eternal, forgotten truth. The Buddha compared his activity with the clearing of a jungle path that had been overgrown owing to neglect of maintenance: he did not claim to have made the path, but rather to have rediscovered it.

In a remarkable story he tells his disciples about some of his predecessors of millions of years ago:

> It is now ninety-one aeons ago, since Vipassī, the Exalted One, Arahant, Buddha Supreme, arose in the world. It is now thirty-one aeons ago, since

> Sikhī, the Exalted One, Arahant, Buddha Supreme, arose in the world . . . It is in this auspicious aeon, that now I, an Arahant, Buddha Supreme, have arisen in the world.[1]

The life history of Vipassī, of ninety-one aeons before, is remarkably similar to his own. The Buddha did not expect his own order to last forever, either: the time would come when the jungle path would overgrow again and a new Buddha would have to arise to clear it.

One common assumption in particular, that of *saṃsāra* and *karma*, the Buddha not only shared with his contemporaries, it was the decisive impetus for his quest:

> If three things were not present in the world the Perfect One would not appear in this world, the Supreme Buddha, the teaching and the order that he announced would not shine in this world. What are these three things? Birth and old age and death.[2]

Saṃsāra, the endless cycle of birth, old age and death is a necessity, a fact which no one can change.

> There are five things which no being in this world, nor a god nor Māra can obtain: that that which belongs to old age does not become old; that that which belongs to death does not die; that that which belongs to sickness, does not fall sick; that that which belongs to decay, does not decay; that that which belongs to time, does not cease.[3]

Every new beginning is the beginning of a death: 'As fully ripe fruit are threatened to fall in the early morning, thus everything that is born is threathened by death.'[4] By contrast, when the texts tell about the achievement of enlightenment by a person, the stereotypical formula says: 'Destroyed is rebirth . . . there is no more return to this world.'

The obvious transience of everything is pressing hard on the Buddhist; the Great Non-Sense of the unceasing round of birth and death is the universal 'ill', the inescapable 'suffering' of all. This universal law, however, is not mechanical, but is working ethically–morally. The mind-frame of a person, the inclinations, the past experiences determine the future.

'Intentionality' is the Buddhist criterion for the creation of *karma*. There are some remarkable stories in the Pāli Canon, in which serious breaches of the *Vinaya* are brought to the Buddha's attention, and *bhikkhus* ask what the punishment should be. The Buddha always asks first whether these offences were committed intentionally. If the answer is in the negative, he rules that there is no offence, no need for a punishment – no bad *karma*. On the other side, intended acts, never executed, bring bad *karma*, though they are not punishable offences according to the rules of the *Vinaya*.

What we are is the fruit of what we have thought and done. As all his contemporaries did, so also the Buddha posits a beginningless chain of *karma*. It is not possible to go back to the time before *karma*, to find a point in time when one was free from desire, not enmeshed in ignorance. However, there is an end to it, if one follows the Buddha's teachings.

The Buddha not only states the universality of the law of *karma*, he sees the connections between the different stages that lead from ignorance to rebirth. This analysis of the conditions of rebirth is quite uniquely Buddhist, and so is the suggested way of eliminating rebirth by reducing its conditions:

> This body is not yours, nor does it belong to someone else. It should be seen as the result of previous *karma*, effected by what had been willed and felt. In this connection the well-trained disciple of the Noble One reflects wisely on conditioned origination: if that is, that becomes. From the origination of this originates that. If that is not, this will not be. Through the cessation of that this will cease.[5]

The great ill, from which the Buddhist seeks liberation, is the eternal cycle of becoming and unbecoming, regulated by implacable *karma*. The aim is to escape from it. This can only be done by finding a position outside *karma*. Only by eliminating all *dharmas* can one get outside the range of *karma*. Freedom can only be gained by dissolving one by one the links of the Chain of Dependent Co-origination, thus escaping from rebirth and re-death.

Dharma (P: *dhamma*)

Dharma or *dharma* (derived from the Sanskrit root *dhṛ*, to sustain, uphold) is one of the most frequently encountered words in Indian religions and it has a great many different meanings in various contexts: law, doctrine, established order, 'element', something irreducible either in thought, language or physical reality. In Buddhism it is used to describe the teaching of the Buddha, the *Buddha-dhamma*, as well as a specific Buddhist teaching about the nature of reality.

Buddhism differs from most other Indian schools of thought in so far as it does not assume the existence of an eternal material or spiritual primary substance out of which the manifold world evolved. Nor does it attempt to explain the world-process by postulating an interplay of a multitude of unchanging entities. The Buddha explains the phenomenal world as 'composite', that is composed of a large (but finite) number of elements, called *dharmas*.[6] The insight into its composite character deprives everything of its apparently substantial individuality. If things are composed of so many interchangeable elements, there is nothing that would make them individual entities. *Dharmas* are colours, sounds, sense faculties, breath, feelings, states of consciousness, good and bad luck, birth, death and so on. A *dharma* is defined as a 'carrier of its qualities', a 'factor of existence', a component of so-called reality. *Dharmas* originate from other *dharmas* in functional dependence and they cease to exist once their energy is exhausted. All *dharmas* – with the exception of *nirvāṇa* (P: *nibbāna*) – are transient, i.e. *duḥkha* (S; P: *dukkha*).

Applied to human existence, the *dharma* theory yields the insight that a human being is a composite of many *dharmas*, none of which is permanent. Personality is not 'in-dividuality', i.e. a being that is indivisible, but 'dividuality', i.e. a bundle of factors of existence whose composition follows a certain pattern.

In detail, the human person is divisible into five groups of *dharmas*, called *skandhas* (bundles, aggregates), namely:

- *rūpa*: 'body'; all perceptible forms;
- *vedanā*: 'feeling'; all feelings of pleasure and pain;
- *saṃjñā* (P: *saññā*) : 'consciousness', all that can be perceived or imagined, including the faculty to discern perceived and imagined objects;[7]
- *saṃskāra* (P: *saṅkhāra*): 'motive forces', the power that produces something as well as that which has been produced. The *saṃskāras* are responsible for the formation of *karma*. They comprise attachment to (bodily) life, desire, delusion, aversion, volition;
- *vijñāna* (P: *vijjāna*): 'consciousness', the element that transmigrates in a new rebirth and is thus responsible for reincarnation.

None of these aggregates, nor the totality of them bundled together, is identical with the 'self', or constitutes an immortal substance called 'soul'. Many have concluded from the Buddha's refusal to ascribe substantiality to any of these factors that he preached a form of nihilism.

Buddhists have at all times rejected this interpretation of *anattā* (S: *anātmā*). As Walpola Rahula insists:

> The Buddha's teaching on *Anattā*, or No-Self, should not be considered as negative or annihilistic [*sic*]. Like Nirvāṇa, it is Truth, Reality; and Reality cannot be negative. It is the false belief in a non-existing imaginary self that is negative. The teaching of *Anattā* dispells the darkness of false beliefs, and produces the light of wisdom. It is not negative: as Asaṅga very aptly says: 'There is the fact of No-selfness (*nairātmyāstitā*)'.[8]

It is one of the most common and dangerous illusions to identify the 'self' with any of the five *skandhas* (P: *khandas*). The disciple has first to learn, therefore, that no *dharma* can be the self. At no place do we read that there is no self – only that it is not identical with any of the transient *dharmas*. As one text has it:

> The well-instructed disciple of the Noble One does not consider the bodily shape as the self, or the self as something that has bodily form, or bodily form as something that exists in the self, or the self as something that exists in bodily form ... He does not consider feeling as the self or the self as something that has feelings ... He does not consider perception as the self, or the self as having perception ... He does not consider motive forces as the self or the self as having motive forces ... He does not consider consciousness as the self or the self as having consciousness . . . He understands each of these aggregates as it really is, that it is impermanent, painful, non-self; composite and leading to decay. He does not approach them, does not grasp them, and does not identify them as 'my self'. The well-instructed disciple sees in bodily form, etc. 'that is not mine, that is not me, that is not my self'. Thus, when bodily form, etc. changes there does not arise in him sorrow, anxiety, suffering, complaint or despair.[9]

Māra

Time and again we meet the figure of Māra in the canonical texts. We have seen Māra approach the Buddha, attempting to confuse him, to prevent him from announcing his *dharma* to the world. In early Buddhism Māra becomes the personification of evil, the Lord of this world. He addresses the Buddha: 'To me belong the eye, all bodily forms, the field of vision ... To me belong the ear, the sounds, the field of audition ... To me belong the nose ... the tongue ... the body ... the mind, the conditions of mind, the field of mind cognition.'[10] The Buddha concedes: 'All this, O evil one, is yours. But where all that is not, you have no access.'

Māra is described as the constant opponent of all who strive for liberation. 'Māra is following you everywhere', the Buddha tells his followers. Māra is in fact the ancient Indian god of death, and at the same time the personification of lust for life, the power of transience that attracts people. Ultimately it is the power that keeps humans within the cycle of becoming. The Buddha wants us to escape from death, from transience, from *saṃsāra*. Only that which can decay can die; and die it must, if it can decay. What is beyond, is outside the sphere of Māra. It is one of the great accomplishments of the Buddha to have defeated Māra on his own ground, to have escaped from his domain into the realm that is no longer under his rule.

HĪNAYĀNA, MAHĀYĀNA, VAJRAYĀNA: BUDDHISM, ONE OR MANY?

Buddhist Origins

The Pāli Canon contains a text[11] that purports to contain the very first public teaching of the Buddha after reaching enlightenment, addressed to the five ascetics who had been living with him in Uruvelā and who had abandoned him shortly before his enlightenment. It is called *Dhammacakkappavattana Sutta*, or the 'Sermon on the Turning of the Wheel of *dhamma*'. Rhys Davids, the first translator, gave it the title 'The Foundation of the Kingdom of Righteousness', because it contains the basic teaching of early Buddhism, the core of the Buddha's messsage.

There are two extremes, the Buddha says, which a person who has renounced the world, is not to follow: the ways of the 'world', i.e. seeking sense gratifications, following the passions, and the way of 'self-torture' – both these ways are 'painful, unworthy and unprofitable'. 'There is a Middle Way', the Buddha says, 'avoiding these two extremes, discovered by the Tathāgata – a path that opens the eyes and bestows understanding, which leads to peace of mind, to the higher wisdom, to full enlightenment, to *nibbāna*.'

And what is that middle way ? It is the Noble Eightfold Path which consists of:

1. right views (*sammādiṭṭhi*);
2. right aspirations (*sammāsaṁkappa*);
3. right speech (*sammāvācā*);
4. right conduct (*sammākamanta*);
5. right livelihood (*sammāājīva*);
6. right effort (*sammāvāyāma*);
7. right mindfulness (*sammāsati*);
8. right contemplation (*sammāsamādhi*).

The Buddha emphasized repeatedly that what he announced to the world as the 'Four Noble Truths', was 'not among the doctrines handed down, but there arose within me the eye, there arose in me the knowledge, there arose in me the understanding, there arose within me the wisdom, there arose within me the light': they constitute the very essence of his enlightenment.

1. 'This is the noble truth concerning suffering (*dukkha*):[12] birth is suffering, decay is suffering, disease is suffering, death is suffering. Union with the unpleasant is suffering; separation from the pleasant is suffering; any desire that is not satisfied is suffering.'
2. 'This is the noble truth concerning the origin of suffering (*dukkha-samudaya*): it is that craving (*taṅhā*; S: *tṛṣṇā*)[13] that causes the entering into a new birth, accompanied by sensual delight which seeks satisfaction here and there, craving for the gratification of passions, craving for a future life, craving for success.'
3. 'This is the noble truth concerning the end of suffering (*dukkha-nirodha*): this is the end, where no passion remains, no craving; the getting rid of craving.'
4. 'This is the noble truth concerning the way which leads to the end of suffering (*dukkha-nirodha-gāminī*): it is this Noble Eightfold Path.'

The Pāli Canon and the teaching it contains belong to the tradition of the Theravādins, 'The Elders'. Besides this very well-documented and well-represented line of transmission of the *Buddha-dhamma*, there are many others that arose in course of time and that competed with it in representing the Buddha's true teaching. We read in the Pāli Canon about the Buddha's concern to maintain unity in the Saṅgha and about his cousin Devadatta's attempt to split the Saṅgha – one of the most serious offences a Buddhist can commit, which is punished by expulsion.

Disagreements as regards the content of the Buddha's teaching and the latitude of interpretation of his rules of discipline arose many times during the Buddha's lifetime, and the Pāli Canon reports many instances where the Buddha corrects misunderstandings. In practical matters he appears to have been very generous in permitting modifications required by different circumstances and climates. After his death it was the Saṅgha's function to settle disputes between members. As we know from history[14] not all disputes could be settled and several major traditions developed within Buddhism that disagreed with each other on points of doctrine as well as discipline.

From the viewpoint of the *Saṃdhinirmocana Sūtra*, several centuries later, the Buddha's sermon in the deer park near Benares was only the first of three turns of the wheel, the beginning of the promulgation of the teaching that was to culminate in the wisdom proclaimed in this very *sūtra*. From this perspective the first teaching, as it appears in the Pāli Canon, was 'minor' compared to the 'major' teachings of the *Prajñāpāramitā* (Perfection of Wisdom) texts; it was dubbed *Hīnayāna*, 'Small Vehicle' as compared to the *Mahāyāna*, the 'Great Vehicle' which contained the full revelation of the Buddha.

The first turning of the wheel produced the teaching of the Four Noble Truths. But, wonderful as it was, it was 'provisional, subject to various interpretations and to disputes'. The second turning of the wheel, 'proclaiming emptiness to those who had correctly entered the Mahāyāna', taught the non-substantiality of all things. This too, was found provisional, subject to various interpretations and to disputes:

> The Bhagavān turned the third wheel of doctrine, very wondrous and amazing, possessing good differentiations for those who have correctly entered all the vehicles, dealing with the lack of entityness of phenomena, that are unproduced, unceased, originally quiescent, and naturally passed beyond sorrow. This wheel of doctrine turned by the Bhagavān is unsurpassed, not provisional, of definitive meaning, it is indisputable.[15]

The Mahāyāna

The reasons for the rise of Mahāyāna are complex and scholars are far from unanimous in their views concerning the origin of this form of Buddhism and of its relation to Hīnayāna Buddhism. For a long time it was believed (a belief supported by weighty arguments from established scholars) that Mahāyāna represented a lay movement within Buddhism that strove for a more egalitarian constitution and a lessening of emphasis on monastic asceticism. It was assumed that the Mahasāṅghikas, who split off from the main body in the Second Council, were the core group out of which the multifarious Mahāyāna developed. While many scholars, especially the Japanese, still hold to the view of the lay origins of Mahāyāna, a group of younger Western scholars,[16] resting their case on archaeological as well as historical arguments, has come to the conclusion that Mahāyāna began as a minority monastic movement within the Saṅgha and remained as such for several centuries, down to at least the fifth century CE.[17] According to them Mahāyāna does not represent an innovation or a drastic change but only an emphasis on specific elements already present in traditional Buddhist teaching as it was codified in the Pāli Canon. G. Schopen, one of the principal advocates of that view, argues that the prominence of texts – specific *sūtras* – suggests a monastic origin. He further proposes that Mahāyāna, far from being an organized movement that set itself up against Hīnayāna, developed locally around the followers of certain *sūtras* that were held in high esteem.[18]

Mahāyāna arose before the final establishment of the Pāli Canon, i.e. before the Theravāda school had finalized its textual tradition of the Buddha teachings. The Mahāyāna *sūtras*, often beginning with *evam mayā śrutam* (thus has been heard by me), claim to be the Buddha's word with the same status (or even more) as the *suttas* of the Pāli Canon. In their later polemics the Mahāyānists not only refuted Hindu and Jain schools of thought, but also Hīnayānists. This, however, should not make us overlook the fact that not only were the words of the Buddha as preserved in the Pāli Canon the foundation of Mahāyāna too, but there is much that Hīnayāna and Mahāyāna have in common, as expressed in a statement by a leading Buddhist scholar, Walpola Rahula, at the World Buddhist Saṅgha Council on 27 January 1967:

- The Buddha is our only Master.
- We take refuge in the Buddha, the Dhamma and the Sangha.
- We do not believe that this world is created and ruled by a god.
- Following the example of the Buddha, who is the embodiment of Great Compassion (*mahā-karuṇā*) and Great Wisdom (*mahā-prajñā*), we consider that the purpose of life is to develop compassion for all living beings without discrimination and to work for their good, happiness and peace; and to develop wisdom leading to the realization of Ultimate Truth.

- We accept the Four Noble Truths, namely *Dukkha*, the Arising of *Dukkha*, and the Path leading to the Cessation of *Dukkha*; and the universal law of cause and effect as taught in the *pratītya-samutpāda* (Conditioned Genesis or Dependent Origination).
- We understand, according to the teaching of the Buddha, that all conditioned things (*saṃskāra*) are impermanent (*anitya*) and *dukkha*, and that all conditioned and unconditioned things (*dharma*) are without self (*anātma*).
- We accept the Thirty-seven Qualities conducive to Enlightenment (*bodhipakṣa-dharma*) as different aspects of the Path taught by the Buddha leading to Enlightenment.
- There are three ways of attaining *bodhi* or Enlightenment, according to the ability and capacity of each individual: namely as a disciple (*śrāvaka*), as a Pratyeka-Buddha and as a Samyak-sam Buddha (Perfectly and Fully Enlightened Buddha). We accept it as the highest, noblest, and most heroic to follow the career of a Bodhisattva and to become a Samyak-sam Buddha in order to save others.
- We admit that in different countries there are differences with regard to the life of Buddhist monks, popular Buddhist beliefs and practices, rites and ceremonies, customs and habits. These external forms and expressions should not be confused with the essential teachings of the Buddha.[19]

There are, however, in numerous Mahāyāna writings instances of negative comparisons with the Hīnayāna. As one of these has it:

> Whosoever, after gaining the thought of enlightenment (*bodhicitta-utpada*) does not study the Mahāyāna scriptures but communicates with the adherents of the Hīnayāna, reads their scriptures, studies them and recites them or teaches them, becomes dull witted and is thrown back on the Road to Wisdom. Whatever wisdom eye he may have gained, it becomes dull and ineffective.[20]

Nevertheless, Hīnayāna continued to flourish in India side by side with Mahāyāna. Both traditions had renowned colleges and monasteries[21] and often Hīnayānists and Mahāyānists lived under the same roof. Both Hīnayāna and Mahāyāna missionaries went out to propagate Buddhism all over Asia. While Hīnayāna became the predominant form of Buddhism in South and South-East Asia,[22] Mahāyāna spread mainly in North and East Asia and proliferated into a great number of schools in

Tibet, China and Japan. However, various Hīnayāna schools also survived in China and Japan.

The Mahāyāna itself is not a homogenous phenomenon. While rejecting the literalism of (some) Theravāda schools, the exponents of a more sophisticated philosophical or mystical understanding of the Buddha's teaching did not reach agreement on some very fundamental issues, and several major schools of Mahāyāna, each with its own sets of preferred *sūtras*, emerged. As the quotation from the *Saṃdhinirmocana Sūtra* (p. 36) would suggest, the adherents of the (Mahāyāna) school of Cittamātra (or Yogācāra), recipients of the 'third turn of the wheel', would consider themselves superior to the adherents of the (Mahāyāna) school of Madhyamaka, who received only the teaching of the 'second turn'. It is not so much a change in Buddhist doctrine that set one school against the other, as a different emphasis on a specific point of generally accepted Buddhist teaching, such as the emptiness and non-substantiality of everything.

It should be made clear that these philosophical differences did not produce a split in the Saṅgha: adherents of the Madhyamaka or the Yogācāra schools continued to be ordained in the same monastic tradition as the adherents of the 'Old School'. Throughout the followers of the Mahāyāna accepted the *Vinaya* of the Hīnayānists and did not produce new monastic codes. Some would insist that Mahāyāna expressed less a difference in doctrine than in attitude: while Hīnayānists supposedly strove to perfect (only) themselves and to attain *arahattā*, Mahāyānists cultivated universal compassion for all suffering beings and were to strive towards complete Buddhahood.

A further, rather interesting difference between Theravāda, Hīnayāna[23] and Mahāyāna is the use of language: while Pāli, a Middle Indian language close to the Māgadhī spoken by the Buddha, is the sacred language of the Theravādins – not only the Pāli Canon itself, but also commentaries on it were composed in that language by the Buddhists of Sri Lanka, whose mother tongue was Sinhalā – Sanskrit, the sacred language of Hindu India, became the preferred medium for writers in the Mahāyāna traditions. By adopting Sanskrit they were able to reconnect with Hindu scholarship and engage in extensive debates with the followers of other systems of thought.

The *Trikāya* (Three Bodies) doctrine is one distinctive development of Mahāyāna as against Hīnayāna. All Buddhists came to believe that Gotama the Buddha, whose life and death were recorded, was only a phenomenal and ephemeral manifestation of some transcendental and eternal reality. They began to distinguish his *rūpa-kāya*, the visible bodily appearance in a human body, from his *dharma-kāya*, the invisible transcendental essence of his enlightenment teaching.[24] The Yogācārins perfected that development by subdividing the *rūpa* into *nirmāṇa-kāya* and *saṃbhoga-kāya*, thus teaching a *trikāya*-doctrine, rather crudely translated as the 'Teaching of the Buddha's Three Bodies'.

The *nirmāṇa-kāya* Buddha is the temporal form, in which the Buddha appears like an ordinary mortal and teaches the *dhamma* through ordinary language. In the view of the Mahāyānists, this is the focus of the Hīnayāna.

The *saṃbhogha-kāya*, the 'Glorious Buddha', is central to Mahāyāna:

> He is the supreme object of faith and devotion, the ultimate dazzling focus into which are concentrated like innumerable converging beams of light, all those incipient strivings and yearnings of the heart, those half-blind impulses to perfection, those mighty soaring flights of love and adoration ... His glorious body adorned with the thirty-two major and eighty minor marks of a Buddha, the illimitable radiance of which fills the entire cosmos, has ever been a favourite subject of Mahāyāna art, and the various transcendental forms in which it dawns sunlike above the horizon of the devotee's meditation have in the course of time been embodied in works of art, which apart from their value as supports of the spiritual life in general and the practice of meditation in particular, are acclaimed as being among the greatest artistic treasures of mankind.[25]

The *dharma-kāya*, the 'essential Buddha', cannot be described, but is the source and ultimate end of all Buddhas and of all efforts towards enlightenment. The *dharma-kāya* can make everything a means of communicating itself to ignorant people. The *Laṅkāvatāra Sūtra* declares that just as there are many words designating one and the same thing (like a hand), there are hundreds of thousands of names under which the Tathāgata can be known – even the names of the Hindu deities such as Brahmā, Viṣṇu, or abstract notions like *nirvāṇa*, *śūnyatā*, *dharma-dhātu*.[26]

The Vajrayāna

From around 300 CE there emerged in some parts of India – in Bengal and Assam in the east and in the district of Uddiyana in the west – a new form of Buddhism, which has been termed 'Tantric'.[27] The word *tantra* originally meant 'loom', or 'thread', but was soon understood as a technical term implying magic and secret rites.[28] Tantra, which did not remain restricted to Buddhism but extended to many forms of Hinduism,[29] did not arise suddenly. It resulted from the growth of magical beliefs and ritual practices in popular religion, and from ideas in some circles of mainstream Mahāyāna Buddhism. What some consider a 'third vehicle', calling it the 'Vajrayāna' or 'Diamond Vehicle', others would hold to be a special form of Mahāyāna. As with Hīnayāna and Mahāyāna, the difference between Mahāyāna and Vajrayāna is not easy to establish, especially since frequently a Buddhist might be ordained in a Hīnayāna tradition, follow a Mahāyāna philosophical school, and practise certain rituals of Vajrayāna.

The Tibetan historian of Buddhism, Bu-ston Rimpoche (1290–1364), flourishing in a Buddhist culture that was permeated with magic and miracles, embellished many biographies of important Buddhist teachers of earlier times with stories of miracles and magical feats. Thus he credited Nāgārjuna (c. 100–60 CE), the great (Mahāyāna) Madhyamaka master, with miraculously providing meals for five hundred monks during the time of a long famine, by means of a gold-producing elixir, and with building ten million Buddhist sanctuaries from a piece of clay obtained from the king of the Nāgas.[30]

Similarly, he reported that Śāntideva (eighth century CE), flourishing at a time when Tantric Buddhism was already openly established, was able miraculously to procure food and drink for a group of three hundred heretical monks during a time of a great disaster, and thus converted them to Buddhism. Śāntideva is also said to have counteracted the magic of a brahman fanatic who wanted to burn down all Buddhist establishments through a so-called 'Magic Circle of Maheśvara in the Sky'. The account of this event is quite dramatic and must have been popular in Buddhist circles.[31]

The use of miracles to spread the Dhamma and the defeat of opponents by means of magic became quite commonplace features in the biographies of Buddhist teachers who established Buddhism in Tibet and China, such as Śāntarakṣita, Bodhidharma and especially the legendary Padmasambhava.

On the one hand, Vajrayāna developed a quite distinct and elaborate system – largely a continuation and sharpening of Madhyamaka metaphysics and Yogācāra meditation – and on the other it gave rise to debased sexual rites that are blamed for the eventual downfall of Buddhism in large parts of India.[32]

One of the distinctive features of Vajrayāna is the worship of the 'five Tathāgatas' or five '*Dhyānī* Buddhas'.[33] Analogous to the five *skandhas* of which the human person is made up, the Buddha himself, now called the Ādi Buddha (The First, or Primary, Buddha), appears to the meditator in five distinct forms:

- Vairocana, 'The Illuminator' or 'The Brilliant';
- Akṣobhya, 'The Imperturbable';
- Ratnasaṃbhava, 'The Jewel-born';
- Amitābha, 'The Infinite Light';
- Amogasiddhi, 'The Unfailing Success'.

'These five Buddhas were introduced about 750 CE and they differ completely from all the other Buddhas known to Buddhism up to then.'[34] The difference is, briefly, that the Buddhas of both Hīnayāna and Mahāyāna had commenced their *bodhisattva* careers as human beings and had had to work up to Buddhahood in hundreds of incarnations. The five Buddhas of Tantric Buddhism began their careers as fully fledged Buddhas. They also constitute the world and each of them corresponds to one part of the universe.

> The Jīnas are Vairocana, Ratnasaṃbhava, Amitābha, Amoghasiddhi and Akṣobhya, whose colours respectively are white, yellow, red, green, and blue and who exhibit Bodhyaṁga (Dharmacakra or Teaching), Varadā (Gift-bestowing), Dhyāna (Meditative), Abhaya (Assurance) and Bhūsparśa (Earth-touching) attitudes of hands respectively.[35]

Since the five Buddhas themselves remain absorbed in meditation they act in the world through their emanations, the five *bodhisattvas*:

- Samantabhadra, 'The Universal Sage';
- Vajrapāṇi, 'The One Who Holds a Diamond in His Hand';
- Ratnapāṇi, 'The One Who Holds a Gem in His Hand';
- Padmapāṇi,[36] 'The One Who Holds a Lotus in His hand';
- Viśvapāṇi, 'The One Who Holds the Universe in His Hand'.

These and a host of further emanations, such as Mañjuśrī and Avalokiteśvara (both emanating from Amitābha and giving rise to other emanations like Simhanāda, etc.), are represented in numerous figures and paintings in Tibet.

The Ādi Buddha in human form is called Vajradhāra (Holder of the Thunderbolt or Diamond) and he is usually shown in embrace with his *śakti* (female counterpart) Prajñā-pāramitā (Perfection of Wisdom) with a *vraja* (thunderbolt, sceptre) in his right hand.

There is a widepread popular tradition that the Bodhisattva Maitreya, who resides in Tuṣita heaven, is to appear in the near future on earth as a mortal Buddha to introduce a lasting reign of peace and justice.

Mañjuśrī (The Soft-Beautied One), embodying learning, is an often mentioned form of the Buddha. His attributes are a lotus and a book. Sometimes he is considered an emanation from Amitābha or Akṣobhya, or of all five Tathāgatas together. He plays a major role in the biographies of many prominent Buddhist teachers. He holds the 'sword of knowledge', destroying ignorance, in his right hand, and the book of saving wisdom in the left.[37]

The most widely worshipped *bodhisattva* is Avalokiteśvara (The Lord who Looks Down from On High). He is an emanation of Amitābha and his *śakti* Pāṇḍarā, and personifies universal compassion. He covers the period between the disappearance of the Gautama Buddha and the appearance of Maitreya. He assumes numerous forms (both male and female) and is variously known as Ṣadākṣarī Lokeśvara (Hundred-Eyed Lord of the World) and Simhanāda (Lion's Roar),[38] among many other names.[39]

Parallel to the development of the five Buddhas and their emanations, the multiple embodiment of *prajñā*, 'wisdom', in the form of the female deity Tārā, 'The Saviouress', took place.[40] Usually distinguished by colours, the 'green Tārā' and the 'white Tārā' are the most popular. They are seen as helpful, graceful and generous and are approached in all kinds of needs.

Vajrayāna became the predominant form of Buddhism in Tibet and strongly influenced the development of Buddhism in China and Japan. Since the occupation of Tibet by China in 1956 and the flight of many Tibetan monks to India and the West, Vajrayāna has become well known and quite popular all over the world. Often it is presented as a synthesis of Hīnayāna scriptures, Mahāyāna philosophy, and Tantric practices. As a matter of fact, the Tibetan and Chinese Buddhist canons are the repository of extensive Hīnayāna and Mahāyāna literatures, in addition to Vajrayāna works, that have been lost in their original languages.

NOTES

1. *Mahāpadāna Sutta*, 4: *Dīgha Nikāya* II, 2.
2. *Aṅguttara Nikāya* V, 144.
3. Ibid. III, 60.
4. *Sutta Nipāta* 576.
5. *Samyutta Nikāya* II, 64.
6. The theory of *dharmas* in the specific sense has been elaborated in the *Abhidharma*, dealt with in Part III of this book. The Theravādins assumed seventy-two, the Sarvastivādins seventy-five *dharmas* that constitute phenomenal existence. The actual instances of those (finite) classes are infinite, as R. Gethin pointed out in *The Foundations of Buddhism*, pp. 209ff.
7. As R. Gethin pointed out in a personal communication, 'the Buddhist exegetical tradition consistently explains *saṃjñā* as performing the function of labelling, noting or marking'.
8. Rahula, *What the Buddha Taught*, p. 66. The reference is to Asaṅga's *Abhisamuccaya*, p. 31.
9. *Samyutta Nikāya* III, 114f.
10. Ibid. I, 114.
11. This text occurs repeatedly in the Pāli Canon. The version paraphrased here is from *Samyutta Nikāya* 56.11 in the Devanāgarī edition. It also occurs in the first chapter of the *Mahāvagga* where it is rendered as the first teaching of the Buddha to the first five disciples. It is therefore also called the *Pancavaggiya*.
12. I have chosen to use 'suffering' as translation of *dukkha* instead of 'pain' (which it also means), because it appears to be the more generic term. As will be seen, *dukkha* is not only the sensation of pain experienced in a bodily or mental hurt, but more generally the sadness and 'suffering' arising out of an acute awareness of the transience and insufficiency of everything.
13. Literally *taṅhā* means 'thirst'; in connection with the 'origin of suffering', 'craving' seems to be a more appropriate translation.
14. For more about the Buddhist councils, the problems they attempted to solve and the factions that emerged, see chapter 3, pp. 49ff.
15. *Saṃdhinirmocana Sūtra*, ch. 7, as translated by D. S. Lopez, Jr in 'Interpretation of the Mahāyāna Sūtras', p. 58.
16. Represented, among others, by Paul Williams, Gregory Schopen, Rupert Gethin and Donald S. Lopez Jr.
17. For a detailed exposition of this view see Gethin, *The Foundations of Buddhism*, pp. 50ff.
18. The argument for and against the lay origin of Mahāyāna is fully discussed in Williams, *Mahāyāna Buddhism*, pp. 20ff.
19. Rahula, *The Heritage of the Bhikkhu*, appendix IV, 'Basic Points Unifying the Theravāda and the Mahāyāna', pp. 137f. Dr Walpola Rahula, Tripiṭakavagīśvarācārya, was at that time Vice-Chancellor of the Vidyodaya University in Sri Lanka. In the text quoted I have left unchanged the spelling and capitalization of Buddhist terms.

20. *Niyatāniyatāvatāramudrā Sūtra*, quoted by Śāntideva in *Sikṣāsamuccaya*, p. 7.
21. According to the testimony of some famous Chinese pilgrims, Mahāyānists continued to live with non-Mahāyānists in the same monastery.
22. This does not mean that Mahāyānist ideas did not also find reception in those countries. As Walpola Rahula (*History of Buddhism in Ceylon*) writes, during the ninth and tenth centuries some major Sri Lankan monasteries were under Mahāyānist administration (pp. 136f). He also attributes the widespread worship of Buddha images in Sri Lanka to Mahāyānist influence. Mahāyāna influence has always been strong in Vietnam.
23. Some other Hīnayāna schools also wrote in Sanskrit, the lingua franca of Indian scholarship.
24. Some Theravādins considered the Pāli Canon to be Buddha's *dharmakāya*.
25. Sangharaksita, *Survey of Buddhism*, pp. 279ff.
26. *Lankāvatāra Sūtra*, pp. 165f.
27. See chapter 9, pp. 190–9 on Tantric Buddhism for more detailed information on *Vajrayāna*.
28. The interpretation of *tantra* as 'thread' is understood to refer to the tradition of teachers and disciples (similar to the Hindu *paraṃparā*) through which these (secret) teachings were transmitted.
29. A scholarly debate is still going on regarding the mutual dependence of Buddhist and Hindu Tantricism. While some scholars claim that Buddhist Tantricism is not an offshoot of Hindu Śaivite Tantric traditions, as had earlier been maintained, A. Sanderson seems to have proved that some of the earliest Buddhist Tantric texts are reworkings of Śaiva *Tantras* (Sanderson, 'Vajrayāna: Origin and Function'). I wish to thank R. Gethin for having brought this reference to my attention.
30. Obermiller, *History of Buddhism by Bu-ston*, vol. II, pp. 124f.
31. Ibid. pp. 164ff.
32. Benoytosh Bhattacharyya, a respected Indian scholar and author of *An Introduction to Buddhist Esoterism* (1931), one of the first major studies of Tantric Buddhism, begins his preface with an unqualified condemnation: 'If at any time in the history of India the mind of the nation as a whole has been diseased it was in the Tantric age, or the period immediately preceding the Muhammedan conquest of India. The story related in the pages of the numerous Tantric works is supposed to be so repugnant that, excepting a few, all respectable scholars have condemned them wholesale and left the field of the Tantras severely alone.'
33. Conze, *Buddhism*, p. 189: 'In European literature they are often called *Dhyanī Buddhas*, but this term, introduced by Hodgson about a century ago, is not only faulty Sanskrit: it has never been found in any Tantric text. It is time to discard it.' However, the term continues to be used in recent Buddhological literature.
34. Ibid. p. 189.

35. B. Bhattacharyya, *Buddhist Iconography*, p. 2.
36. He is also called Avalokiteśvara.
37. On Mañjuśrī see Williams, *Mahāyāna Buddhism*, pp. 238ff.
38. Simhanāda is invoked to cure leprosy.
39. See Williams, *Mahāyāna Buddhism*, pp. 231ff.
40. See D. C. Bhattacharya, *Studies in Buddhist Iconography*, ch. 2, 'The Goddess Tārā' and chapter 9, pp. 190–9 below.

3 THE CONTENT OF THE *BUDDHA-DHAMMA*

Given the distance in time between now and the time of Gotama the Buddha, and considering that it took several centuries before the oral Buddhist tradition was committed to writing (that is, at a time when there already existed numerous sects of Buddhists maintaining different teaching traditions) it is not possible to identify with certainty the authentic word of the Buddha himself, the *Buddha-vācana*. On the other hand, we have a very well recorded history of transmission of the *Buddha-dhamma* and strong agreement between the various branches of Buddhism on certain essentials, such as the Four Noble Truths and the Eightfold Path.

There are formulae which are repeated over and over again in the Buddhist scriptures and which are attributed to the Buddha himself. They differ from the teachings of other Indian religions while sharing certain presuppositions with them. Some of these assumptions have been dealt with in chapter 2 on the background to the *Buddha-dhamma*.

What we today call the *Buddha-dhamma* is not necessarily what the Buddha said in these very words, but what the Buddhist community preserved as his teaching and what it considered the ideal practices of a follower of the Buddha. According to Buddhist tradition the only concern of the Buddha was *nibbāna* and all his teaching was about ways of reaching this ultimate condition.

The present chapters details the contents of the *Buddha-dhamma*, especially the *Dhammapada* and the *Milindapañha*, which are summarized later in the chapter. Part II of the book considers further the systematic presentation of the way to *nibbāna*, Buddhist meditation, and

THE MIDDLE PATH

These two (dead) ends, monks, should not be followed by one who has gone forth. Which two? That which is, among sense-pleasures, addiction to attractive sense-pleasures, ill, un-arian, not connected with the goal; and that which is addiction to self-torment, ill, un-arian, not connected with the goal.

Now monks, without adopting either of these two (dead) ends, there is a middle course, fully awakened to by the Truthfinder, making for vision, making for knowledge, which conduces to calming, to superknowledge, to awakening, to *nibbāna*.

And what, monks, is this middle course fully awakened to by the Truthfinder, making for vision, making for knowledge, which conduces to calming, to superknowledge, to awakening, to *nibbāna*? It is the aryan eightfold Way itself, that is to say: right view, right thought, right speech, right action, right mode of living, right endeavour, right mindfulness, right concentration. This, monks, is the middle course, fully awakened to by the Truthfinder, making for vision, making for knowledge which conduces to calming, to super-knowledge, to awakening, to *nibbāna*. (From the Sermon in the Deer Park at Benares, trans. I. B. Horner in *The Book of the Discipline (Vinaya Piṭaka)*, vol. IV (*Mahāvagga*), SBB, vol. XIV, p. 15.

the *bodhisattva* path, and the various schools of Mahāyāna. The present chapter deals first with the history of the preservation of the Buddha-word and its spread throughout the world, as well as its study by modern Western scholars.

THE BUDDHIST COUNCILS

Because the Buddha's teaching had been entirely by word of mouth, the Dhamma initially existed only in the memories of his immediate disciples. Even during his lifetime the Buddha had to correct misunderstandings of his teachings and had to intervene regarding deviations from the regulations that he had issued for his followers. Preserving the fruit of over forty years of incessant teaching was a colossal task which only the community of disciples as a whole could undertake in a collective effort, in a 'council' (*saṅgīti*, recital) of all members in good standing.

Since the councils acquired such an important status in the transmission of the words of the Buddha, a kind of canonical history of the councils developed, which was to buttress claims to have preserved the original teaching. Modern critical scholarship has thrown doubts on many aspects of this traditional history of the councils.[1] In the following we shall first summarize the traditional account as found in the Pāli sources[2] and then mention the points at which critical scholarship disagrees with it.

The First Council[3]

Shortly after the Buddha's death, when some voices such as those of the rebellious Subhadda were heard expressing relief at the death of the Buddha, who had insisted on observing hundreds of regulations, some of the older and more disciplined monks under the leadership of Mahākassapa agreed to convene a meeting of five hundred monks in order to recite and rehearse the Buddha's teaching and preserve it in its purity for posterity.[4] They were supported in this effort by King Ajataśatru of Magadha, who offered facilities in his capital Rājagriha.

Mahākassapa began the proceedings by asking questions about the *Vinaya* from Upāli, a highly respected senior *bhikkhu*. His information concerning discipline was considered correct and was accepted by the council. Next Mahākassapa asked Ānanda, who had been closest to the Buddha for many years, about the *suttas*. Ānanda was to supply information about the occasion of a sermon, the location and the persons addressed. His account too, was accepted as the true teaching of the Buddha.

As a side issue, the assembled monks also undertook a trial of Ānanda, who had apparently made enemies through some of his actions. He was accused of having allowed women to see the dead body of the Buddha, permitting them to desecrate his body with their tears, of not having requested the Buddha to remain alive and teach for a whole world-age, of having on one occasion stepped on the Buddha's cloak while repairing it, and – worst of all – of having (successfully) pleaded with the Buddha for the admission of women to the Saṅgha.

Modern critical scholarship throws doubts on the very fact of there having been a First Council in the rainy season following the Buddha's death, as well as the presence of five hundred *arahants* to constitute the entire *Vinaya* and the *Sutta Piṭaka*.

The Second Council[5]

The Second Council, according to Buddhist tradition, was held at Vaiśālī about a century later in order to settle a dispute between the monks of the Vajji country, who had declared 'Ten Points or Indulgences', and Yaśa, who considered these contravened the rules. They included *siṅgiloṇa-kappa*, 'the practice of carrying salt in a horn', which was judged to go against the canonical prohibition on storing food; *dvaṅgula-kappa*, 'the practice of taking meals when the shadow is already two fingers broad', which was considered to contravene the injunction not to eat after midday and *gāmantara-kappa*, 'the practice of going to another village (for a second meal)', which violated the rule against overeating.

The other seven infringements had to do with such practices as holding *uposatha* ceremonies in different parts of one and the same parish, drinking palm wine, taking buttermilk after meals and, most seriously, accepting gold and silver, which was expressly forbidden to monks. The decision of the assembled elders against the Vajjian monks appears to have led to the first major split of the Buddhist community.

The Third Council[6]

According to Theravāda tradition, the Third Council was held at Pāṭaliputra c. 240 BCE under the patronage of the famous emperor Aśoka, who supported the spread of Buddhism not only in India, but also abroad. The council was presided over by Tissa Moggaliputta and was intended to correct corrupt practices that had crept into the Saṅgha. Because Buddhism received state patronage under Aśoka and had become prosperous, many who had no faith in the *Buddha-dhamma* and were not prepared to abide by its rules had joined the order. The council was to renew Buddhist practice and eliminate those who did not belong. It also authorized Buddhist missions to various countries in Asia, Africa and Europe.

By now, what later came to be known as the Pāli Canon[7] had been established.[8] The presiding monk at the Council, Tissa Moggaliputta, is credited with having composed the fifth book of the *Abhidhamma Piṭaka*, the 'Points of Controversies' (*Kathāvatthu*), thereby bringing the Pāli Canon to a close.

Those who had opposed the Theravādins at the Second Council called themselves *Mahāsaṅghikas*, the adherents of the 'Greater Community', and went their own ways in interpreting and developing the original teachings of the Buddha. It has been suggested that the 'innovators' who brought about a split were not the Mahāsaṅghikas but the Theravādins, who introduced at that council stricter regulations and a more narrowly defined teaching.

The Fourth Council[9]

A council was called by Emperor Kaniṣka around 100 CE and was held either in Kashmir or in Jalandhar, north-western India. It is not recognized by the Theravādins. Emperor Kaniṣka wanted to settle differences of interpretation of Buddhist teachings and engaged five hundred monks to produce commentaries on the Canon. They are reported to have written one hundred thousand *ślokas* on each of the Three Baskets, most of which did not survive.

Regional Councils[10]

Regional councils of the Theravādins were held throughout the following centuries in Sri Lanka, Thailand and Burma (Myanmar), countries which for a long time became the most important strongholds of the tradition of the Elders (Theravāda). These councils served to standardize the (Pāli) Canon, to arrange the commentaries, and to commission the writing of the Canon (done under the leadership of Mahāthera Rakkhita in the first century BCE).

Two councils held in Burma, in 1871 and 1954–6 (in commemoration of the 2,500th anniversary of the Buddha's *parinirvāṇa* according to the traditional reckoning), are accepted by the Theravādins as 'full' councils. They were concerned with establishing the authentic text of the (Pāli) Canon, which was incised on 729 marble slabs in 1871, and committed to print in 1954–6. This latter version, the so-called Chaṭṭha Saṅgāyana edition, has become the accepted Buddhist version of the Pāli Canon, from which was published the first Pāli Canon in Devanāgarī in India (1956–61).

THE SPREAD OF BUDDHISM

From its very beginnings Buddhism was a religion on the move. The Buddha encouraged his early followers to travel into distant regions to make the good news of the enlightenment known to all (see figure 3).

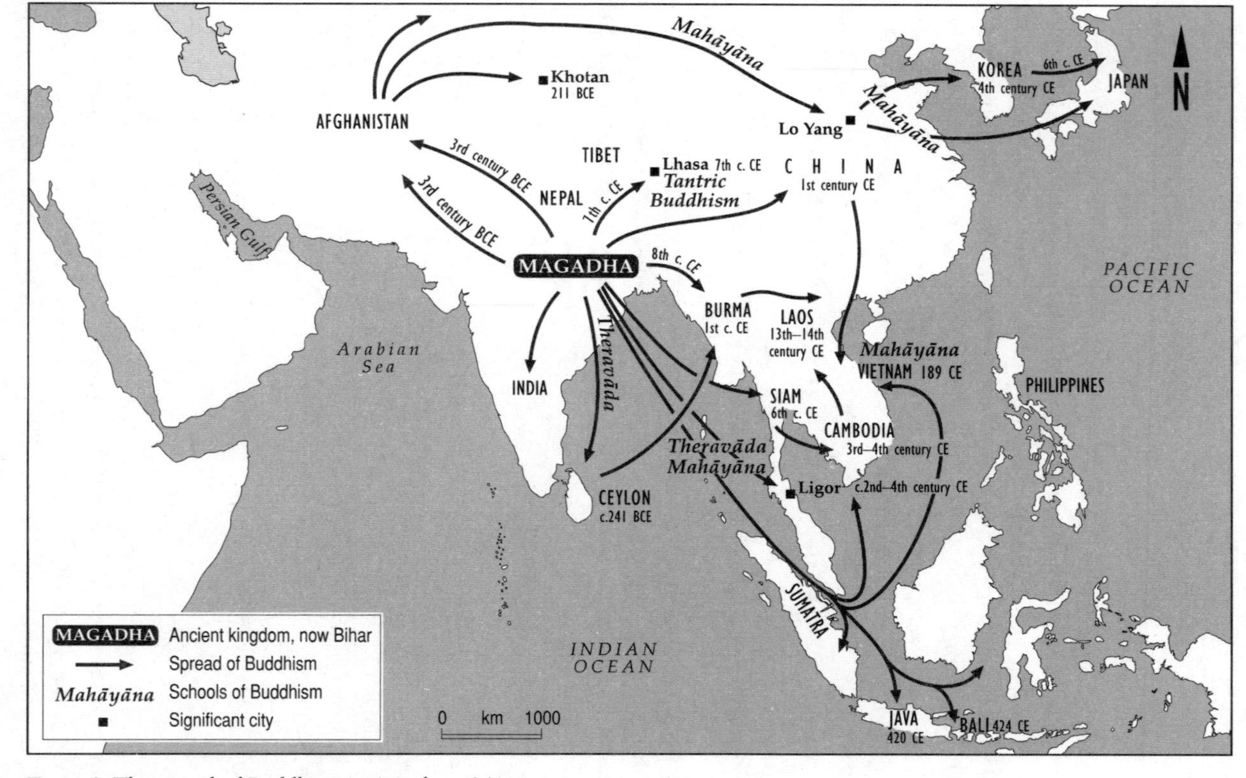

Figure 3 The spread of Buddhism in Asia from 241 BCE

Buddhist tradition has it that Emperor Aśoka sent Buddhist missionaries east and west as ambassadors to kings and princes. In particular, one of his sons, by name of Mahinda, who had become a Buddhist monk, and one of his daughters who had become a Buddhist nun, were sent in 246 BCE to Sri Lanka to establish Buddhism in that island kingdom, which for many centuries was to be one of the major monastic and scholastic centres of the Buddhist world.

The Sinhalese consider themselves the Buddha's chosen people; in their histories (especially the ancient *Dīpavaṃsa*) they claim that the Buddha travelled to their island three times during his lifetime and predicted the great role which Sri Lanka would have in the development of the faith. Sri Lanka has preserved the Theravāda tradition over more than two thousand years. It was also here that around 80 BCE, at a time of crisis and breakdown of order, the Pāli Canon was committed to writing in order to preserve it intact for posterity at a time when fewer and fewer monks who had memorized it could be found.

Burmese tradition, too, claims that Gotama Buddha had visited the country during his earthly life and that it received the *dhamma* from Buddhist missionaries sent out by Aśoka in the third century BCE. Burma in fact has often rivalled Sri Lanka in importance for the maintenance of Theravāda, especially in recent times, and two important councils were held there which were recognized by all Theravādins.

While it was mainly Theravāda Buddhism that spread in South and South-East Asia, various forms of Hīnayāna as well as Mahāyāna Buddhism found entry in Northern and Eastern Asia. In the first century CE Buddhist missionaries went to China, beginning a large enterprise of translating Buddhist scriptures into Chinese. By the fourth century CE Buddhism had reached Korea, by the fifth Java and Sumatra, by the sixth Japan, and by the seventh Tibet.

For many centuries Buddhism was the predominant religion in the whole of Asia, inspiring a great outburst of art, attracting millions of people to the monastic life and profoundly shaping the cultures of most Asian countries generally. In its homeland, India, Buddhism flourished for about a thousand years. By the fifth century CE, with the patronage of the Gupta dynasty, brahmanic Hindus launched a counter-attack and eventually succeeded in gaining majority status again.

When the Muslims invaded India, destroying the large Buddhist universities of Taxila and Nālandā, which they considered bulwarks of resistance, many Buddhist monks and nuns were killed. The rest fled to northern, mountainous regions not yet occupied by Muslims. Many ended up in Tibet, bringing with them texts they had saved. Thus it came about that Tibet became the stronghold of Buddhism in an age when it was threatened in much of the rest of Asia by Hindu missions and Muslim conquests. Much of Buddhist literature would have been lost forever but for the libraries of Tibetan monasteries which preserved originals and translations of many rare books.

European colonial conquests from the early sixteenth century onwards had two quite contrary effects. While the Dutch and the Portuguese tried to convert the Buddhist inhabitants of Sri Lanka to Christianity (and succeeded up to a point), the British, who occupied Sri Lanka and Burma in the early nineteenth century, left the Buddhists in peace. Among the British officials who worked in Sri Lanka there were some who openly sympathized with Buddhism.

MODERN WESTERN BUDDHIST SCHOLARSHIP

After a period of dormancy and decay Buddhism is flourishing again in many countries in the East. It also has found followers in many Western countries, where it has become the subject of intense and sympathetic study. In Asia, the revival of Buddhism was part of the rising nationalism of the nineteenth century. European colonial and Christian missionary expansion provoked a reaction: a new national consciousness began to dawn, and with it a new appreciation and a revival of indigenous traditions. Some European scholars and seekers, disillusioned with their own culture and religion, were instrumental in reviving Buddhism.

One of the most remarkable of these is Henry Steel Olcott (1832–1907), an American Protestant who took the Three Refuges and became the founder and organizer of several Buddhist revival movements. His memory is still celebrated in Sri Lanka every year on 2 February, Olcott Day.[11] While more of an organizer and reformer than a scholar, Olcott authored the *Buddhist Catechism* (authorized by the influential Buddhist scholar-monk Hikkaduve Sumangala) which even during his lifetime had already been reprinted in dozens of editions.

From the early nineteenth century, Western Indologists studied, edited and translated Buddhist texts, both Sanskrit and Pāli, together with other Indian manuscripts and inscriptions.[12] In 1826 Eugene Burnouf and C. Lassen published an essay on the Pāli language. In 1844, in his *Introduction to the History of Indian Buddhism*, Burnouf offered translations of substantial passages of Buddhist Sanskrit works. In 1852 he published a French translation of the *Saddharmapuṇḍarīka*, one of the most important Mahāyāna works. In 1855 the Danish scholar Vincent Fausböll published the Pāli *Dhammapada* together with a Latin translation, and an English translation of the *Sutta Nipāta* in 1881 in the *Sacred Books of the East* series. He also published an edition of the *Jātakas* in six volumes.

Hermann Oldenberg (1854–1920) is another major figure in Buddhist scholarship. This German scholar had gained a reputation in Vedic studies and through translations of brahmanical texts. He also edited the entire *Vinaya Piṭaka* in three volumes between 1879 and 1883 and in collaboration with T. W. Rhys Davids published an English translation of substantial portions of this in three volumes of the Sacred Books of the East Series (1881–5). His monograph *Buddha*, published in 1881, was based entirely on Pāli sources. It immediately became a standard work, republished and re-edited many times in German and also translated into other languages.

Nobody, however, did more to propagate and popularize Buddhist studies in the West than the English scholar T. W. Rhys Davids (1843–1922) and his wife C. A. F. Rhys Davids (1858–1942). T. W. Rhys Davids went to Sri Lanka in 1864 as a member of the Ceylon Civil Service. He was keenly interested in Buddhist culture and started learning Pāli. Returning to England in 1872 he devoted himself to Buddhist scholarship. In 1881 he founded the Pāli Text Society[13] to which he gave most of his talent and energy for the rest of his life, as did his wife. Together they edited and translated dozens of canonical and extra-canonical Pāli works, and sought out fellow scholars for editing and translating still more. By the time of T. W. Rhys Davids's death almost the entire Pāli Canon had been edited, together with a large number of Pāli commentaries on canonical works, and most of the Canon had been translated into English. His wife continued with the work. As president of the Pāli Text Society she not only encouraged other scholars to edit and translate important Pāli works, but also contributed herself a large number of texts and translations. She translated some of the most difficult texts and contributed illuminating introductions to many others.[14] C. A. F. Rhys Davids authored several important monographs, such as *Sākya or Buddhist Origins* (1931).

The First World War with its enormous devastation of lands and minds was instrumental in the growth of popular interest in Buddhism.

In many Western countries Buddhist societies emerged, dedicated to promoting non-violence, freedom from greed and peaceableness. The history of Buddhism and its teachings were favourably contrasted with the history of Christianity, with its support for war and violence, as shown by the utterances of church leaders in the combatant countries.

In the last eighty years hundreds of scholars in East and West have taken up the study of Buddhism in its entirety: literature in dozens of Asian languages has been edited and translated and hundreds of monographs and thousands of papers have been published. Bibliographies on Buddhism fill shelves in libraries and courses of Buddhist studies have been established at many universities.

THE *BUDDHA-DHAMMA* AND FEMINISM

Contrary to the brahmanism of his time, the Buddha taught the essential equality of the possibilities for liberation available to all, regardless of gender, race or caste. When asked whether women could reach enlightenment he emphatically affirmed it. There is nothing in the basic teachings that is gender specific. By not demanding extreme forms of asceticism the Buddha did not shut the door to women as others had done. His regulations for the order of nuns, while hierarchically subordinating it to the order of monks, were of such a nature as to recognize the specific needs of women, while granting them every advantage that the Dhamma offered to its followers.

In the modern West, many women have been attracted to Buddhism and both among the scholars and the practitioners there are a large number of women. Buddhism's overall gentleness, humaneness and inoffensiveness are features that many women have found attractive. To assert that 'Buddhism is Feminism', however, presupposes a Western feminist background that will be hard to establish in traditional Buddhism.[15] Buddhism de-emphasizes everything that might be used to create lasting 'identities', be they male or female, and points towards the impersonal realities of Dhamma and *nibbāna*.[16]

In an environment like that of the West at present, where gender issues are taken very seriously, Rita Gross's 'androgynous reconstruction of Buddhism' sounds attractive. For her 'the Dharma is both male and female'.[17] Others may disagree. While some may feel a need to adapt the *Buddha-dhamma* to a changed and changing world, others will have it the other way round. Edward Conze, both a scholar and a practitioner of

Buddhism, is one of those Westerners who would opt for such a strategy. Referring to his experience in teaching Buddhism to American students, he recalls 'a remark that so endeared [me] to [my] students at Berkeley'. 'Asked what Buddhism should do to become more acceptable to Americans, I used to enumerate with a smile a few concessions one might perhaps make respectively to the feminist, democratic, hedonistic, primitivistic and anti-intellectual tendencies of American society.' In Conze's opinion, 'it is not so much a matter of the Dharma adjusting itself to become adaptable to Americans, but of Americans changing and transforming themselves sufficiently to become acceptable to the Lord Buddha'.[18]

The Buddha himself was constantly adapting the Dhamma in the light of suggestions and complaints arising out of new situations. He reportedly said shortly before his death that all the major and minor regulations could be changed or abolished, if that was found necessary in order to persue the overall aim. However, *nibbāna*, the aim, and the only means[19] to reach it, the Eightfold Path, were non-negotiable. If latter-day Western sympathizers with Buddhism equate *nibbāna* with 'wholeness and balance, tranquillity and deep peace'[20] and reduce the Eightfold Path to 'basic psychological grounding, deep sanity, and peace with ourselves'[21] one would have to question whether this is the *Buddha-dhamma* as transmitted in the succession of Buddhist teachers.

Buddhism cannot be dissociated from the Four Noble Truths and the search for *nibbāna*. If these are found unacceptable for whatever reasons, one has to find an alternative, but one should not call it the *Buddha-dhamma*. The *Buddha-dhamma* is the answer to the questions which the Buddha confronted, not necessarily to all the questions which someone today may raise. Not everyone has the sensibility for the universal *dukkha* which drove Gotama the Buddha to his search for enlightenment.[22] Questions of peaceful co-existence, sanity and satisfactory relationships are on a different level and need different answers. They are important issues, but they are not the issues that the Buddha considered paramount. Antibiotics are excellent remedies against bacterial infections and they have saved many lives; they do not provide immortality, however. The *Buddha-dhamma* does not protect against bacterial infections, but it claims to lead to *nibbāna*, a condition beyond suffering. The Buddha considered it the only remedy against the sickness of bodily existence, a sickness for which only those who feel afflicted by it will seek a remedy. The Buddha never claimed to be able to make all unhappy people happy under the circumstances they lived in, or to provide palatable answers to all human questions about life and fate. He invited those who shared his view of the world to join the Saṅgha and to practise the Dhamma.

BUDDHIST EDUCATION

When complaints reached the Buddha about followers of his who had misbehaved and were ignorant of the Dhamma, he gave the following ruling:

> I allow, O *bhikkhus*, a preceptor.[23] The preceptor should arouse in the one who shares his cell the attitude of a son; the one who shares his cell should arouse in the preceptor the attitude of a father. Thus these, living with reverence, with deference, with courtesy towards one another, will come to growth, to increase, to maturity in this Dhamma and discipline.[24]

The text continues, specifying the mutual duties. The student is to serve the preceptor in everything he requires but he is also to admonish him when he deviates from the true Dhamma. The preceptor is to take care of the student in every respect and teach him both the theory and the practice of the Way.

There are also hints at problems that arose in the shared life of student and teacher. The text deals with some very specific complaints from students as well as teachers, and advises how to handle these conflict situations. The Buddha ruled on many of these and established criteria to be followed with regard to the dismissal of students by teachers.

Essentially, for several generations, instruction of new members of the order was on a one-to-one basis and concerned training in monastic etiquette and repeating the teachings of the Buddha. This was an appropriate method for monks who were mostly moving from one place to another, at a time when the three months of the rainy season retreat were the only opportunity for any kind of systematic instruction.

When the first monasteries evolved, where monks resided on a year-round basis, they became training centres for future monks. The need to answer objections from the adherents of other religious groups made it necessary to develop a systematic and more sophisticated reflection on the Dhamma, which we see emerging in the *Abhidhamma* texts. In course of time this became a regular ingredient of training. When a sufficient number of teachers was available, they specialized in teaching doctrine (*suttantika*), discipline (*vinayadhara*) and philosophy (*dhamma kathika*). A Buddhist innovation in traditional Indian education was the encouragement given to students to challenge their teachers when they had doubts about their orthodoxy.

With the development of large-scale monastic institutions education also expanded to include courses in various branches of Buddhism and in the teachings of other religions, as well as subjects necessary for the efficient administration of the monastic establishments, such as architecture and agriculture. Monasteries received gifts from kings and merchants; often the revenues of whole villages were made over to them. Eventually lay people and foreigners could also attend Buddhist schools. Libraries developed and all members of the Saṅgha were expected to devote considerable time to study.[25]

Foreign visitors, mainly Buddhists from China,[26] who came to India between the fifth and eighth centuries CE to visit the holy places associated with the Buddha and to study at the by-now world-famous Buddhist universities such as Nālandā and Taxila, have left fairly detailed descriptions of the facilities and the curricula of these institutions.

Nālandā, situated in what is today Bihar, in north-east India, was apparently already an institution of learning in pre-Buddhist times. The Buddha is said to have visted the place several times and Ānanda preferred it to Pāṭaliputra as a more suitable place for the Buddha's *parinibbāna*. It was the reputed birthplace of Sāriputta, one of the Buddha's most learned disciples.

When Buddhist kings began patronizing Nālandā, building colleges and endowing chairs, it became the foremost Buddhist academy. Some of the greatest names in Buddhist learning, such as Nāgārjuna, Vasubandhu, Dinnāga, Śāntarakṣita, Śāntideva and others are associated with Nālandā. In the words of H. D. Sankalia, the renowned archaeologist who excavated parts of it, it became not only an international university, frequented by students and teachers from the entire Buddhist world, but a 'university of universities', i.e. a place of advanced learning, to which the graduates from other institutions came in order either to complete their education in some special subject or to upgrade their qualifications with a degree from this most famous of all Indian schools.

While not much written evidence about the history of Nālandā exists before the description offered in the travel diaries of Hiuen Tsang[27] and I-Tsing,[28] archaeological excavations have revealed that the latest buildings were erected on top of the ruins of earlier ones. It appears that Nālandā was destroyed and rebuilt several times before its final destruction by the Muslims in the twelfth century.

From the reports of Chinese pilgrims, who spent several years in India, we learn that not only the kings of Māgadhā, but also those from other parts of the country endowed colleges and libraries in Nālandā. Descriptions of the physical facilities at Nālandā emphasize the beauty and the great extent of the buildings. Nālandā had three libraries called Ratnodadi (Ocean of Jewels), Ratnasāgara (Lake of Jewels) and Ratnarañjaka (Adorned by Jewels) – the first reportedly had nine storeys and must have housed hundreds of thousands of manuscripts. Copying manuscripts was one of the tasks students were expected to do; Hiuen Tsang carried hundreds of copies of manuscripts back to China. Hiuen Tsang identifies eleven large colleges, each populated by several hundred students. Several sizeable villages were donated to the colleges and hundreds of villagers were entrusted with the task of preparing food for teachers and students. In the seventh century Nālandā reputedly had fifteen hundred teachers and ten thousand students.

The basic curriculum for undergraduates comprised the following five subjects:

- śabdavidyā: Sanskrit grammar and lexicography;
- śilpasthānavidyā: arts and crafts;
- cikitsāvidyā: medicine;
- hetuvidyā: logic and dialectics;
- adhyātmavidyā: philosophy, metaphysics.

The Chinese pilgrim-scholars mention by name many Sanskrit works that they had to study. Graduate students – and these seem to have been the vast majority, especially among the foreign students – specialized in a great variety of subjects and texts, very often spending years with a particular teacher who was an expert in that speciality.

Hiuen Tsang mentions that each external student had to pass examinations set by the gatekeepers, who were usually famous scholars in their own right. He also mentions that seven or eight out of ten applicants failed, and that many of those that were admitted did not complete their degrees. Apparently, Nālandā degrees were as difficult to obtain as they were prized by their possessors.

Most of the teaching was apparently done on a tutorial basis. A student was assigned to a specific teacher with whom he studied a specific subject or text. However, there were also frequent public debates between the teachers, with hundreds of students attending, which provided instruction on controversial points of teaching. At many occasions public lectures were also given and the periodic public examinations were not only stimuli to study for those who were examined, they were also occasions to learn for the audience. In these examinations students were not only tested on memorized matters – studying a work usually meant learning it by heart – but also on their own creations, which presumably had to contain a certain amount of original thinking.

Students at Nālandā, while being trained in the intellectual aspects of Buddhism and in academic studies in general, were also expected to progress morally, and they had to participate in the ritual activities of the institution. A great many Buddha figures were found in the ruins of Nālandā. In the time of its greatest fame it had been a Mahāyāna institution and ritual worship was probably part of its routine. Hiuen Tsang was as much impressed by the spirit and morale of the body of teachers and students of Nālandā as he was by their industry and intelligence.

Taxila (Takṣaśīlā), in what today is Pakistan, had probably been an ancient Indian seat of learning before it became a Buddhist institution. Pāṇini, the famous grammarian, reportedly studied there. Jīvaka, the physician of King Bimbisāra, a contemporary of the Buddha, received his education there and several *Jātakas* report that the Bodhisattva in one of his several earlier births had gone to Taxila for his studies. The *bodhisattva* of the Bhīmasena *Jātaka* studied the three Vedas and the

---

THE FOUR REFUGES OF THE BUDDHIST SCHOLAR

1. The Dharma is refuge, not a person (*puruṣa*);
2. The Spirit is refuge, not a letter (*vyañjana*);
3. The *sūtra* of precise meaning (*nithārtha*) is refuge, not that which requires interpretation (*neyārtha*);
4. *Jñāna* is refuge, not *vijñāna*.

(From the *Catupratiśaraṇa Sūtra*)

---

eighteen Vidyās in Taxila; one of these was archery, in which he excelled. Fa-Hien, one of the famous Chinese Buddhist pilgrims, visited and described the place as he saw it in the mid-fifth century CE.

One new university development which took place after the time of the visits of the famous Chinese travellers was at Vikramaśīla, established by the Pāla rulers of Bengal in the late eighth century CE. Within two centuries it had outstripped Nālandā and became the centre for the new wave of Tantric Buddhism and the major link between India and Tibet. A galaxy of famous teachers taught there, such as Ratnākaraśānti, Śāntibhadra and Maitripi. The most famous of them was Dīpaṅkara Śrījñana, also called Atiśa (980–1053 CE). He was the chief scholar and administrator of Vikramaśīla, in charge of 108 temples.

Vikramaśīla was the favourite place of study for students from Tibet, and Tibetan students carried the message of Atiśa's fame into their homeland. Several unsuccessful attempts were made to persuade him to go to Tibet. He finally relented, and after a journey lasting several years, he reached the Sam-ye *vihāra* (monastery) in central Tibet, which had been founded by Śāntarakṣita from Nālandā two centuries earlier. Atiśa found a rich store of manuscripts in the library and spent the rest of his life translating, with the help of Tibetan scholars, hundreds of texts from Sanskrit into Tibetan.

Vikramaśīla, like Nālandā and the other large and famous Buddhist universities in India, succumbed in the twelfth century to the onslaught of Muslim invaders and nothing but fields strewn with rubble and ruins remains today. However, the scholar monks who had to flee India found new homes in neighbouring countries.

In the following centuries Tibet developed a unique Buddhist theocracy in which scholarly monastic institutions became the focus of cultural and political life. The Tibetan scholar Bu-ston Rimpoche (1290–1364) wrote an extremely valuable work, the *History of Buddhism*, which he prefaced with a book-length essay on the study of the Dhamma, specifically dealing with the qualifications and activities of teacher and student. He notes that both studying and teaching bring merit and quotes the *Bodhisattva Piṭaka*: 'One who studies comes to know the Dharma. One who studies will abstain from sinful deeds. One who studies will reject all that is vain. One who studies attains *Nirvāṇa*.'[29] Similarly, the teaching of the Dharma is 'the highest means of worshipping the Buddha, the Teacher, is superior to material gifts; it secures a good memory and intellectual power, it augments virtue and leads to Enlightenment'.[30]

Summarizing the opinions of many authorities on the qualifications required in a teacher he says: 'The teacher must be well versed in the doctrine that is to be expounded; skilful, as regards the ways of expressing himself; experienced as concerns his behaviour.'[31] A teacher must be motivated by supreme compassion and the desire to lead all to enlightenment, without regard for compensation.

In parallel with enumerating the qualifications of a teacher, Bu-ston also deals with the qualifications (and disqualifications) of a student. He quotes the *Vyākhyayukti* which says that 'arrogance, absence of desire to study, distraction, apathy and lassitude are the defects in a student'.[32] By way of contrast the good student is characterized as 'one who is sincere, desirous to study and intelligent'.[33] Bu-ston goes into great detail with regard to the various degrees of intelligence a student may have, the preparations for and results of study of the different subjects, and warns that mere intellectual appropriation of the doctrine without appropriate moral life is worthless.

Sri Lanka, Burma (Myanmar) and Thailand maintained in their great *vihāras* the traditions of Buddhist learning and the village temples were traditionally also institutions of learning, both religious and secular: Buddhists have been open to modern science, in which many have seen an affirmation of age-old Buddhist insights.

Buddhism, built on insight and understanding, requires and supports serious study and intellectual endeavour. It is essential to understand the Dhamma and to appropriate it intellectually in order properly to practise and promulgate it. This study resulted in some of the most sophisticated philosophical systems the world has seen, as will be shown.

THE WHEEL OF BECOMING

The Wheel of Becoming (*Bhāvacakra*) is one of the most popular and concise representations of the 'Chain of Dependent Co-origination' (*pratītya samutpāda*). It is found not only in Hīnayāna but also in Mahāyāna teaching and appears, with minor variations, on countless Tibetan *thaṅgkas* (painted scrolls or wall hangings). It represents the universe as seen through the eyes of the Enlightened One, seated on a lotus seat outside the world of becoming (see figure 4).

The whole world, represented by a large disc, is in the clutches of a black demon, representing all-devouring time (*kāla*) adorned with five skulls, symbolizing 'that which neither gods nor humans can give:

Figure 4 The Wheel of Becoming

freedom from old age, from sickness, from death, from decay and from rebirth. The three eyes symbolize impermanence, ill and not-self, under whose domain everything is placed.

The centre of the wheel is occupied by three animals that chase each other and make the wheel turn: a pig, representing *lobha* (greed), a peacock, representing *moha* (delusion), and a snake, representing *dveṣa* (anger, hatred). They are ultimately responsible for keeping the wheel of becoming in movement. Their death means liberation (*nirvāṇa*).

The rim adjacent to the centre depicts the series of rebirths: the dark half shows the downfall into ghostly existences from which liberation cannot be gained; the bright half shows the ascent into human existences, the presupposition for gaining liberation.

The next rim shows the six realms that are subject to the law of *karma*: the realm of the gods (*devas*), the demons (*asuras*), the ghosts (*pretas*), of denizens of hells, of animals and humans.

The outer rim, divided into twelve sections, illustrates the *pratītya samutpāda*, the most central of all Buddhist teachings, the essence of Buddha's enlightenment. The twelve sections are usually interpreted as covering three successive lifetimes: sections 1 and 2 refer to the previous life; 3 to 10 to the present life; 11 and 12 to the next life. Beginning in the lowest left-hand field, moving clockwise, the images are as follows:

1. man with a stick, representing ignorance (*avidyā)*;
2. potter with wheel and pots, representing *karma* formations (*saṃskāra*);
3. monkey, representing 'name-and-form' (*nāma rūpa*; individuality);
4. ship with passengers, representing the five mental aggregates (*skandhas*), namely form (*rūpa*), sensation (*vedanā*), perception (*samjñā*), volition (*saṃskāra*), consciousness (*vijñāna*);
5. empty house with windows, representing the body with the six senses (*ṣaḍāyatanāni*);
6. man and woman embracing, representing touch (*sparśa*);
7. man with an arrow in his eye, representing sensation (*vedanā*);
8. woman offering a drink to a man, representing craving (*tṛṣṇā*, thirst);
9. man gathering fruit from a tree, representing grasping (*upādāna*);
10. woman with child, representing becoming (*bhāva*);
11. woman in childbirth, representing (new) birth (*jāti)*;
12. old man carrying a corpse to funeral, representing old age and death (*jarā-maraṇa*).

THE *DHAMMAPADA* AS A COMPENDIUM OF THE *BUDDHA-DHAMMA*

The most popular book of the entire Pāli Canon is certainly the *Dhammapada*, 'The Path of the Law', an anthology of 423 sayings of the Buddha, culled from various sources and thematically arranged. Although it is largely restricted to offering ethical advice and deals less with the higher ranges of meditation and wisdom, many consider it the epitome of Buddhism as such. Even today, Buddhists frequently memorize it and quote freely from it. It is worth noting that it was not only appreciated by the Theravāda school, but also by followers of Mahāyāna schools. Thus there exist four Chinese translations, evidently from a Sanskrit original, and a Tibetan version, also apparently made from a Sanskrit version called *Udānavārga*. Fragments of versions in other Central Asian languages have also been found.[34]

Its popularity in ancient times is attested by the numerous commentaries that were written on it. The most famous is the one by an unidentified fifth- or sixth-century Buddhist scholar-monk of Sri Lanka, who reworked a mass of materials then existing in Sinhalese only and translated them into Pāli. This is a massive work compared to the text of the *Dhammapada* itself: while the translation of the text covers only about thirty pages, the translation of the commentary takes more than eight hundred! It also has a life of its own and often uses a stanza from the *Dhammapada* only as a peg for a story that is largely independent.

The Dhammapada

The *Dhammapada* is divided into twenty-six *vaggas* (chapters, cantos) with titles that do not always reveal much about the content. It begins with 'twin verses', or 'pairs'; so called because each verse is followed by a parallel verse that repeats the content of the first in a slightly modified form.

The first pair, the very opening of the *Dhammapada*, begins with the brief statement: *manopubbaṅgamā dhamma manoseṭṭhā manomayā*. There exist dozens of English translations, widely differing from each other and exhibiting widely different conceptions of the key term *mano* (mind).

The translation by N. K. Bhagwat, published by The Buddha Society Bombay (n.d.), reads thus:

> All our tendencies of character are the offspring of consciousness, dominated by consciousness, and made up of consciousness. If a man speaks or acts with a sullied consciousness, then suffering follows him, even as the wheel of the wagon follows the hoof of the bullock.
>
> All our tendencies of character are the offspring of consciousness, dominated by consciousness, and made up of consciousness. If a man speaks or acts with an unsullied consciousness, then happiness follows him ever, just as his shadow.[35]

By comparison, the most recent scholarly translation, by J. R. Carter and M. Palihawadana has:

> Preceded by perception are mental states, for them is perception supreme, from perception they have sprung. If with perception polluted, one speaks or acts, thence suffering follows as a wheel the draught ox's foot.
>
> Preceded by perception are mental states, for them is perception supreme. From perception they have sprung. If with tranquill perception, one speaks or acts, thence ease follows as a shadow that never departs.[36]

Compare with that Juan Mascaro's translation, as it appeared in the Penguin Classics series:

> What we are today comes from our thoughts of yesterday, and our present thoughts build our life of tomorrow: our life is the creation of our mind. If a man speaks or acts with an impure mind, suffering follows him as the wheel of the cart follows the beast that draws the cart.
>
> What we are today comes from our thoughts of yesterday, and our present thoughts build our life of tomorrow: our life is the creation of our mind. If a man speaks or acts with a pure mind, joy follows him as his own shadow.[37]

The next translation is by Sarvepalli Radhakrishnan, world-famous Indian philosopher and former president of the Indian Republic:

> (The mental) natures are the result of what we have thought, are chieftained by our thoughts, are made up of our thought. If a man speaks or acts with an evil thought, sorrow follows him (as a consequence) even as the wheel follows the foot of the drawer (i.e. the ox which draws the cart).
>
> (The mental) natures are the result of what we have thought, are chieftained by our thoughts, are made up of our thoughts. If a man speaks or acts with a pure thought, happiness follows him (in consequence) like a shadow that never leaves him.[38]

The simplest and clearest translation may be that by Max Müller, published in the Sacred Books of the East series:

> All that we are is the result of what we have thought: it is founded on our thoughts, it is made up of our thoughts. If a man speaks or acts with an evil thought, pain follows him, as the wheel follows the foot of the ox that draws the carriage.
>
> All that we are is the result of what we have thought: it is founded on our thoughts, it is made up of our thoughts. If a man speaks or acts with a pure thought, happiness follows him, like a shadow that never leaves him.[39]

The key term, which leads to so many different translations, is *mano/manas*. The Pāli Text Society dictionary[40] tells us that it 'represents the intellectual functioning of consciousness' and 'the rendering with "mind" covers most of the connotations; sometimes it may be translated as "thought"'.

Having illustrated the difficulty rendering key Pāli terms into idiomatic English, we can proceed with a summary of the *Dhammapada*, highlighting some of its sayings in the hope that the reader will pick up a copy of the *Dhammapada* and read it all. In the discussion that follows I largely rely on the Pāli text and my own translations, although I have consulted some of the many published translations.

The verses following the first pair are as famous and often quoted as the opening:

> 'He abused me, he beat me, he defeated me, he robbed me' – those who harbour such thoughts will never appease their anger/hatred.[41]
>
> 'He abused me, he beat me, he defeated me, he robbed me' – those who reject such thoughts will appease their anger/hatred.
>
> Never in this world can anger/hatred be appeased by anger/hatred; it will be appeased only by non-anger/non-hatred.

It was one of the endeavours of the Buddha to teach people to overcome hostile feelings and to find inner and outer peace. This requires not harping on past injuries but forgetting and the creation of sentiments that neutralize negative feelings. It is as dangerous to give in to anger and hatred as it is to yield to temptation and lust, to greed and grasping – the Buddha warns against these too and advises restraint and moderation.

The next section, entitled 'Wakefulness', begins with the verse: 'Wakefulness is the way to immortality; heedlessness is the way to death; those who are wakeful die not, the heedless are already dead.'

This is followed by *Citta-vagga*, the 'Mind Chapter'.[42] The human mind is described as fickle and crooked by nature, needing 'straightening out', restraining, educating.

In the 'Chapter on Flowers' a number of sayings are collected that refer to Buddha, the Dhamma and the Saṅgha in terms of gardens and blossoms. A chapter called 'The Fool' identifies various ways of being foolish, including that of a *bhikkhu* who aspires to fame and a high position in the order. Similarly under the caption 'The Wise' various praiseworthy attitudes and actions are mentioned.

An interesting statement occurs in the chapter 'The Holy One': 'He is supreme among men who is without belief and without duties and who has cut the knot of doubt. He has removed the conditions of desire.' 'Belief' and 'duties' imply dependence on someone else's intellect and will. The truly free person has found insight independently and has become his or her own source of understanding and action. That this does not mean amorality or arbitrariness is implied in the 'removal of the conditions of desire'. The 'cutting of the knot of doubt' also cuts through the dark recesses of the mind where desires, the root of all evil, reside.

In the 'Chapter of the Thousands' we read: 'It is better to live one day seeing the Law Supreme, than to live for a hundred years not seeing the Supreme Law.' The 'Law Supreme' is specified in the preceding verses as the life of meditation, the pursuit of knowledge, strong endeavour and contemplation of the origin and cessation of all component things as well as of the deathless state. This is the content of a meaningful life and makes life worthwhile, even if discovered only late in life. The very notion that we are under a 'Law', and that recognizing and following it is our 'being', our 'freedom', and our 'fulfilment' is something which may appear strange to many. It is diametrically opposed to the popular notion of freedom consisting of unlimited choice, pursuit of self-interest and the gratification of all impulses.

Other chapters have various sayings relating to sin, old age, happiness, wrath, hell and craving – they do not teach anything that would be new to the Buddhist, but offer precise and ready-to-use couplets on these central matters. One often-quoted verse is found in a chapter called *Atta-vagga*: 'Self is the Lord of self; what higher Lord could there be? When a man subdues well his self, he will have found a Lord very difficult to find otherwise.' And: 'The evil done by self, conceived by self, made possible by self, will crush the evildoer as a diamond crushes another diamond.'

There is no possibility of making 'the other' responsible for one's moral failings: it is the self that makes evil possible, executes it and reaps its rewards. This is an ultimate challenge to personal responsibility. 'Evil and liberation depend on oneself – no man can purify another.' For a tradition that supposedly teaches 'no-self' this is a strong assertion of individual responsibility. Obviously, *anattā* does not mean what outsiders make of it. What crushes and elates is not what others – society, history, circumstances – do to us but what we have done to ourselves. We are, in an ultimate sense, responsible for our lives and our fates.

In the *Buddha-vagga* we find what may be the shortest epitome of Buddhism: 'Abstain from all evil, do what is good, purify your thought – this is the teaching of all the Buddhas.' The chapter on happiness suggests that the highest happiness consists in finding *nibbāna*: 'Health is the greatest acquisition; contentment is the greatest wealth; confidence is the best of relations; and *nibbāna* is the highest happiness.'

The *Magga-vagga* tells us:

> Of all Paths, the Eightfold Path is the best; of Truths, the Four Noble Truths are the best; of all conditions, freedom from desire is the best; of men the One who Sees is the best . . . You yourself must exert yourselves; for the Tathāgatas are only signposts . . . 'Impermanent (*anicca*) are all component things', 'Involved in suffering (*dukkha*) are all component things', 'Unsubstantial (*anattā*) are all component things'. He who perceives this with insight becomes thereby immediately impervious to suffering.

Liberation is hard work at one's own character: nobody can do it for anyone else. It involves great insights, like seeing the impermanence of all things, and seemingly trifling matters like getting up early from bed and using one's time and talents properly. Also, one has to 'cut down the forest of lust, including its undergrowth', the tree of egotism, the false reliance on property and other people.

The *Taṅhā-vagga* advises: 'Renounce what lies in the future, give up what lies in the past, and surrendering the present, cross to the other shore. With a mind thus entirely freed you will no more fall into birth and death.' The Buddha suggests eliminating time from all one's considerations in order to be free, in order not to be reborn again. This too is in stark contrast to the attitude of many people today who wish to extend their earthly life indefinitely. What would the Buddha say to those who have their dead bodies preserved in liquid nitrogen so as to be able to be 'resurrected' if and when technology is sufficiently advanced to revive their old bodies?

The *Bhikkhu-vagga* defines the essence of a monk's life as self-control (*saṃvara*):

> To control the eye is good; to control the ear is good; to control the nose is good; to control the tongue is good; to control the body is good; to control speech is good; to control the mind is good; good is control on every side. A *bhikkhu* who is thus controlled on every side is freed from all suffering.

The very last section is called *Brāhmaṇa-vagga*: it describes brahmanhood, the highest social status in India, not in terms of lineage and birth, but in terms of ethical perfection:

> I call not a man a brahman because he is born of a brahman mother: he, who is without worldy belongings and free from attachment, him I call a brahman. Him I call a brahman, who has severed all fetters and is thus without cares; who has transcended all ties, and is totally unshackled ... Him I call a brahman, who is free from anger and faithfully keeps his observances; who follows the moral precepts and is without craving; who has subdued himself and who wears this body for the last time ... Him I call a brahman, from whom lust, ill-will, pride and envy have fallen off.

The Buddhist ideal is one of unflinching pursuit of what is considered the highest spirituality: freedom from craving, from ill-will, from delusion is valued much higher than material goods, so-called rights or any kind of self-assertion. It looks despicable to those for whom possessions, self-assertion and gratification of sense-desires are everything, but the Buddhist ideal may in the end win out: it is the witness to the eternal.

The Dhammapada *commentary*

While it was for some time assumed that the great Buddhaghosa, the most prolific of commentators of Pāli literature, had also composed the commentary to the *Dhammapada*, it is now certain that 'neither Buddhaghosa nor Dharmapala can be regarded as the author of the *Dhammapada Aṭṭhakathā*'.[43]

The commentary consists of two components: (1) a word-for-word paraphrase, explaining all elements of the text; and (2) a collection of (traditional) stories intended to elucidate the moral of each verse. The first of these is of little interest to the general reader. It is very helpful to the serious student and the translator of the texts, but not very exciting to read. The second constitutes by far the largest portion and often has only a tenuous connection with the first. While quoting extensively from most books of the Pāli Canon, it is most closely related to the *Jātakas*, from which it draws much inspiration and material.

Most of the stories are concerned with informing the listener about the fruits of past deeds and rebirths. Many of these tales are quite humorous: they describe the absurd consequences of miserliness, pride and drunkenness. Other stories deal with the lives of well-known Buddhist saints and with ghosts and spirits. The main point of all of them, like that of the *Jātakas*, is to dissuade the hearers from committing sins and to motivate them to perform good deeds. A few examples are offered as an invitation to read the collection, or at least some of the stories, in its entirety.

After quoting the first verse of the *Dhammapada* ('All that we are is the result of what we have thought', etc.) the commentator tells a story of events that are supposed to have happened at Sāvatthi during the lifetime of the Buddha. The narrative is very circumstantial and takes a long time to come to the point. Mahā Pāla, the son of Mahā Suvaṇṇa, a rich householder in Sāvatthi, and the brother of Culla Pāla, after listening to the Buddha, becomes a monk at an advanced age. While practising meditation, as instructed by the Buddha, his eyesight gets worse and worse; no medicine is of any avail. He achieves *arahattā* but becomes completely blind. Having succeeded, after many adventures, in getting to the place where the Buddha resides, one day, after heavy rain, he takes a walk and tramples many insects underfoot. Other *bhikkhus* report him to the Buddha. The Buddha excuses him and says that he had not committed an offence, because he was blind and neither saw the insects nor intended to harm them.

When asked why Mahā Pāla, although destined for *arahattā*, had become blind, the Buddha tells them a story: a long, long time ago a wandering physician had been approached for help by a woman whose eyesight was failing. He offered to treat her and asked what she would give him in return. The woman promised to make herself, her son and her daughter his slaves. The physician gave her an ointment. With a single application she regained her eyesight.

She then regretted having made her earlier promise to the physician, and when he came to collect his reward, she complained that her eyes had become worse, not better. The physician, recognizing the deception, prepared another ointment for her. Applying it to her eyes, the woman turned totally blind. The physician, the Buddha tells us, was Mahā Pāla, in a previous life. The law of *karma* demanded that he atone for his crime by suffering blindness himself.

Within the main story there are many digressions which allow a teacher to add moral instructions on matters not directly related to the central issue. Thus we are told that when Mahā Pāla, after having become blind, wanted to meet the Buddha he sent for his brother Culla Pāla to accompany him. Culla Pāla sent a novice, who, by holding the tip of Mahā Pāla's staff, guided him along. Once, close to a village, they heard a woman singing while gathering firewood, and the novice fell in love with her. This is an occasion to quote a Buddha-saying: 'Bhikkhus, I know of no other sound which so completely takes possession of the heart of a man as this, namely the voice of a woman.'[44]

The novice asks the blind monk to wait for a moment. 'The elder thought to himself: "Just now I heard the sound of someone singing, and it was none other than a woman's voice. The novice tarries; he must have violated the law of chastity."'[45] After being questioned by the elder, the novice admits to his failing, and the elder refuses to continue being led by him. The young man takes off his robes and tells the elder that he has become a layman again, so they may set forth. The elder replies: 'An evildoer is an evildoer, be he layman or novice' and refuses to accept his services. He would rather face the risk of being attacked by wild beasts and robbers than continue in the company of the sinner. In the end Indra, the king of the gods, moved by the power of Mahā Pāla's virtue, adopts an appropriate disguise and accompanies the elder into the presence of the Buddha.

Another story that has the ring of historical truth is offered to illustrate a couplet from the last section, the *Brāhmaṇa-vagga*, which says: 'Him I call a brahman, who is free from anger . . .' The elder Sāriputta, making the alms round with five hundred *bhikkhus*, comes to the door of his mother's house. She invites him in, lets him have a seat and gives him food. Then she starts abusing him: 'You leftovers eater! If you don't get leftovers of rice gruel at home, you go from house to house to strangers and lick the back of the ladle with which rice gruel has been stirred. And for this you renounced a vast inheritance and became a monk!' She also feeds his entourage, but scolds them likewise: 'Eat, you scoundrels, who have made my son your own page-boy!'[46]

Sāriputta takes the food and without saying a word, returns to the monastery. The Buddha, questioning Rāhula about his alms round, learns what has happened. The other monks approvingly tell each other about the incident. The Buddha, to conclude the story, then utters the couplet: 'Him I call a brahman, who is free from anger . . .'

Conclusion

There is a great similarity between the *Dhammapada* commentary and the *Jātakas*, the tales about Buddha's previous births. Likewise, a great similarity exists between the *Dhammapada* and some other books of the Pāli Canon such as the *Udāna* (Uplifting Verses) and *Itivuttaka* (Thus it was said). The *Udāna* prefaces each of its moral sayings with a story, similar to those in the commentary to the *Dhammapada*. The *Itivuttaka* consists of brief sermons by the Buddha which are then summarized in verse form. They are arranged in ones, twos, threes and fours, referring to the number of objects mentioned in each. In the first section, for instance, the Buddha teaches *sīla-kosalla* (S: *sila kausalya*), 'the diligence in virtuous deeds', as 'the one thing which practised brings gain in this world and the next'; in the second he teaches, amongst other things, 'two conditions of *nibbāna*', namely 'that with basis remaining and that without basis'; in the third section he teaches that there are 'three profitable ways of thinking', namely thinking about renunciation, goodwill and harmlessness, which 'are conducive for *nibbāna*'; in the fourth section he mentions 'four grounds for the arising of craving in a monk', namely 'craving for alms-food, for lodging, for success, for failure' and concludes with the verse: 'Freed from craving let the monk, ungrasping, mindful wander forth.'[47]

KING MILINDA'S QUESTIONS

Among the post-canonical Pāli works the *Milindapañha*[48] stands out as an early and greatly respected summary of Buddhist teachings.[49] It purports to record questions (P: *pañha*) of King Milinda (supposedly a Bactrian King Menander who ruled in the middle of the second century BCE in north-west India) addressed to Nāgasena, a learned Buddhist *bhikkhu*, of whom nothing else is known to us. The questions reflect the problems which a newcomer to Buddhism would typically have, and the answers are often given with the help of homely images and down to earth explanations to which everybody can relate.

The question–answer part proper is preceded by a lengthy introduction[50] that familiarizes the reader with the background of both the protagonists. It leads us back to the time of the Buddha Kassapa, who had lived thousands of years before Gotama. Both Milinda and Nāgasena had then been members of the Saṅgha: Milinda as a novice, Nāgasena as his preceptor. Nāgasena had punished Milinda with a broomstick for disobeying an order to remove a dust heap. Both, however, individually utter wishes for their future which are going to come true.

Gotama the Buddha is described as seeing them before his mental eye, prophesying that they would reappear five hundred years after his passing away and explain the Dhamma through questions and similes. When the former novice was reborn as King Milinda, he proved to be a learned, wise and just ruler, accomplished in all arts and sciences, very fond of debate and always on the lookout for a discussion partner. His questions were so incisive and subtle that he silenced all the well-known scholars of his day. Nobody could answer him and he made the *bhikkhus* insecure by his probing, 'heretical' questions.

The situation became so serious that the gods in heaven became involved: the king of the gods, Sakka, approached Mahāsena, who had a reputation for scholarship and learning, and tried to persuade him to go back to earth. After refusing at first, and declaring that he had no inclination to go back to the world of humans with all its vexations, he finally agreed and was reborn in a pious and learned brahman family.

It was to this family that a Buddhist monk by the name of Rohana was sent as a penance[51] to beg his food. For seven years he was refused not only food but even a greeting. He graciously bore this humiliation and when once asked to look for food at the neighbour's house (which was the customary way of declining a monk's request), he announced this event as a great gift. The brahman, astounded and surprised, recognized the great virtue of the *bhikkhu* and henceforth offered him daily food.

Meanwhile the brahman's little boy, the reincarnated Mahāsena, had reached the age of 7: the time when schooling traditionally began. In no time he had mastered the Vedas and the Vedāṅgas, but reviewing what he had learnt 'he found no value in it anywhere at all. And he exclaimed in bitterness of soul: "Empty, indeed, are these Vedas, like chaff. There is in them neither reality, nor worth, nor truth."'[52]

Rohana witnessed this in his mind and approached the unhappy boy. At the sight of Rohana he gladdened and began enquiring about the life of a *bhikkhu*. He so much liked what he heard that he asked his parents for permission to join the order, accepting the name Nāgasena. Very soon he had mastered the *Abhidhamma*, the most abstract and difficult portion of the Pāli Canon. At the age of 20 he received the higher ordination and became a full member of the Saṅgha. He became well known for his grasp of the Dhamma and his facility of expression.

He often heard about King Milinda 'who harrassed the brethren by putting puzzles to them of a heretical tendency'.[53] He fearlessly offered to meet him and solve all the puzzles. After studying with some other learned monks and achieving arahantship, he was ready to face the heretical-sounding monarch. Milinda, meanwhile, bored by the lack of suitable discussion partners ('All India is an empty thing, it truly is like chaff. There is no one capable of discussing with me and dispelling my doubts') had heard about Nāgasena and his great reputation, and resolved to meet him. Thus begins the discussion portion of the *Milindapañha*.

Even before Nāgasena could demonstrate his learning and astuteness in answering King Milinda's questions, he had a tremendous reputation in his own circles: he was the head of a body of disciples, the teacher of a school, famous and highly esteemed by the people. He was learned, wise and able; a skilful expounder, of subdued manners, full of courage, well versed in tradition, master of the three *Piṭakas* and erudite in Vedic lore. He also was in possession of the highest insight. A skilled debater and an eloquent preacher, he had the reputation of being 'a confounder of the followers of other masters, and a crusher of the adherents of rival doctrines'.[54]

This Nāgasena, seated amidst five hundred *bhikkhus*, is now facing the king, who has arrived with a retinue of five hundred. At his sight the king is overcome by feelings of fear and anxiety; he feels like 'a snake caught in a basket, or a fish in a net, like a man who has lost his way in a dense forest haunted by wild beasts'.[55]

The Questions

THE CHARIOT SIMILE

The first meeting between King Milinda and Bhikkhu Nāgasena, prepared with due pomp and circumstance at the capital city Sāgala, raises an important issue even at the stage of the initial mutual introductions. The king, politely enquiring about Nāgasena's name, is given his first lesson in the Buddhist doctrine of *anattā*. Nāgasena replies to Milinda's question by saying: 'I am known as Nāgasena, and it is by that name that my brethren in the faith address me. But although parents give such a name as Nāgasena, this is only a designation used: for there is no permanent individuality (*puggala*) involved.'[56]

The king shows himself truly amazed at this denial of individuality and retorts with a practical counter-argument:

> Who, then, is it who gives you monks your robes, your food, your lodging and what you need? To whom is it given, and who devotes himself to a life of righteousness and meditation? Who wins arahantship and who commits a sin, by destroying life? If what you say were true, a man would not commit a murder by taking someone else's life and there would be no teachers in the Saṅgha and the ordinations would be void.[57]

The king just cannot understand how somebody sitting in front of him can deny the existence of the personality ascribed to him. If the name Nāgasena does not denote a person, what does it denote? Nāgasena's hair? His nails, teeth, his kidneys, his heart, his brain or any other part of his body? Nāgasena denies all that. He also denies that his outward form, his sensations, his ideas or his consciousness are denoted by the name Nāgasena.

By now, Milinda sounds rather frustrated: 'Then I can detect no Nāgasena; Nāgasena is a mere sound. Who is it, whom I see before me?' And he accuses him of having uttered an untruth rather than a word of wisdom.

Instead of giving an answer to the king's questions, Nāgasena begins questioning the king in his turn. He innocently asks how the king had come to the meeting place, whether on foot or in a chariot. Almost offended, Milinda answers that, of course, he had come in a chariot, as befits a king. Now Nāgasena goes into details: what is the chariot? Is it the pole, the axle, the wheels, the framework, the ropes, the spokes of the wheel? The king has to say no to all these questions. If, Nāgasena concludes, neither all the parts nor anything outside the parts are the chariot, the chariot does not exist, it is a mere word. And he accuses the king of having spoken an untruth by asserting that he had come in a chariot that did not exist.

While the king's entourage applauds the cleverness of Nāgasena, Milinda himself tries to extricate himself from this situation by stating that the composite of all the things mentioned by Nāgasena is commonly understood as a 'chariot' – and that is what he came in. Nāgasena approves of the king's grasp of the matter: the same, he says, applies to the term 'individuality'. It is a conventional designation for the aggregate of components mentioned in connection with a name.

To give the conclusion the appropriate form and authority, Nāgasena quotes a canonical statement made by 'our Sister Vajirā in the presence of the Blessed One: "Just as it is by the condition precedent of the co-existence of its various parts that the word 'chariot' is used, so it is, that when the *khandhas* are there, we talk of a "living being."' The king sees the point and congratulates Nāgasena: 'Were the Buddha himself here, he would approve your answer.'[58]

WHY DOES ONE BECOME A MONK?

Before entering into another round of discussion on similar matters Nāgasena wishes the king to clarify a question of procedure: would the king debate with Nāgasena as a scholar or as a king? If the former, Nāgasena was ready for it; if the latter, Nāgasena would decline.

The king wants to hear from Nāgasena the difference between a scholarly and a royal debate. Nāgasena enlightens him: when pandits (traditional scholars) talk over a matter with one another, there is the development of an argument in which eventually one of them admits having been wrong and acknowledges it; assertions are made as well as counter-assertions, and nobody is angered by this process of to and fro. When a king discusses a matter and somebody argues against him, he is apt to have the opponent fined and punished. The king agrees to discuss like a pandit.

This discussion is to be held in the king's palace and Nāgasena is invited to bring as many companions with him as he wishes. He arrives with his entire entourage and all are given a meal and robes. The meal finished, the king asks Nāgasena to stay on with only ten of his brethren and to talk with him, seated on the same level as the *bhikkhus*, about no less a matter than truth.

The king wants to know about the objective of the *bhikkhus*' 'going forth' (*pabbajā*) and their 'ultimate goal' (*paramattha*). Nāgasena answers: 'Our going forth is for the ending of *dukkha*, and our ultimate aim is *parinibbāna*.'[59] When questioned, Nāgasena admits that not all members of the Saṅgha have joined for such high reasons: 'Some have left the world in terror of the tyranny of kings. Some have joined us in order to be safe from robbers, some harassed by debt, some to gain a livelihood.' Questioned about his own motives, Nāgasena tells the king:

> I was received into the Order when I was a mere boy. I then did not know about the ultimate aim. I thought that these Buddhist monks were wise scholars who would be able to teach me something. I have been taught by them and now I both know and understand the reason for and the advantage of the going forth.[60]

The king enquires about each of the 'five good qualities' that bring about the transformation of the *bhikkhu*: good conduct (*sīla*), faith (*saddhā*), perseverance (*viriya*), mindfulness (*sati*) and concentration (*samādhi*). Nāgasena gives fairly exhaustive lectures on these subjects, illustrated by comparisons and similes relating to the king's sphere of experience.

Faith, Nāgasena says, has the effect of calming and aspiring. Faith makes the heart calm and clear, freeing it from hindrances (to inner freedom) such as lust, malice, sloth, pride and doubt. It can, in this capacity, be compared to a water-clearing gem that a royal servant immerses in water that has been muddied by the crossing of an army, so as to make it fit for the king to drink. 'The water is the heart; the royal servants are the recluse; the mud, the sand, the particles of plants are the evil dispositions; and the water-clearing gem is faith.' It can further be compared to a guide who is capable of leading to higher ground people who have been marooned by a flood, on account of his knowledge of the terrain. 'This is the kind of way in which the *bhikkhu* by faith aspires to leap, as it were by a bound, into higher things.'[61]

He explains the other five qualities in similar ways, to the king's satisfaction. When the king, at the end, wonders, how these very different qualities can bring about one and the same result, Nāgasena replies they do so because they all put an end to evil dispositions. 'They are like the various parts of an army – elephants, cavalry, war chariots, archers – who all work towards one end, namely to conquer the opposing army in combat.'

WAS THE BUDDHA REALLY ENLIGHTENED?

Somewhere during the course of the discussions the king converts to Buddhism and choses Nāgasena as his *kalyāṇa mitta*, his spiritual guide. He practises the remembrance of the Buddha, does penance and takes the eightfold vow. No longer does he demand that Nāgasena come to him to discuss matters that interest him; he himself now approaches Nāgasena 'with downcast eyes and measured words, gentle in manner, collected in thought, glad and pleased and rejoicing in heart'.[62] He has faith in the Buddha but he also has his doubts: doubts concerning the Buddha's omniscience, supposed to be part and parcel of his enlightenment – and 'there are apparent contradictions in the word of the Conqueror'.[63]

Nāgasena, after affirming that the king possesses the ten virtues required of a good Buddhist lay disciple, encourages him to come forward with his questions.

The first question concerns the honours paid to the Buddha, apparently a point of debate between Buddhists and their opponents. Here is the dilemma: if the Buddha still accepts honours and gifts, he must somehow still be in connection with this world and cannot have entirely passed away. If he has entirely passed away, he cannot accept honours and gifts and Buddhists who continue providing these are doing something foolish and pointless.

Not so, says Nāgasena. The Buddha is entirely set free, and he does not accept any gifts. If people put up a building to house his relics they benefit themselves, not the Buddha, and acquire merit that results in either a human rebirth, a rebirth in heaven or arahantship. 'Acts done to the Tathāgatha, who has passed away and neither accepts nor rejects them, are not empty and vain but are of value and bear fruit.'[64]

Nāgasena, as usual, illustrates his teachings with striking similes, comparing the coming and going of the Buddha with that of a mighty fire, a great wind or a huge sound: these come and go, not affected by smaller fires, by lighter winds or the ordinary sounds which people may make.

The second dilemma concerns the omniscience of the Buddha: the Buddha, according to tradition, had to reflect in order to understand certain things. Milinda, probably echoing anti-Buddhist opinions, concludes: 'The Buddha cannot have been omniscient, if his all-embracing knowledge was reached through investigation.'

Before answering the question directly, Nāgasena provides an excursus on the seven classes of mind and their ways of understanding. The epistemology that is offered is closely tied to the spiritual condition of each person: the lowest, slowest kind of thinkers are the unconverted, uncontrolled. The second class are the converted, who are beginning their life as Buddhists. The third class are those who have reduced their lust, ill-will and delusion to a minimum: they are agile thinkers on the lower level, not, however, on the higher level. Above them are those who have come to the point of no return; they still 'act slowly' in the higher regions. The next are the *arahants* and the *pacceka-buddhas*, each more perfect than the other. The highest class are the 'complete Buddhas' who possess all knowledge and 'whose thinking powers are on every point brought quickly into play'.

A homely simile helps to explain the point: imagine a fruit tree, laden with ripe fruit, but none of it yet fallen from the tree. With little effort, one could obtain as many fruits as one wanted. Certainly such a tree would not be considered 'barren'. Thus, 'though reflection is a necessary condition of the knowledge of the Tathāgatha, yet on reflection he perceives whatever he wants to know'.[65]

A dilemma that must have vexed the Saṅgha was how to reconcile the Buddha's presumed omniscience and compassion with his admitting Devadatta, who was to bring about a schism in the order, and thereby earn for himself hellish punishments for untold ages. Nāgasena asserts that the Buddha knew, when admitting Devadatta, that he would cause a schism; but by becoming a *bhikkhu* Devadatta reduced the evil *karma* that otherwise would have led him into even longer and greater torments.

Milinda retorts:

> The Buddha first wounds a man and then pours oil on the wound, first throws a man down a precipice and then reaches out to him an assisting hand, first kills him and then seeks to give him life, first gives pain and then adds a subsequent joy to the pain he gave.

Nāgasena agrees – but qualifies the king's version:

> The Tathāgatha wounds people but to their good, he casts people down but to their profit, he kills people, but to their advantage. Just as mothers and fathers hurt their children and even knock them down, thinking the while of their good, so by whatsoever method an increase in the virtue of living things can be brought about, by that method does he contribute to their good.[66]

In the case of Devadatta the Buddha foresaw that if Devadatta had not entered the Order he would have accumulated as a layman much worse *karma* than that he earned through his sin of splitting the Saṅgha. 'It was at the thought that by renouncing the world according to his doctrine Devadatta's sorrows would become finite that, in his mercy, the Buddha adopted that means of making his heavy sorrow light.' In addition, at the hour of his death Devadatta took refuge in the Buddha for the rest of his rebirths. The merit from this act will result in his becoming a *pacceka-buddha* under the name of Aṭṭhissara at the end of this *kalpa* (world-age, aeon). The Buddha is the skilled physician who, in order to prevent worse, uses scalpel and caustic substances to treat fatal wounds.

THE END OF THE TRUE DHAMMA

Milinda contrasts two Buddha-words that appear to contradict each other. In the one the Buddha says that the true law (*saddhamma*) will last five hundred years. In the other he declares that the world will never be bereft of *arahants*. One of these statements has to be false, if the other is true. Nāgasena attests the authenticity of both Buddha-words. But – while the Buddha made the first statement in connection with the admission of women to the Order, declaring a diminishing of its duration, a reduction, as it were, of the reservoir of the *saddhamma* – he did not foretell a disappearance of the true law. The continued good deeds of the children of the Buddha will keep the now reduced reservoir brimming over with the fresh cool water of the practice of virtue and morality.

DID THE BODHISATTVA VIOLATE THE DHAMMA?

The *Milindapañha* accepts *Jātaka* stories as true in the same sense as the other accounts concerning the Buddha in earlier parts of the Pāli Canon. King Milinda points out a number of discrepancies between the actions of the *bodhisattvas* and the Buddha's teaching. The answers which Nāgasena gives, not denying either the comparability or the reliability of the *Jātaka* stories, are most interesting.

A traditional saying attributed to the Buddha states that even as a *bodhisattva* he did not inflict pain on living beings. On the other hand one of the *Jātakas* tells us that when the Bodhisattva was born as the Ṛṣi Lomasa Kassapa he had hundreds of living beings slain, offering the blood of many animals as a 'Drink of Triumph'.

Nāgasena, again, does not question the authenticity of both sayings – apparently it had become very important by that time to accept the canon as a whole as authoritative and then to attempt to reconcile apparently contradictory statements. Nāgasena excuses the Bodhisattva by saying that what Ṛṣi Lomasa Kassapa did was an act of madness committed when he had insanely fallen in love with Princess Candavatī.

And an 'evil act, done by one out of his mind, is even in the present world not considered a grievous offence, nor is it so with respect of the fruit that it brings about in a future life'.[67]

The king agrees that contemporary practice did not even provide punishment for an insane man who committed murder: he would be beaten and set free. Analogously, the deed of Ṛṣi Lomasa Kassapa did not result in a sin, but his subsequent return to the life of renunciation earned for him a rebirth in Brahmaloka.

A great variety of additional dilemmas are placed by Milinda before Nāgasena, who unfailingly has an answer to all of them. The questions apppear to reflect the doubts which ordinary people entertained with regard to the Buddha and his Dhamma; the answers show centuries of scholastic reflection and sophistication. The satisfaction shown by Milinda after receiving Nāgasena's answers seems to be a sign of broad acceptance of the solution to those often quite serious objections to certain Buddhist teachings.

Even at that time, a few centuries after his life, the question was raised as to whether the Buddha had ever really lived. Nobody among those present had seen him; nor had their teachers. Who can prove that the Buddha, to whom these teachings are ascribed, ever lived? Nāgasena's 'proof' is the only one possible: in the same way in which the hereditary insignia legitimate King Milinda's rule, although neither he nor his immediate ancestors had seen the founder of the dynasty, so the Buddha's 'royal insignia' are still around as a testimony to his life. The Noble Eightfold Path, his teaching of mindfulness and the life of the Saṅgha testify to his existence.

A telling simile is employed to illustrate this: the City of Righteousness (*dhamma nāgara*). As a well-built and well-maintained city testifies to the existence and talent of the architect and master-builder who conceived and built it, so the Buddha's Dhamma City is testimony to the Buddha's existence and deep intelligence.

> The Blessed One's *dhamma nāgara* has righteousness for its rampart and fear of sin for its moat, knowledge for its battlements over its city gate and zeal for the watchtower; it has faith for the base of its pillars and mindfulness for a watchman at the gates. It has the *suttāntas* for a marketplace and the *Abhidhamma* for its crossroads, the *Vinaya* for its court building and constant self-control as its main street.

It has a great many bazaars as well: a flower bazaaar and a fruit bazaar, a medicine bazaar and a nectar bazaar, a bazaar for gems and for all kinds of goods.[68]

The blooms in the flower bazaar, Nāgasena explains, are the subjects for meditation made known by the Buddha: the idea of impermanence and insubstantiality of everything, the idea of impurity and of danger connected with the body, the idea of freedom from passion and of the transience of all things, and so on.

The perfume bazaar offers a great variety of virtues, the fruit bazaar displays attainments like *arahattā*, and so on. A verse at the end sums it all up:

> Long life, good health, beauty, rebirth in heaven,
> High birth, *nibbāna* – all are found for sale –
> There to be bought for *kamma*, great or small –
> In the great Conqueror's world-famed bazaar.
> Come; show your faith, o brethren, as the price,
> Buy and enjoy such goods as you prefer.[69]

The *dhamma nāgara* simile allows the author to lay out the whole of Buddhist doctrine – the most convincing proof of Buddha's existence.

THE *ARAHANT* AS UNIVERSAL BEING

In the last section of the *Milindapañha*, King Milinda asks about the qualities which a *bhikkhu* needs in order to become an *arahant*. Nāgasena marshalls the whole of nature and tells the king that he needs the virtues and qualities found in animals and plants, in the elements and in the planets, in all kinds of people and of all kinds of things in order to be a true *arahant*, a 'complete being'.

Everything a *bhikkhu* sees should become for him a lesson to be learned: the cock's constant scratching and searching for food should remind the *bhikkhu* continually to examine himself, the panther's preference for lonely places should tell the *bhikkhu* to look for solitude, the *sal* tree's deep root-system should instruct the *bhikkhu* about the need to lay deep foundations for his meditation effort; when he sees a ship he should remind himself of his duty to ferry many people across the ocean of *saṃsāra*. There is quite literally no end to this learning, and the author is wonderfully inventive in pointing out in everything the qualities that a Buddhist *bhikkhu* needs to reach the perfection of *arahattā*.

As for Milinda, he is filled with joy of heart after listening to everything that Nāgasena has to teach. He ceases to have any doubts, and asks Nāgasena to accept him as a supporter of the faith, a true convert. Eventually he hands over the rule of his kingdom to his son and becomes a *bhikkhu* himself, attaining *arahattā* in this life.

NOTES

1. The most extensive such critique is to be found in E. Lamotte, *Histoire du Bouddhisme Indien* (Louvain 1958), now also available in an English translation (see bibliography).
2. The account in Bu-ston Rimpoche's famous *History of Buddhism* is quite different in many details and much more circumstantial. Since he is a Mahāyānist, he emphasizes the importance of the later councils (not recognized by Theravādins).
3. The traditional report is found in the *Mahāvaṃsa* and the *Cullavaṃsa*.
4. There is a curious incident reported in connection with the First Council. Only 499 *arahants* could be found. Ānanda, the closest associate of the Buddha, had not yet found *arahattā* but was deemed close to it. So he was sent away for a short retreat during which he achieved *arahattā*. In all likelihood there was a party which wanted to exclude Ánanda from the council but given his standing in the community, he had to be included after some arguing.
5. The traditional account is found in the *Cullavaṃsa*.
6. This was no longer an 'ecumenical council' but an assembly of the Sthaviravādins or the Vibhajjavādins only.
7. For the content of the Pāli Canon see appendix 1.
8. Pāli originally meant 'line', i.e. the line that separated an original text from the commentary that was written underneath. The text would be called *Pāli-bhāṣa*, a designation that was later used to name the language in which it was written. Pāli is one of the Middle Indian languages, close to Māgadhī, the language in which the Buddha is believed to have taught. It was one of the Buddha's innovations, and one of the reasons for his great popular success, to use the vernacular for his teaching instead of Sanskrit, which only the educated could have understood.
9. There is no account of this council in the Pāli sources.
10. For details see B. Jinananda, 'Four Buddhist Councils'.
11. For a full treatment of Olcott's role in reviving Buddhism and his activities as president of the Theosophical Society see Prothero, *The White Buddhist*.
12. Norman, 'Pāli Studies in the West' mentions that 'the first Westerner to study Pāli was a French missionary named Laneau, who in a report dated 1680 is said to have studied Pāli in 1672 and to have written a Grammar and a Dictionary of Pāli'. Both are lost.
13. For a list of text editions and translations published by the Pāli Text Society see appendix 2.

14. For more about the work of the Pāli Text Society see 'Pāli Studies in the West' by K. R. Norman, its then president.
15. See Gross, *Buddhism After Patriarchy*, pp. 130ff.
16. That there was a gender issue in some Buddhist circles is made clear by the widespread (but not universal) conviction that the Buddha could only appear as a male and that a female *bodhisattva* would undergo a change of body before becoming a Buddha. On the other hand, in Mahāyāna Buddhism there is not only acceptance of a number of female *bodhisattvas* as teachers of the true Dharma, but the grammatical gender of Prajñā-pāramitā (Perfection of Wisdom) is also taken as an expression of the female nature of the 'Mother of all Buddhas'. Several important Mahāyāna texts are ascribed to female *bodhisattvas* and there is recognition of the irrelevance of gender in questions concerning the true Dharma.
17. Gross, *Buddhism After Patriarchy*, pp. 207ff.
18. Conze, preface to the US edition of *Perfection of Wisdom in Eight Thousand Lines*, p. xix.
19. Vasubandhu in the *Abhidharma-kośa-bhāṣya* (ch. IX) offers this telling dialogue: Q: 'Is there any liberation outside of *Buddha-dharma*?' A: 'No, there is not.' Q: 'What is the reason for this?' A: 'Because other doctrines are corrupted by a false conception of the soul.'
20. Gross, *Buddhism After Patriarchy*, p. 288.
21. Ibid.
22. The *Abhidharma-kośa* has a revealing comment on the designation *āryasatya* for the Buddha's teaching: 'what the *āryas* call happy (i.e. *nirvāna*), others call painful; what others call happy, the *āryas* call painful' I, 6, 2.
23. The Pāli text says: *anujanāmi upajjhāyam* and could be translated 'I allow a preceptor' or 'I prescribe or advise a preceptor'. For the sake of the integrity of I. B. Horner's translation I have left it unchanged.
24. *Mahāvagga*, I, 25 trans. I. B. Horner in *The Book of the Discipline*, SBB, vol. IV (*Mahāvagga*), pp. 58f.
25. For details see Dutt, 'Buddhist Education', p. 161. A large amount of relevant information is also given in the article 'Education, Buddhist', by H. W. P. Guruge, in the *Encyclopedia of Buddhism*, vol. V. fasc. 1 (1990), 22a–35b.
26. According to Professor Liang Chi-chao the names of 162 such scholar-pilgrims from China are known; the reports of three of them, Fa-Hien (405–411 CE), Yuan Chwang (629–646 CE) and I-Tsing (671–695 CE) have been translated into English. See Beal, *Si-Yu-Ki*.
27. Also known as Yuan Chwang, born in 602 in Lo-Yang, northern China. Following the example of his elder brother he became a Buddhist monk and soon excelled in debates. Disquieted by the different teachings of the many schools of Buddhism, he desired to go to the sources and visit India. The emperor denied him permission to go but he left nevertheless in 628 CE. After a perilous journey of several years through deserts and over mountain passes he reached India. He kept a diary and described all the places he visited. He spent about fifteen months (636–7) in Nālandā,

studying Yogācāra with the famous Śīlabhadra, who at that time was the president of Nālandā. Hiuen Tsang had apparently built up a great reputation by then and he was royally treated at Nālandā. His long stay in Nālandā and his careful reporting make his account a very valuable source both for the history of Nālandā and its operation in the mid-seventh century. After further travels in India he returned to China in 645 and was received with great honour. He refused an appointment as minister and preferred to remain a teacher of Buddhism. He died, highly respected in 664 CE.

28. Born in 635 CE I-Tsing was admitted to the Buddhist order at the age of 14. A few years later he wanted to travel to India like Hiuen Tsang, but did not get an opportunity till 671 CE. He spent twenty-five years travelling through thirty countries, returned to China in 695 and died around 710 CE. He spent ten years at Nālandā, after his return translating many manuscripts which he had taken back to China with him.
29. Obermiller, *History of Buddhism by Bu-ston*, p. 9.
30. Ibid. p. 11.
31. Ibid. p. 64.
32. Ibid. p. 78.
33. Ibid. p. 80.
34. For more details see *Dhammapada Aṭṭhakathā*, trans. E. W. Burlingame, *Buddhist Legends*, vol. I, pp. 25f. J.R. Carter and M. Palihawadana (trans.), in *The Dhammapada* (Oxford: Oxford University Press, 1987), p. 3 also mention a *Gandhāri Dharmapāda* in Prakrit and the *Patna Dharmapāda*, 'which is in a language close to Pāli'.
35. N. K. Bhagwat (trans.), *The Dhammapada* (Bombay: The Buddha Text Society, n.d.), p. 1.
36. Carter and Palihawadana, *The Dhammapada*, p. 13.
37. J. Mascaro (trans.), *The Dhammapada: The Path to Perfection* (Harmondsworth: Penguin, 1973), p. 35.
38. S. Radhakrishnan (trans.) *The Dhammapada* (Oxford: Oxford University Press, 1954), p. 1.
39. SBE, vol. X (Oxford: Oxford University Press, 1881), p. 3.
40. *Pāli–English Dictionary*, p. 520.
41. The Pāli word *vera* means both anger and hatred.
42. The Pāli dictionary tells us that *citta* is 'the subjective part of consciousness'.
43. Carter and Palihawadana, *The Dhammapada*, p. 418, n. 1.
44. *Aṅguttara Nikāya* I, 1.
45. *Dhammapada Aṭṭhakathā*, trans. Burlingame, vol. I, p. 155.
46. Ibid. vol. III, p. 289.
47. *Itivuttaka* IV, 4.
48. Pāli text in Devanāgarī published by Swami Dwarikadass Sastri, vol. XIII in the Bauddha Bhāratī Series (Varanasi: Bauddha Bharati, 1979); English translation by T. W. Rhys Davids, SBE, vols. XXV and XXVI (1890). All page references in the text are to this translation. The wording of the translation has sometimes been slightly modified.

49. T. W. Rhys Davids thinks that the *Milindapañha* is not only an important Buddhist document but 'undoubtedly the master-piece of Indian prose and indeed the best book in its class, from a literary point of view, that had then been produced in any country' (SBE, vol. XXV, introduction, p. xlviii).
50. Called *Bāhira-kathā*, 'Outside narrative'.
51. Rohana was so absorbed in meditation at the time when the other *bhikkhus* went to appeal to Sakra that he missed joining them. The leader of the *bhikkhus* reproached him by saying: 'When the religion of the Buddha is in danger of crumbling away, have you no eyes for the work of the Order?' (14). For his inadvertence the penance described is imposed upon him.
52. *Milindapañha* I, 18.
53. Ibid. 23.
54. Ibid. 35.
55. Ibid. 38.
56. Ibid. 40.
57. Ibid. 41f.
58. Ibid. 45.
59. Ibid. 49.
60. Ibid. 50.
61. Ibid. 56.
62. Ibid. 138.
63. Ibid. 143.
64. Ibid. 147.
65. Ibid. 162.
66. Ibid. 164f.
67. Ibid. II, 19.
68. Ibid. 212.
69. Ibid. 230.

4 THE SAṄGHA

The third 'Jewel' in which a Buddhist takes refuge is the Saṅgha, composed of four 'assemblies': the *bhikkhus* (monks), the *bhikkhunīs* (nuns), *upāsakas* (male lay followers) and *upāsikas* (female lay followers). The Saṅgha, the community of all the followers of the Buddha, is divided into *saṅghas*, smaller local communities that over time developed their own characteristics and interpretations of the Buddha's teachings. While members of all four assemblies are true Buddhists, there is a gradation with regard to both requirements and spiritual expectations. Those who are single-mindedly striving for *nibbāna* will seek to become (ordained) monks and nuns; those who for whatever reason are satisfied with lay status hope through good deeds to merit a rebirth that will bring them closer to *nibbāna*. This view is also expressed in the famous *anupubbi kathā*, the 'gradual instruction' that occurs at several places in the Pāli Canon:

> The Blessed One gave a gradual teaching, a discourse on giving, a discourse on ethics, a discourse on heaven, explaining the peril, futility and baseness of sense pleasures and the advantage in renouncing these. When the Blessed One realized that the hearer's mind was prepared and free of hindrance, he taught the full Dhamma of the Blessed Buddhas: the Four Noble Truths, suffering, its origin, its extinction and the path leading to its extinction.

Someone desirous of joining the Buddha's following and prepared to accept his Dhamma, could either ask to become a lay follower or request ordination. The former choice was expressed by taking refuge in the

Three Jewels and the request to be accepted as lay follower. Lay followers were instructed to submit to the *pañca-sīla*, the 'Five Moral Restraints': not to take life, not to steal, not to commit unchastity, not to lie and not to take intoxicants. The main duty of the laity was to support the monks and nuns, who were forbidden from doing any gainful work.

The choice of joining the assembly of monks and nuns was originally sealed immediately by ordination. Following his request to the Buddha, the prospective monk would be summoned with the call: 'Come monk; the Dhamma has been well taught, practise purity to end all suffering.' Even during Buddha's lifetime changes were introduced to make becoming a monk more difficult and more dependent on meeting certain conditions. The 'going forth' (*pabbajjā*), the leaving home, through which one became a *sāmaṇera/ī* (novice), and the 'ordination' (*upasampadā*), the full incorporation into the assembly of *bhikkhus*, were separated and conditions were attached to both. A minimum age of 8 was required for one to take *pabbajā* and a minimum age of 20 for *upasampadā*. Certain physical as well as social conditions were attached to receiving ordination – if these were not met, ordination was declared invalid. Nobody who did not have an appointed novice-master (*upajjhaya*) and teacher (*ācariya*) could apply for ordination and the request for ordination had to be supported by five ordained members of the *saṅgha* with at least ten years' standing. The person who was to confer ordination had to address the following questions to the candidate:

> Are you afflicted with leprosy? boils? consumption? fits?
> Are you human? a male? a freeman?
> Are you free from debts? from royal service?
> Have your father and mother given consent?
> Are you fully twenty years old?
> Are your alms-bowl and your robes in good condition?
> What is your name?
> What is your preceptor's name?[1]

The ordination was conferred in an open assembly and any objections against conferring it could be voiced. If after three announcements the community remained silent, the officiant declared the ordination valid.[2]

Like all spiritual masters of his time, the Buddha thought that liberation was only attainable after cutting the ties with ordinary social life: liberation work was full-time work, not compatible with caring for a family. Quite naturally, he sought his first audience among ascetics, people who had left the world in order to find liberation, people who had already gone far on the way towards enlightenment.

In spite of proclaiming a Middle Way that avoided extremes of asceticism, the Buddha never repudiated the ascetic ideal as such: his rules for his community quite clearly advocate self-control, restraint and high ethical standards. The Eightfold Path, the core of the Buddha's message, can only be followed fully by people who have disengaged themselves from social and economic obligations, people who have become full-time seekers. The emphasis on meditation in particular, the very core of Buddhist 'exercises', demands freedom from everything else that might intrude upon one's time.

The spreading of the Dhamma throughout the world, one of the tasks the Buddha had imposed on his disciples, demanded complete independence:

> Released am I, monks, from all ties, whether human or divine. You also are delivered from fetters, whether human or divine. Go now and wander for the welfare and happiness of gods and men. Let not two of you proceed in the same direction. Proclaim the Dhamma that is excellent in the beginning, excellent in the middle, excellent in the end.[3]

The Buddha's preaching met with success from the very beginning: the original five ascetics, whom he had known from his time in the Uruvelā forest, became his followers after the first instruction and the community grew very quickly. Both the joy and the pain of having a large family – and the Buddha did consider his followers his 'offspring' – were part of the experience of the historical Buddha. His practical wisdom shows in the pragmatism with which he approached the task of guiding his followers through challenges both mundane and spiritual.

While according to the accounts in the Pāli Canon the first disciples reached *arahattā* immediately on being accepted into the fold, the majority of the later adherents either took a long time to reach it or did not attain it at all during the lifetime of the Buddha. Thus it became necessary to lay down rules for those who were not yet enlightened and to provide a firm framework of regulations reflecting the ideals of Buddhist life. Whereas the first and foremost concern of the Buddha was the teaching of *nibbāna*, there were practical considerations *vis-à-vis* the laity who supported the community of monks and whose opinions could not be disregarded. The life of the Buddhist *bhikkhu* had not only to be focused on enlightenment, it had to be structured in such a way as not to interfere with the socio-economic order of the country. Such concerns found expression in the Buddha's forbidding his monks and nuns to wander about during the rainy season (lay followers had complained that they trampled down the crops) and in his not admitting slaves or soldiers into the order (a king had warned the Buddha that he could not vouchsafe his security if there were no police to keep criminals in check).

While the Saṅgha was on principle open to everyone and disregarded many traditional barriers of caste, sex or ritual purity, it nevertheless excluded certain categories of people who were considered unfit even to enter the path, namely:

- those who had committed deeds bad enough to merit hellish existences;
- those who belonged to heretical outfits that would lead to animal existences;
- those whose *karma* had not matured sufficiently and who needed to go through other human lives before being fit;
- those who had no faith in the Buddha, and who were without energy and insight.

Someone desirous of becoming a novice had to be prepared to accept as binding the ten rules of the *sikkhā-padāni*:[4]

1. not taking life;
2. not taking what was not given;
3. not engaging in sexual activity;
4. not lying;
5. not using drugs or intoxicants;
6. not eating after midday;
7. not attending public entertainments;
8. not using ornaments, perfumes etc.;
9. not using a luxurious bed;
10. not handling money, gold or silver.[5]

The candidates also understood that by entering the order of the *bhikkhus* and *bhikkhunīs* they had to leave the laity to provide the necessities of life (*nissaya*) for them, such as food, clothing, shelter and medicine and that they could not engage in economically gainful activity.

As an outward sign of membership in the assembly of *bhikkhus* and *bhikkhunīs* the head was shaved and lay dress exchanged for monastic

REASONS FOR EXPULSIONS FROM THE SAṄGHA

I allow you, monks, to expel a novice who is possessed of ten qualities: if he is one who makes onslaught on creatures, if he is one that takes what is not given, if he is one who is unchaste, if he is a liar, if he is a drinker of strong drink, if he speaks dispraise of the Buddha, if he speaks dispraise of the Dhamma, if he speaks dispraise of the Saṅgha, if he is a holder of false views, if he is a seducer of nuns. I allow you, monks, to expel a novice who is possessed of these ten qualities. (*Mahāvagga* I, 61, trans. I. B. Horner, SBB, vol. XIV, p. 108)

robes. While originally Buddhist monks and nuns were supposed to wear only dress discarded by other people, it soon became customary to accept robes made specifically for use by monks and nuns, donated by the laity. Providing food and robes to the order became the favourite means of gaining merit.

One of the permanent obligations of an ordained member of the Saṅgha was participation in the fortnightly gatherings (*uposatha*) at which the recitation of the 'mirror of virtues (and vices)' (*Pātimokkha*) took place.

THE *PĀTIMOKKHA*

The *Pātimokkha* (leaving aside for the time being its etymology)[6] designates the list of rules by which all members of the Saṅgha had to abide, which were recited at the fortnightly gatherings (*uposatha*) of all the monks and nuns of a district. The ability (and obligation) to hold an *uposatha*, a gathering of all ordained members of the Saṅgha living in a defined area is tantamount to demonstrating the vitality of the Dhamma in this region.

The *Pātimokkha* defines the essence of Buddhist monastic life, i.e. of Buddhism as a profession. While there is some scholarly debate about the exact date by which the *Vinaya* in its present form was fully formulated, there is no doubt that both the *uposatha* and the core of the *Pātimokkha* go back to the earliest stages of Buddhism and are formative of the Saṅgha.

Several branches of Buddhism developed their own modifications of the *Pātimokkha*. The Theravādins possess a separate *Pātimokkha* for *bhikkhus* containing 227 rules and one for *bhikkhunīs* containing 311 rules. The Mūlasarvāstivādins' *Pātimokkha*, used by Northern Buddhists, has 258 rules for monks and 366 for nuns, whereas the Dharmaguptaka's *Pātimokkha* used in East Asia has 250 rules for monks and 348 for nuns.[7]

All monks and nuns of a (previously defined) constituency (*sīmā*) (the minimum number was five) were to meet on full moon and new moon days for an assembly (*uposatha*) at which their leader was to recite the *Pātimokkha*. Anyone present who had committed a breach of the rule or had observed another member breaking a rule had to speak up and confess, and accept the appropriate penance. Silence was interpreted as expression of innocence. Each rule was mentioned three times. If after the third time no answer was received the Saṅgha was presumed to be pure with regard to it.

The rules are structured according to severity of breaches. The first group of four are called *pārājika*, '[those acts which bring about] defeat', i.e. which automatically exclude a member from the Saṅgha. Since they are so important, and since every circumstance mentioned seems equally important, the full text in the stately translation of Rhys Davids and Oldenberg, made more than a century ago, is offered here:

> 1. Whatsoever Bhikkhu who has taken upon himself the Bhikkhus' system of self-training and rule of life, and has not thereafter withdrawn from the training, or declared his weakness, shall have carnal knowledge of any one, down even to an animal, he has fallen into defeat, he is no longer in communion.
>
> 2. Whatsoever Bhikkhu shall take, from village or from wood, anything not given – what men call 'theft' – in such manner of taking as kings would seize the thief for, and slay, or bind, or banish him, saying, 'Thou art a thief, thou art stupid, thou art a fool, thou art dishonest' – the Bhikkhu who in that manner takes the thing not given, he, too, has fallen into defeat, he is no longer in communion.
>
> 3. Whosoever Bhikkhu shall knowingly deprive of life a human being, or shall seek out an assassin against a human being, or shall utter the praises of death, or incite another to self-destruction, saying 'Ho! my friend! what good do you get from this sinful, wretched life? death is better to thee than life!' – if so thinking, and with such an aim, he, by various arguments, utter the praises of death or incite another to self-destruction – he too, is fallen into defeat, he is no longer in communion.

> 4. Whatsoever Bhikkhu, without being clearly conscious of extraordinary qualities, shall give out regarding himself that insight into the knowledge of the noble ones has been accomplished, saying, 'Thus do I know', 'Thus do I perceive': and at some subsequent time whether on being pressed, he, feeling guilty, shall be desirous of being cleansed from his fault, and shall say, 'Brethren! when I knew not, I said that I knew; when I saw not, I said that I saw – telling a fruitless falsehood,' then, unless he so spake through undue confidence, he, too, has fallen into defeat, he is no longer in communion.[8]

The text seems clear enough; however, commentators have added many pages of detailed explanation of each term.

The next category of regulations, called *Saṅghādisesā*, contains rules whose violation requires a formal meeting of the Saṅgha and the imposition of an appropriate fine. They range from contact with women, solicitation and procuring, to claiming personal property and offending other *bhikkhus* or laity by words or bad example. Penance includes periods of probation and certain disciplines.

The bulk of the regulations (many no longer observed) concern internal matters of the order, dress codes, the unity of the Saṅgha, the etiquette of eating and of moving about.

A major part of the *Vinaya* is taken up with providing casuistic evidence for the regulations contained in the *Pātimokkha*: *bhikkhus* and *bhikkhunīs*, and also laity or people not belonging to the Buddhist community, are reported approaching the Buddha with questions relating to the proper behaviour of monks and nuns and the Buddha would give a decision. In those decisions the Buddha shows himself flexible and pragmatic; he grants exceptions to general rules, accommodates to the needs and sensibilities of all concerned, and allows interpretations of principles.

The life of the Buddhist monk is structured from morning till night, from the beginning of the year to the end; nothing is left to whim and improvization. The monk has to rise early, make his daily begging round for food, complete his one and only meal before noon, and devote most of his time to meditation and to study or to giving instruction. Twice a month he has to appear for *uposatha* and for three months every year during the rainy season he has to go into retreat. While the monk has no 'social function' his life itself serves to remind society of the Dhamma. And, as E. Lamotte has it: 'The ruling which imprisons the monk in a network of detailed prescriptions tends to make him a fully self-denying person: gentle and inoffensive, poor and humble, continent and perfectly trained.'[9]

WOMEN AND THE SAṄGHA

The Pāli Canon reports that at a time when the Buddha visited Kapilavatthu, his home town, Mahāpajāpatī Gotamī, his aunt and foster mother, approached him and said: 'Lord, it would be fine, if women were allowed to renounce their homes and enter the homeless state under the *dhamma* and *vinaya* of the Tathāgata.'[10] The Buddha refused her request outright not just once, not twice, but three times.

He then travelled on to Vesālī. Mahāpajāpatī cut off her hair, put on orange-coloured robes, and travelled together with a number of like-minded women to Vesālī as well. Ānanda, the Buddha's closest associate, saw her and addressed her: 'Why do you stand here, outside the porch, with swollen feet, covered with dust, sad, sorrowful and weeping?' Mahāpajāpatī explained that it was because of the Buddha's refusal to admit her to the monastic order. Ānanda sympathized with her and took her plea before the Buddha. Not once, not twice, but three times – and the Buddha refused again.

So Ānanda changed his tactic: instead of asking the Buddha to grant permission to women to become members of the order, he asked the Buddha whether women were capable of arahantship. The Buddha gave an affirmative answer: yes, they were capable. Reminding the Buddha of the care and affection he had received from Mahāpajāpatī, he repeated her request and this time the Buddha agreed.

However, he put restrictions on the *bhikkhunīs* that made them dependent on the *bhikkhus*. He allowed Mahāpajāpatī to become a *bhikkhunī* under condition that she accepted the *aṭṭha garu dhamma* (Eight Heavy Rules):

1. even the seniormost *bhikkhunī* had to show signs of respect to the juniormost *bhikkhu*;
2. no *bhikkhunī* was allowed to spend the rainy season in a district in which there was no *bhikkhu*;
3. the *bhikkhunīs* had to ask the *bhikkhus* every fortnight about the date of the *uposatha* ceremony and the time of the *bhikkhus*' sermon;
4. the *bhikkhunīs* were to confess before their own as well as before the *bhikkhus*' *saṅgha* any transgressions;

5. any penance imposed on a *bhikkhunī* for a transgression had to be be undergone before both *saṅghas*;
6. after training for two years a *bhikkhunī* novice had to ask both *saṅghas* for ordination;
7. a *bhikkhunī* was never to revile a *bhikkhu*;
8. a *bhikkhunī* was not allowed to admonish a *bhikkhu*, but *bhikkhus* were allowed to admonish *bhikkhunīs*.

Mahāpajāpatī happily embraced the Eight Heavy Rules and thus became initiated into the monastic order. The Buddha, in spite of his enlightenment, very much a child of his age and his culture, somewhat spoilt it by commenting that if women had not been allowed to become *bhikkhunīs*, the order would have lasted a thousand years; now it would only last half that long. He even stated generically, using various homely examples to make his case: 'Under whatever doctrine and discipline women are allowed to go out from the household life into the homeless state, that religion will not last long.'

Later the Buddha also agreed to let *bhikkhunīs* receive the *upasampadā*, the higher ordination, but they had to be ordained by *bhikkhus*, not by *bhikkhunīs*. When asked for reciprocity in the honours given and taken between *bhikkhus* and *bhikkhunīs*, the Buddha refused: 'This is impossible and unallowable.' And he exhorted the *bhikkhus*: 'You are not to bow down before women, to rise up in their presence, to stretch out your joined palms towards them, to perform any service to them. Whoever does it, will be guilty of an offence.'

Out of regard for popular sentiment the Buddha ordered that *bhikkhunīs* should recite the *Pātimokkha* for *bhikkhunīs* in a *uposatha* ceremony separate from that of the *bhikkhus*, and *bhikkhunīs*, not *bhikkhus*, should hear the confessions of *bhikkhunīs*. The numerous questions brought up before the Buddha with regard to the lifestyle of the *bhikkhunīs*, the changes that had to be made in their rules as against the rules for the male members of the order, and the many incidents reported concerning *bhikkhunīs*, make us realize that it must have been a difficult beginning and a way of life beset with constant vexations.[11] Nevertheless, during the Buddha's lifetime the *bhikkhunī saṅgha* flourished and brought forth a great many learned and pious women who were highly regarded by all.[12]

One book in the Pāli Canon, the *Therīgāthā*, 'Psalms of the Elder Sisters', upon which a commentary was later written by Dharmapāla,

ANOPAMĀ

Daughter of Treas'rer Majjha's famous house,
Rich, beautiful and prosperous, I was born
To vast possessions and to lofty rank.
Nor lacked I suitors – many came and wooed;
The sons of Kings and merchant princes came
With costly gifts, all eager for my hand.
And messengers were sent from many a land
With promise to my father: 'Give to me
Anopamā, and look! whate'er she weighs,
Anopamā, thy daughter, I will give
Eightfold that weight in gold and gems of price.'
But I had seen th'Enlightened, Chief o'the World,
The One Supreme. In lowliness I sat
And worshipped at his feet. He Gotama,
Out of pity taught to me the Norm.
And seated even there I touched in heart
The Anāgamī-Fruit, Third of the Paths,
And knew this world should see me ne'er return.
Then cutting off the glory of my hair,
I entered on the homeless ways of life.
'Tis now the seventh night since first all sense
Of craving dried up within my heart.

(*Therīgāthā* LIV, trans. C. A. F. Rhys Davids, PTS, vol. I, pp. 86f)

contains hymns composed by *bhikkhunīs* and was apparently accepted by the entire Saṅgha.[13] A contemporary witness speaks of over five hundred *bhikkhunīs* who had achieved *arahattā*. However, due to a variety of circumstances, in several countries where the *bhikkhunī saṅgha* had once been established, the line of succession was broken and for several centuries no *bhikkhunī saṅgha* has existed in the heartlands of Theravāda Buddhism, Sri Lanka and Burma (Myanmar). Only in our century have efforts been undertaken to re-establish the *bhikkhunī* order there again.[14] In East Asia the *bhikkhunī* tradition continued through the centuries and there are a fair number of fully ordained Buddhist nuns in China, Japan and Korea.

THE SAṄGHA AND THE *SAṄGHAS*

The Saṅgha was always composed of *saṅghas*, smaller communities of monks and nuns, who lived in a certain area and who came together for the *uposatha* celebrations. It happened not infrequently that within these smaller groups differences developed that were serious enough to prevent all the members of the group coming together for an *uposatha*. Since it was mandatory that a group of ten (later five) monks recommended a novice for higher ordination, *nikāyas*, ordination lineages, not unlike the Hindu *guru paraṁparā*, developed and became important. Thus present-day Theravāda Buddhism in Sri Lanka is composed of various fairly exclusive *nikāyas*. Rifts among existing *nikāyas* often lead to a situation in which the *uposatha* cannot be held for years, for lack of a quorum.[15] Given the central function that the *Pātimokkha* is intended to fulfil, both for the continuity of the Saṅgha and for the discipline of the individual member, its non-performance for years must have a serious effect.

NOTES

1. *Mahāvagga* I, 76, 1.
2. *Vinaya* I, 22, 56.
3. *Mahāvagga* I, 11. English translation in SBB, vol. XIV, p. 28.
4. In order to avoid confusion with what will be dealt with as the 'ten components of a noble character', the *dasa-sīla* proper, I am not using this term here, although the *sikkhā-padāni* are often referred to as *dasa-sīla* both in Pāli sources and secondary literature.
5. *Mahāvagga* I, 56.
6. The word is written both *pātimokkha* and *paṭimokkha*. The following meanings for the former are given in the Pāli dictionary: (1) a purgative, a sort of remedy and (2) obligatory, binding, for the latter: 'that which should be made binding'. The translators of the *Pātimokkha* in the Sacred Books of the East series (vol. XIII, *Vinaya Texts*, I, trans. T. W. Rhys Davids and H. Oldenberg) render it 'Words of Disburdenment'.
7. Harvey, *Introduction to Buddhism*, p. 225.
8. *Vinaya Texts*, I, SBE, vol. XIII, first published in 1881, pp. 3–5.
9. Lamotte, 'The Buddha, His teachings and His Saṅgha'.
10. *Cullavagga* X.
11. There is a section called the *Bhikkhunī Vibhaṅga*, 'The Nuns' Analysis', in the *Vinaya* that deals exclusively with problems relating to *bhikkhunīs*. See SBB, vol. XXV, pp. 80–122.
12. Although belonging to a much later time and reflecting a different branch of Buddhism, the *Gandavyūha Sūtra*, which describes fifty-seven *kalyāṇa mitras* (religions mentors) visited by Sudhana, contains the description of twenty-four women teachers, almost half of the total.

13. It is noteworthy that the translation of the *Therīgāthā* was the first volume in the Pāli Text Society's Translation Series: *Psalms of the Sisters*, trans. C. A. F. Rhys Davids, first published in 1909.
14. This has lead to a major controversy in Sri Lanka. Most *bhikkhus* hold with Piyadassi Mahathera (*Mahabodhi*, April–June 1988, p. 99) that 'the *Bhikkhunī Sāsana* or the Order of the Nuns has ceased to exist, and in the absence of a Buddha and the *bhikkhunīs* the order cannot be resuscitated'. Feminist Buddhist scholars and practitioners, however, demand the re-establishment of the *bhikkhunī sāsana*, and believe it just patriarchal bias on the side of the *bhikkhus* not to allow this. Sister Khema (German-born Ilse Ledermann) was ordained a nun in Sri Lanka by Narada Thera at Vajorarama and founded Parapuppu-diwa Nun's Island, Dodanduwa. It has to be kept in mind, however, that in East Asia there are and always have been numerous ordained Buddhist nuns.
15. See Carrithers, *The Forest Monks of Sri Lanka* for concrete examples.

Part II

THE BUDDHIST PATH

Buddhism aims at liberating those who are bound into a transient existence by their delusion, anger and desire. The Buddhist Dhamma is all comprehensive: it envisages a total transformation of life in all its aspects. Buddhism is a life-programme that demands the full attention of its followers. In the course of time Buddhists have systematized the teaching regarding Buddhist practice in various ways, insisting that by following the path, the ultimate goal will be found. Since the liberating insight of the Buddha concerned the nature of the universe and the interdependence of everything in it, a central element in the Buddhist path is the endeavour to arrive at this liberating insight through meditation.

This section will describe first the path that leads to *nibbāna*, the ultimate goal of Buddhism, and to the state of the *arhat*, the enlightened. It then focuses on Buddhist meditation, a very elaborate practical science that has been developed along several branches. Finally, the path of the *bodhisattva* will be described, a path that aims to emulate not only the Buddha's wisdom, but even more his compassion for all living beings. In the process we shall read excerpts from one of the greatest works in spiritual literature, the *Bodhicaryāvatāra*, the description of a Buddhist's initiation to the *bodhisattva* path, the beginning of a truly cosmic journey through all levels of existence that play such a great role in later Buddhist literature.

5 THE WAY TO *NIBBĀNA*

> At a time when the Exalted One dwelt in the *siṃsapā* forest at Kosāmbī, he took some *siṃsapā* leaves into his hand and spoke to his disciples: 'What do you think, *bhikkhus*, what is more, those few *siṃsapā* leaves which I hold in my hand or the leaves outside in the forest?' 'The leaves which the Exalted One has taken into his hand are few, and many more are the leaves outside in the forest.' 'Thus, what I have come to know and did not tell you is much more than what I told you. And why did I not tell you? Because it does not profit you, it does not further the life of holiness, it does not lead to aversion from the world, to the demise of all passion, to the cessation of the impermanent, to peace, to enlightenment, to *nibbāna*: therefore I did not announce it to you.[1]

The Buddha's only goal in teaching the Dhamma was to lead everyone willing to listen to *nibbāna*, the kind of liberation he himself had experienced in his enlightenment. He condemns the 'thicket of opinions, the wilderness of opinions, the congestion of opinions',[2] the endless theorizing about everything, of which the philosophers are so fond. He refuses to answer questions concerning the eternity or temporality of the world, its infinity or limits, questions concerning the identity or non-identity of body and soul, existence or non-existence after death, questions which constituted the main interest of philosophers. He keeps silent, because answering these questions does not lead to *nibbāna*, does not further liberation:

> I do not know an end to suffering without reaching the end of this world. But I tell you: within this ensouled body, only three cubits tall, there is the world, and the origin and the cessation of the world, and the way to its

dissolution.'[3] And at some other place he announces: 'As the great ocean has only one flavour everywhere, the flavour of salt, so the Dhamma has only one flavour, the flavour of *nibbāna*'.[4]

WHO CAN REACH *NIBBĀNA?*

The Buddha's compassion was aroused when he contemplated the eternal and endless cycle of birth, death and rebirth in which unenlightened humanity was caught. He was considering how difficult a task it would be to communicate such a subtle and difficult message to crude and unprepared people. Brahmā, the highest god of traditional religion, encouraged him to teach the Dhamma by reassuring him that there were some people already quite close to enlightenment, for whom the Buddha's teaching would lead to *nibbāna*.

The Buddha shared the common Indian opinion concerning *karma* and rebirth, according to which bad deeds result either in a rebirth in one of the many hells or in an animal incarnation. References to hells are numerous in Buddhist writings, the *Jātakas* in particular offering colourful descriptions of the tortures which sinners have to undergo.

The threat of hell provides most people's first motive for avoiding evil deeds. It is very difficult to return to a human existence after having earned a rebirth in hell or as an animal. However, and this is a ray of hope to all, existence in hell is not eternal. After some time all sins have eventually been atoned for and a new chance to win *nibbāna* offers itself.

Good *karma* can lead to a rebirth in heaven. This too is common Indian opinion. Heavenly existence, again, is only temporal and will come to an end. The *Jātakas* tell us about the delights and limitations of the heavens in which the Bodhisattva dwelt before reaching enlightenment on earth.

The way to *nibbāna* for most people is long and arduous, and some are even excluded from entering it altogether. The Buddhist scriptures identify four categories of people who are barred from even entering the path to *nibbāna*:

1. those who are prevented on account of evil deeds, such as matricide, parricide, murder of an *arahant*, intentional violation of a Tathāgata, causing a schism in the order: such deeds inexorably lead to a hellish existence;

2. those who are prevented on account of mental obstruction, such as entanglement in the false opinions of nihilism, scepticism and fatalism which result in a denial of a moral world-order: such behaviour leads to an existence in animal bodies;
3. those who are hindered by their ripening *karma*: mental, moral or bodily defects are indications of bad deeds in former existences and these people simply have to wait for their *karma* to work itself out in the present existence in order to get a chance in the next life;
4. those who are without faith in the Buddha, without energy and insight. There is, however, hope for these latter: 'In the discipline of the Holy One it is progress to admit one's fault as fault, to endeavour to atone for it, and to refrain from it in future.'[5]

Eventually all will reach enlightenment, but at any given time there will never be more than a few who attain it, when all the circumstances are auspicious.

Altogether, there are ten fetters (*saṃyojanas*) that bind a person into *saṃsāra*, namely:

1. belief in a permanent individuality (*sakayadiṭṭhi*);
2. doubt (*vicikicchā*);
3. clinging to rituals (*sīlabbataparāmāsa*);
4. sensuality (*kāma-rāga*);
5. viciousness (*vyāpāda*);
6. desire for existence in the sphere of pure forms (*rūparāga*);
7. desire for existence in the sphere of no-forms (*arūparāga*);
8. pride (*māna*);
9. irritation (*uddhacca*);
10. ignorance (*avijjā*).

People bound by all ten fetters are *puthujjana*, 'ordinary people', i.e. people without higher aspirations. One who has cut the first three fetters is a *sotāpanna*, someone who has 'entered the stream', someone who is on the way to liberation. They are assured of being exempt from bad rebirths (in hell, as animals, ghosts or demons), but they have to undergo seven more human rebirths before reaching enlightenment. That stage has four phases (*aṅgas*), namely faith in the Buddha, the Dhamma, the Saṅgha, and the noble *sīlas*. *Sotāpanna* is the conversion proper for a Buddhist, the guarantee of eventual enlightenment.

The 'once-returners' (*sakadāgāmin*) will only be reborn once as humans and then become *arahants*.

The next group are the 'no-returners' (*anāgāmin*). They have cut the first five fetters and are destined to be reborn in heaven and to enter *nibbāna* from there.

The highest are the *arahants*, people who have achieved the highest end in this life. They have cut all the ten fetters. When the Buddha was alive, hundreds, if not thousands, reached *arahattā*, often at the very first hearing of the Dhamma. In the course of time there were fewer and fewer. 'Truly happy are the *arahants*. No desire can be found in them. The pride of "I am" has been rooted out, the net of delusion has been torn. They have become free from passion, their mind is clear and luminous. They are undefiled, they have become Brahma, they are wholly pure.'[6]

THE PATH TO *NIBBĀNA*

The Buddha proclaimed the Noble Eightfold Path as the only path to liberation: it was the criterion by which he judged the teachings of other schools and found them wanting. His entire teaching can be organized around the individual items of the Eightfold Path.

Buddhaghosa, in his systematic description of the Path of Purification, follows another traditional method of describing the Path as consisting of three steps: *sīla* (virtue, morality), *samādhi* (meditation, mental culture), and *paññā* (wisdom, enlightenment). The Eightfold Path is subsumed in such a way that the third (right speech), fourth (right action) and fifth steps (right livelihood) of the Eightfold Path are treated under *sīla*; steps six (right endeavour), seven (right mindfulness), and eight (right concentration) are considered under *samādhi*; steps one (right views) and two (right intention) under *paññā*. This seems to be a more logical method and it will be adopted in this discussion.

Sīla

'Virtue' is the first step on the Path: it is important, indispensable and detailed. As it is written:

> First he taught the merit of giving, then good deeds and as a reward the rebirth in a heavenly world. Then he explained the misery, the baseness, the defilement of sensual enjoyments and extolled the advantage of renunciation. When he realized that the listeners were mature enough, he

> revealed the Buddhas' special teaching of Dhamma, of the Origin of Suffering and of the Cessation of Suffering.[7]

Those who enter the way to *nibbāna* have first to cleanse themselves from the gross impurities of bad deeds, words and thoughts, then from the middling impurities of sensual, unkind and cruel thoughts, and finally of the subtle impurities of thoughts of the family, of home and of recognition by others. After that is done, the impediments of the thoughts that are related to the *dhammas* arising with the *jhānas* (stages in a trance) have to be overcome.[8]

The first step on the way to enlightenment consists of good deeds: even if one were only to empty the remnants of one's eating bowl into the ditch at the entrance of a village in order to feed the creatures which live in it, it would bring about an increase in good *karma*; all the more would this be the case if one did good to humans.[9] Verse 183 of the *Dhammapada* has been considered the very essence of Buddhist ethics: 'Abstention from all evil, doing of good, purification of one's thought – this is the rule (*sāsana*) of the Buddhas.'[10]

The Buddha rejected ascetic rigour as well as the mediating role of the brahmans. In his eyes ethical purification was the sole condition for liberation. As is well known, the Buddha was accused by his erstwhile companions of having abandoned the search when he began breaking his suicidal fast. Even Māra tried to confuse him after his enlightenment by suggesting that he had given up the practice of *tapa* through which young brahmans purified themselves: 'the impure, who has missed the pass of purification, considers himself pure'. The Buddha replied to him: 'When I recognized that all the endless mortification was useless, that it did not bring any gain, like a ship's rudder on dry land, I reached the highest degree of purity by practising *sīla*, *samādhi* and *paññā*, the path that leads to enlightenment.'[11]

The Jains, known for the most rigorous ascetic practices, considered the Buddha a 'softie' and composed a ditty to ridicule his path: 'A night rest on a soft bed, a good drink in the morning, dining at noon, tippling again in the evening, munching sweets before falling asleep – in the end liberation has been won, thus has taught the Sākya son.'[12]

The basis of Buddhist morality are the *dasa-sīla*, the 'ten components of good character', described as 'a sort of preliminary condition to any higher development after conforming to the teaching of the Buddha'.[13] In their general form the *dasa-sīla* enjoin:

1. abstaining from taking life;
2. not taking what is not given to one;
3. abstaining from unlawful sexual relations;
4. abstaining from lies;
5. abstaining from slander;
6. abstaining from harsh speech;
7. abstaining from frivolous gossip;
8. abstaining from covetousness;
9. abstaining from malevolence;
10. abstaining from heretical views.

The *pañca-sīla* is a shortened version of the *dasa-sīla* which contains numbers 1–4 and, as a fifth rule, the abstention from intoxicants.

A different organization of the same *dasa-sīla* rules classifies the 'tenfold misconduct' (*ducarita*) into groups of verbal, bodily and mental misdeeds, to be avoided and counteracted by 'tenfold wholesome behaviour' (*sucarita*).

The *ducarita* can be:

- verbal (*vācī*)
  1. lying (*musāvāda*);
  2. slander (*pisuṇāvācā*);
  3. rudeness (*pharusavācā*);
  4. gossip, idle chatter (*samphappalāpa*).
- bodily (*kaya*)
  5. taking of life (*pāṇavadha*);
  6. taking what is not given (*adinnādāna*);
  7. promiscuity (*kāmesu micchācāra*);
- mental (*manas*)
  8. covetousness (*abhijjā*);
  9. malevolence (*vyāpāda*);
  10. false views (*micchādiṭṭhi*).

The *sucarita*, by contrast, consists of:

1. giving (*dāna*);
2. morality (*sīla*);
3. meditation (*bhāvanā*);
4. honouring;
5. giving service;
6. surrendering what was given (*pattidāna*);

7. reflecting with delight on the attainment of merit;
8. listening to the Dhamma;
9. preaching Dhamma;
10. setting one's views straight.

With reference to the Eightfold Path *sīla* comprises the following:

- right speech: i.e. the avoidance of lies, calumnies, abuses, empty gossip and the duty to 'speak at the right time, truthfully, softly, purposefully and in a friendly way';[14]
- right action: i.e. the abstention from killing, stealing, unlawful sexual activity and other bad deeds, and the performance of good deeds;
- right livelihood: i.e earning one's living in such a way as not to offend against the precepts (e.g. not to engage in the profession of hunter, butcher, liquor distiller, etc.).

For *bhikkhus*, *sīla* includes a number of further precepts such as the guarding of the senses, contentment with their way of life, restraint in eating, watchfulness and alertness.[15]

Samādhi

The second stage can only be reached after the first has been successfully mastered.[16] It comprises the last three steps along the Eightfold Path: right endeavour, right mindfulness and right concentration.

Right endeavour consists of the mental effort directed towards the avoidance of the production of bad *dhammas*, and the removal of those already existing. It is also the positive effort of bringing good, wholesome *dhammas* into existence, and, if they have arisen, preserving, augmenting and perfecting them. The means to this are mental discipline and contemplation.

Right mindfulness involves the contemplation of the body, the sensations, thinking and the objects of thought. One has vividly to portray before one's eyes the composition of the body and to realize that mind is either full of, or free from, desire, hatred and deception, the main hindrances to liberation. In this connection we find many systematic meditations, especially meditations on the impurities, designed to evoke repulsion against the body. The *bhikkhu* is asked to go to the burning grounds outside the village and meditate on the corpses in their various stages of decay, and to apply what he sees in others to his own body.[17]

The *bhikkhu* is also asked to contemplate the components of his own, living body:

> which is enclosed by a skin and is full of impurities, from the soles of the feet up to the crown of his head and downwards again. Parts of the body are hair on the head, hairs on the body, nails, teeth, flesh, sinews, bones, kidneys, heart, liver, spleen, innards, stomach, excrements etc.[18]

Important for this exercise is also mindfulness of breath and of bodily posture. There follow the 'four great contemplations', constituting a whole complex of considerations relating to the body, feelings, moods and the wholesome *dhammas*. The purpose of these contemplations is vividly to place before one's eyes the contingency and transience of the body, the feelings and all other contents of consciousness.

The aim of the stage of right concentration consists in achieving a state of singlemindedness in which all objects except one are excluded. Chapter 6, on Buddhist meditation, will supply more detail on this important subject.

The stages of *samādhi* proper, the so-called *jhānas*, are again subdivided into several steps. The first four *jhānas* lead to an overcoming of the lower spheres and to a progressive movement into the region of pure forms. The texts describe the experiences by identifying the *dhammas* manifesting themselves at each stage[19] as they affect concentration and other mental powers.

At the first stage, there is reflection, comprehension and the experience of joyful excitement and happiness. The text compares the meditator's state of being, permeated with that feeling of bliss, to a barber's sponge that is saturated with soap.

The second stage brings the experience of inner peace. The text compares the meditator's feeling of bliss to a lake through which a cool spring is flowing.

At the third stage the meditator experiences equanimity, awareness and attention, and is compared to a lotus surrounded by cool water.

The feeling of bliss makes room in the fourth stage for the complete overcoming of all sense of happiness and sorrow. The meditator's mind is compared to a figure wholly covered with white cloth.[20] At that stage, complete physical immobility ensues; at the psychic level there is a complete cessation of all feelings.

Above these four *jhānas* are four more that belong to the 'region of no forms': a fifth stage in which the meditator experiences the sphere of infinity of space; a sixth stage, in which there is experience of the sphere of infinity of consciousness; a seventh stage, of experience of the sphere of no-thingness and an eighth stage in which experience of the sphere of 'neither discernment nor non-discernment' is attained. Sometimes a ninth stage is added, in which the temporary cessation of consciousness and sensation is experienced.

According to Buddhist tradition, immediately before his death the Buddha went through all the stages of *jhāna*, up to the ninth and then back to the first. Ascending again to the fourth, he departed from there into *nibbāna*.[21] This is how the *Mahā-parinibbāna Suttanta* reports it: after the Buddha had spoken his last words to his *bhikkhus* – 'Decay is inherent in all composite things! Work out your salvation with diligence' – he entered into the first *jhāna*; rising out of the first he went into the second, the third and the fourth:

> Rising out of the fourth *jhāna* he entered into the state of mind to which the infinity of space alone is present. And passing out of the mere consciousness of the infinity of space he entered into the state of mind to which the infinity of thought is alone present. And passing out of the mere consciousness of infinity of thought he entered into a state of mind to which nothing at all was specially present. And passing out of the consciousness of no special object he fell into a state between consciousness and unconsciousness. And passing out of the state between consciousness and unconsciousness he fell into a state in which the consciousness both of sensations and of ideas had wholly passed away.

At that point Ānanda thought that the Buddha had died, but his colleague Anuruddha corrected him: the Buddha had now entered 'into that state in which both ideas and sensations have ceased to be'. From that state, however, the Buddha returned to the previous ones, down to the first *jhāna*. He then moved again from the first up to the second, the third, the fourth 'and passing out of the fourth *jhāna* he immediately expired'.[22]

The training in reaching these higher states of consciousness occupies most of the 'working time' of the *bhikkhu*. As a side-effect of higher stages of meditation, the emergence of supernatural powers (*iddhis*) is discussed by Buddhaghosa in a special chapter of the *Visuddhimagga*.[23] The five extraordinary faculties are the various supernatural powers (*iddhividhā*) and the four kinds of supernatural knowledge, that is the divine ear (*dibbasota*), the penetration of minds (*cettopariyayanana*), the recollection of past lives (*pubbenivāsānussati*) and the knowledge of the passing away and the reappearance of beings (*sattānam cutūpapāta*).

Among the first is the ability to multiply oneself, to be at the same time at different places, to grant miraculous protection in difficult circumstances, to travel through the air like a winged bird, to have extraordinary wishes fulfilled, to appear and to vanish and to see into infinite distances. For all these miraculous powers examples are adduced from Buddhist literature, largely miracles performed by the Buddha himself.

The meaning of the 'four kinds of supernatural knowledge' is quite clear: again, all these were attributed to the Buddha. Through them, the Buddha could listen to distant conversations, read the thoughts of other people and make himself present in many places simultaneously – the Pāli Canon provides numerous instances of these.

Paññā

Paññā (S: *prajñā*), or wisdom, is closely connected with *samādhi*: 'There is no meditation (*jhāna*) where there is no wisdom (*paññā*) – and there is no wisdom where there is no meditation. One who possesses meditation and wisdom is near to *nibbāna*.'[24] Here the two methods of *bhāvanā* (meditation), Samatha and Vipassanā (which will be explained in greater detail in the next chapter) find application.

The content of *paññā* is again threefold: remembrance of former births; knowledge of the law of *karma*; knowledge of the four holy truths. Buddhaghosa deals extensively with all these. Since, ultimately, ignorance is the basic root of *saṃsāra*, knowledge in the highest sense is the means to *nibbāna* and in itself already *nibbāna*. When the disciple of the Buddha has realized the Four Noble Truths, when he possesses them as his own, not just as instructed by someone else, then his consciousness has withdrawn, as it were, to an extra-mundane point. Then he has nothing more to do with the world and the disciple realizes: 'Overcome is rebirth, the holy path has been completed, all duty is done. There is no return to this world.'[25] Thus he has reached *arahattā*.

NIBBĀNA

The ultimate goal of all Buddhist endeavour is *nibbāna*. The commonest meaning of the word is the 'going out' of a lamp or a fire. For Buddhists it means the dying out of the threefold fire of anger, desire and delusion, and subsequently a condition of spiritual well-being, of security, emancipation, peace, bliss and salvation:

> *Nibbāna* is purely and solely an ethical state to be reached in this birth by ethical practices, contemplation and insight. It is therefore not transcendental. The first and most important way to reach *nibbāna* is by means of the Eightfold Path, and all expressions which deal with the realisation of emancipation from lust, hatred and illusion apply to practical habits and not to speculative thought. *Nibbāna* is realised in one's heart: to measure it with a speculative measure is a wrong standard. *Nibbāna* is the untranslatable expression of the Unspeakable, of that for which in the Buddha's own saying there is no word, which cannot be grasped in terms of reasoning and cool logic, the Nameless, Undefinable. Yet it is a *reality*, and its characteristic features may be described, may be grasped in terms of earthly language, in terms of space.[26]

'*Nibbāna* is bliss',[27] 'peace of soul',[28] 'incomparable certitude',[29] 'the peaceful place'.[30] Buddhists of all times and all schools speak without reservation of the 'bliss of *nibbāna*.' *Nibbāna* is the conscious condition of perfection, the end of the way, the consciousness of having left behind all that can pass away, all sorrow.

> *Nibbāna* is the *summum bonum* of Buddhism and the ultimate of all that a Buddha taught or would teach. Buddhism is in essence a proclamation of the truth of *nibbāna*, a clear statement of the truth about *nibbāna*, a search for *nibbāna*, and a sure path leading to *nibbāna*. *Nibbāna* is the free state of consciousness, the tranquil state of our internal nature, and the highest emotional state of spirituality and blessedness. It consists essentially in subduing the haughty spirit, the perfect control of thirst, the paralysing of the very storage of creative energy, the arrest of the course of *saṃsāra* as regards the fate of an individual, the rare attainment of the state of the void, the waning of desire, the dispassionate state, and the cessation of all sense of discordance![31]

Quite often one hears from non-Buddhists that *nibbāna* is 'nothingness', but there is enough textual evidence to show that *nibbāna* is not only not 'nothing' but reality in the ultimate sense. The Pāli Canon explicitly asserts:

> There is, *bhikkhus*, that sphere, in which there is neither extension nor movement, nor the infinite ether, nor that of perception or non-perception, neither this world nor another one, neither moon nor sun. Here I say that there is neither going nor coming, neither staying nor

parting, neither becoming nor ceasing for this itself is without a support, without continuity, without an object – this itself is the end of suffering.

There is (*atthi*), *bhikkhus*, an unborn, un-caused, un-created, un-composed and if there were not, O *bhikkhus*, that un-born, un-caused, un-created, un-composed then there could not be shown a way out from that which is born, caused, created and composed of parts. And because there is an unborn, un-caused, un-created, un-composed of parts (indivisible!) therefore a way out can be shown for that which is born, created, caused, and composed of parts.[32]

Professor T. R. V. Murti comments on this passage:

Buddha did not doubt the reality of *nirvāṇa* (the absolute) – he just did not allow it to be described and defined by empirical concepts like being, non-being, his silence can only be interpreted as consciousness of the undescribable nature of un-conditioned reality.[33]

If we remember that the analysis of the human situation found its expression in the Chain of Dependent Co-origination then we understand that the real stands beyond 'conditions' and 'causes' – it must be 'uncaused' and 'unconditioned'. In one place we are briefly told: 'The cessation of becoming is *nibbāna*.'[34] The worlds of becoming and reality are radically different – between *saṃsāra* and *nibbāna* there is no inner connection. *Saṃsāra* is under the law of *kamma* (*karma*) – *nibbāna* is outside and beyond *kamma*.

It is said that the Buddha once took a bit of cow-dung in his hand and addressed his monks thus: 'If there were only that much of a participation in a Self, which is unchanging, constant, eternal, incorruptible and not subject to the law of change, then the holy way for the destruction of sorrow would not be possible.'[35]

Nibbāna is 'deathlessness', but there is no reason at all to give it a nihilistic interpretation. It just has nothing to do with the fleeting 'reality' which we perceive. 'There is no measure for one who has gone to rest, there is no word which could be said about him. Where all appearances have ceased, all paths of speech are removed.'[36]

Nibbāna is described in mainly negative expressions, because it lies beyond all empirical categories. Those who want positive answers are told that they are bad philosophers, because they do not know about the limits of human knowing: 'Friend, now you have transgressed the questioning, you could not grasp the limit of your questioning.'[37]

The nihilistic interpretation of *nibbāna* is due in part to a lack of understanding of metaphysical realities and in part to those passages in the Pāli Canon which speak of an 'extinguishing', a 'disappearing'. 'The steadfast are extinguished like this lamp.'[38] 'The extinction of the flame itself was the liberation of the spirit.'[39] The extinction of the flame is not its annihilation but its return to its own (permanent) immaterial and invisible condition, which cannot be described in empirical categories.

'It is true that the Lord has shown to his disciples with hundreds of reasons the way to the realization of *nibbāna*, but he has not shown a reason for *nibbāna* ... *Nibbāna* cannot be caused, therefore no cause for *nibbāna* is shown.'[40]

The Pāli Canon distinguishes a twofold *nibbāna*: one in this life and one after death.

> There are two kinds of *nibbāna*: the *nibbāna* in which the five *khandhas* still exist and the *nibbāna* in which they do no more exist. These two kinds of *nibbāna* have been shown: the first kind belongs to the here and now – it has still the *khandhas*, though the channel of becoming has been destroyed. But the *nibbāna* without *khandhas* belongs to the future – in it all becoming ceases.[41]

Nibbāna in body is not yet a permanent condition.

After his enlightenment the Buddha had resisted the temptation of Māra to enter straight into the final *parinibbāna*, because he wanted first to preach to humankind the doctrine of salvation from suffering. 'Verily, this world is doomed, if the heart of the perfect one, the holy supreme Buddha would be inclined to remain in peace and not to preach the doctrine.'[42]

There is a widespread popular opinion in Sri Lanka today that it is no longer possible to attain *nibbāna* in this life[43] and that the best one can do is to lead a good life, hoping to be reborn in a higher state and eventually, after several births, to reach *nibbāna*. Contemporary observers report that a great commotion broke out in Sri Lanka in 1973 when it became known that one monk had reached the stage of *sotāpanna* (stream-enterer), the guarantee that within one more rebirth he would find *nibbāna*.[44]

THE *ARAHANT*

The term *arahant* was known in pre-Buddhist times as an honorific (Your Worship) used as a title of respect for all ascetics. The Buddhists made it the proper designation for those who had achieved enlightenment. The abstract noun *arahattā*, 'arahantship', designates the condition of the one who has reached perfection, in other words entered *nibbāna*. *Arahattā* does not know of any restriction with regard to age or sex. The Pāli Canon reports the *arahattā* of a 7-year-old child, and many women *arahants* are mentioned by name. Of the roughly four hundred *arahants* known most are *bhikkhus*, though are also some twenty lay *arahants* mentioned in the Canon.

The characterization of *arahants* is given in many formulae.[45] The *arahant* is *sukha* (blissful), has no *taṅhā* (thirst, desire), is free from egotism (*ahaṁkāra*), free from delusion (*moha*), from lust and from conceit. The *arahants* practise the seven elements of liberation (*bhojjaṅgas*): mindfulness (*sati*), study (*dhammavicaya*), energy (*viriya*), joy (*pīti*), serenity (*passadhi*), concentration (*samādhi*) and equanimity (*upekkhā*). Their *citta* (mind) is clear. They are knowers of the five *khandas*, have fully comprehended the Buddha's teaching of *anattā*, they 'roam the seven fields of good' (*satta-saddhamma-gocara*). They come close to achieving *pāramitā* (supreme virtue) and possession of 'the sevenfold gem' (which includes enlightenment). Called 'true sons of the Buddha', they are trained in the 'threefold higher training' (*adhisīla*, *adhicitta*, *adhipaññā*). They are free from fear and dread and possess 'the ten powers'. They are *asekha* (beyond further training). They let forth 'the lion's roar' (i.e. declare to the world that the Buddha is supreme).

Arahants have found liberation (*nibbāna*) and enlightenment (*bodhi*), are morally impeccable, free from needs and have developed insight (*vipassanā*) and calm (*samatha*). They possess the six higher kinds of knowledge: magical powers, divine eye, ear and mind, they know former existences and they have overcome *āsava* (influx of *karma*). The first of these accomplishments is called *lokiya* (this-worldly, natural), the last *lokottara* (other-worldly, transcendental).

The occasions described in the Pāli Canon for winnning *arahattā* are manifold, such as hearing the Buddha preach the Dhamma, imminent death, entering the Saṅgha, witnessing a person dying, or almost any other incident: the crumbling of a bowl, seeing a shrine, listening to a song.

The Canon lists five favourable (*kusala*) and four unfavourable (*akusala*) conditions for winning *arahattā*. The favourable ones are: faith in the Tathāgata, good health, sincerity, energy (*viriya*), wisdom (*paññā*) and discrimination (*nibbedhika*). The unfavourable conditions are:

thinking one's teacher (other than the Buddha) omniscient, following a (non-Buddhist) tradition, following rational analysis (*takka*) only, and accepting a stupid teacher.

Claiming to have achieved *arahattā* without in fact having reached it was one of the major faults (*pārājika*) for which a monk or nun could be expelled from the order. The testing of a claimed *arahattā* took place in two ways: external and internal.[46] The external examination consisted of the candidate being asked questions about things seen, heard, sensed and intellectually understood about the elements (*dhamma*). The candidate then had to relate the process by which that state was allegedly reached. The internal examination involved mind-reading (*catasā ceto paricca*) by a monk proficient in *jhānas*, *iddhis*, and *abhiññā*.

This testing acted as a deterrent, and fewer and fewer monks declared *arahattā*. According to the Buddha, an increase in precepts would be accompanied by a decrease in *arahants*. After the Buddha's death a council of 500 *arahants* was to meet to recite his teaching, but only 499 were found. Ānanda, the Buddha's favourite disciple, who had not yet achieved *arahattā*, was given a 'retreat' and attained *arahattā* just in time for the council to begin.

ARAHATTĀ AND BUDDHAHOOD

The *arahant* was supposed to be an enlightened one, 'knowing' what the Buddha knew. The Buddha was a kind of *primus inter pares*: he became to others the occasion to gain enlightenment; his status was not qualitatively different from that of an *arahant*. Enlightenment being the highest ideal, its attainment was identified with the fulfilment of all aspirations: everything else, at best, was preparatory.

The enlightened embodied the highest qualities of mind and heart; all their endeavours were by definition selfless, compassionate, right and universally helpful. Liberation meant the freeing of one's energies from their fixation on an imagined self, and a radiating of friendliness, compassion, joy and equanimity into the world just as the sun, while transforming helium into hydrogen and thereby generating heat does not intentionally 'do good', but by radiating light and warmth into the universe, it benefits planet earth and the myriads of living beings on it.

It is a measure of their recognition of the difficulty of arriving at the insight and wisdom which define *arahattā* and the entering into *nibbāna*, that for several centuries the Buddhists of Sri Lanka have believed that it is no longer obtainable by contemporaries.[47] Thus it was meant and perceived as a challenge to established Buddhist opinion when in the 1950s a Sri Lankan *bhikkhu* by the name of Jīnavaṃsa put up a sign over the entrance to his meditation training centre in Galduva with the legend: 'Buddhism still leads to Nibbāna'.[48] The whole forest monk movement of Sri Lanka in our century is a challenge to an interpretation of Buddhism that had emphasized the monks' administrative and pastoral roles, an attempt to go back to the roots and to do what the Buddha had taught his disciples: to become lamps unto themselves and to the whole world by becoming enlightened ones. Enlightenment does not come easily but is the fruit of meditation, the end-point of a long process of self-transformation.

NOTES

1. *Saṃyutta Nikāya* V, 437.
2. *Majjhima Nikāya* I, 485.
3. Ibid.
4. *Udāna* V, 5 and *Cullavagga* IX, 1.
5. *Dīgha Nikāya* II, 99f.
6. *Saṃyutta Nikāya* III, 83.
7. This is the so-called *anupubbi-kathā* (also spelled *ānupubbikathā*), the 'step-by-step-teaching' which occurs many times in the Pāli Canon, e.g. *Vinaya* I, 15; *Dīgha Nikaya* I, 110; *Majjhima Nikāya* I, 379.
8. *Aṅguttara Nikāya* III, 100.
9. Ibid. III, 57.
10. The expression *sāsana* has been explained as consisting of the teachings (*pariyatti*), their application in practice (*patipatti*) and the fruits of sainthood (*pativedha*).
11. *Saṃyutta Nikāya* I, 103 (*Mārasamyutta*: *Tapokammasuttam*: I, 4,1, p. 103).
12. Quoted by Oldenberg in *Buddha*, p. 186.
13. The Pāli Text Society's *Pāli–English Dictionary* (1966) under *sīla* (p. 712b).
14. *Aṅguttara Nikāya* 10, 44, 9.
15. Ibid. 10, 5, 4.
16. Terminology and descriptions are not uniform throughout the Pāli Canon. See entry *samādhi* in PTS *Pāli–English Dictionary* pp. 685a f. Generally it comprises the guarding of the senses, self-possession, contentment, emancipation from the five hindrances and attainment of the four *jhānas*.
17. See *Visuddhimagga* III, 104ff.
18. *Majjhima Nikāya* I, 58–63 (*Sattipatthāna Sutta*).
19. Ibid. III, 25.
20. *Dīgha Nikāya* II, 75–82.
21. Ibid. II, 156: *Mahaparinibbāna Suttanta* VI, 10.

22. *Mahāparinibbāna Suttanta* VI, 8–9; *Dīgha Nikāya* II: *Mahavaggo* 3, 23, 72 trans. (modified) T. W. and C. A. F. Rhys Davids.
23. *Visuddhimagga* XII: *Iddhividha-nidesa.*
24. *Dhammapada* 372.
25. *Dīgha Nikāya*: *Sīlakkandavagga* 4,4,19.
26. See entry *nibbāna* in PTS *Pāli–English Dictionary*, pp. 362a–365a.
27. *Dhammapada* 204.
28. *Sutta Nipāta* 79 and 425.
29. *Dhammapada* 23.
30. Ibid. 114.
31. Law, '*Nirvāṇa*', p. 547.
32. *Udāna* 80–1.
33. Murti, *Central Philosophy of Buddhism*, p. 48.
34. *Aṅguttara Nikāya* 11, 1, 2.
35. *Saṃyutta Nikāya* 22, 96, 106.
36. *Sutta Nipāta* 1076.
37. *Majjhima Nikāya* 44.
38. *Sutta Nipāta* 235.
39. *Dīgha Nikāya* II, 47.
40. *Milindapañha* IV, 7, 15.
41. *Itivuttaka* 38f.
42. *Majjhima Nikāya*: *Mulapaññasakam* 26, 4, 15.
43. In South-East Asia, however, quite a few monks are believed to have reached *nirvāṇa* in this century. Thus Ñyāṇaponika Thera, in *The Heart of Buddhist Meditation*, writes of U Nārada, who died on 18 March 1955, at the age of 87: 'Many believe that he attained final Deliverance (*arahattā*)' (p. 86).
44. Carrithers, *The Forest Monks of Sri Lanka*, p. 242.
45. *Samyutta Nikāya* III, 83f.
46. Based on Weeraratne, 'Arahant' and Rahula, *History of Buddhism in Ceylon* ch. 13.
47. According to an old Sinhalese tradition the last person who achieved arhathood in Sri Lanka was Maliyadeva Thera who died long ago.
48. Carrithers, *The Forest Monks of Sri Lanka*, p. 222.

6 BUDDHIST MEDITATION

The term used by Buddhists that we translate as 'meditation' is *bhāvanā*: it literally means bringing something into existence, producing or cultivating something, applying oneself to something, developing something. In the Buddhist context it means the bringing about of the states of mind conducive to liberation, cultivating the attitudes and virtues required for achieving *nibbāna*. Ideally the *bhikkhu* or the *bhikkhunī* would spend most of his or her time practising *bhāvanā*; meditation is only interrupted by work required for physical upkeep and by the teaching of Dhamma to the laity. Even these activities should be done in a meditative mood. Those who take their Buddhism most seriously become forest hermits, avoiding all involvement with the outside world as far as possible, devoting themselves full-time to meditation.

There are teachings in the Pāli Canon ascribed to the Buddha, like the *Satipaṭṭhāna Sutta*, that go into details of meditational practice and there are also important later non-canonical works, like Buddhaghosa's *Visuddhimagga*, that synthesize and systematize the canonical teachings on meditation.[1] The *Visuddhimagga* has been used for almost 1,500 years as a manual by meditation teachers. There also are, of course, many modern works, in which *bhāvanā* is described and explained.[2]

PREPARATION FOR MEDITATION

Meditation is the most central and most typical of the activities of a Buddhist. It is serious business requiring extensive preparation, and cannot be undertaken casually by anyone at any time or any place. As was explained in chapter 5, *sīla*, moral endeavour, is a necessary antecedent to, and prerequisite for, *samādhi* (trance). In addition to cultivating virtues, the monastic who meditates participates in the fortnightly *Pātimokkha* ceremony and has to be free from major transgressions of the rules. He also has to practise restraint of the senses and to pay attention to the 'purity of requisites' with regard to clothing, eating, dwelling and medicine.

Palibodhā *(the cutting out of impediments)*

Successful meditation needs a suitable environment, free from disturbing elements. Buddhaghosa identifies ten impediments which must be 'cut out' before beginning meditation. They concern:

- abode (*āvāsa*);
- family (*kula*);
- gain (*lābha*);
- group (*gaṇa*);
- activities (*kamma*);
- travel (*addhāna*);
- relations (*jātī*);
- illness (*ābādha*);
- study (*gaṇtha*);
- supernatural faculties (*iddhi*).

Some of these impediments do not need explanations: it is obvious that someone living in a crowded house, surrounded by family and friends, worrying about income, busy with all sorts of things, would not be able to engage in meditation. Interestingly, study (literally, 'books') and supernatural faculties are mentioned, which many would count among commendable 'religious' activities. Since they engage faculties other than the meditative mind, though, they have to be 'cut out'.

The kalyāṇa mitta*: the search for a good friend or teacher*

Given the central place of meditation and the great variety of backgrounds from which the members of the Saṅgha come, it is of the utmost importance to find a spiritual guide to introduce a novice to the inner life: the *kalyāṇa mitta*, the 'good friend', described in the *Visuddhimagga* as 'dearly loved, revered, a counsellor, a patient listener, a speaker of profound words, one who does not waste a student's efforts'.[3] In short, the *kalyāṇa mitta* is the personal advisor of a budding *bhikkhu*, the one in charge of his formation and inner growth. Since in the process of meditation there occur all kinds of physical and psychological experiences, the novice meditator needs the advice and support of someone who has been through this for himself. Buddhist tradition maintains that the Buddha himself gave to each newcomer a meditation topic suited for the particular individual and enquired about his progress.

TYPES OF MEDITATORS

In the course of centuries of experience Buddhists developed a fairly systematic psychology of human types and of suitable meditation topics for each one. They relied largely on their own interpretation of body language to find out to which type a candidate belonged: 'By the posture, by the action, by eating, seeing and so on, by the kind of states occurring, may temperament be recognized.'[4]

Buddhaghosa, while mentioning other classifications that distinguish up to fourteen temperaments, adopts a sixfold schema, grouped into two sections, each made up of three types.

SECTION I: PERSONS DOMINATED BY EMOTIONS

1. *rāga-carita* (greed type; symbolized by peacock), characterized by deceit, craftiness, conceit, ostentation, discontent, fickleness, etc.;
2. *dosa-carita* (hate type; symbolized by snake), characterized by anger, bearing grudges, envy, meanness, etc.;
3. *moha-carita* (delusion type; symbolized by pig), characterized by sloth, torpor, worry, perplexity, obstinacy, excitability, etc.

SECTION II: PERSONS DOMINATED BY INTELLECT

4. *saddhā-carita* (faith type), characterized by generosity, desire to see holy people, to hear the Dhamma, guilelessness, a serene confidence, etc.;
5. *buddhi-carita* (intelligence type), characterized by gentleness, capacity for friendship with good people, moderation, mindfulness, wise effort, etc.;
6. *vitakka-carita* (argumentative type), characterized by talkativeness, brooding, aimlessly rushing around, dislike for discipline, fondness for company, etc.

As an example of a diagnosis of the first three types from the way each walks the following quotation from the *Visuddhimagga* may be of interest: 'The step of one of the greed type will be springy; the step of one belonging to the hate type will be dragging; the step of a delusion-type person will be jerky.'[5] Buddhaghosa also offers hints as to how to recognize these types from the way they eat, clean their room and react to certain sights, although he warns that the ascriptions should not be taken too dogmatically: people classified under one category may also exhibit features of another, i.e. there are 'mixed types'.

According to the temperament ascertained, each candidate should be given appropriate housing, clothing, alms rounds, resting places and meditation subjects. This latter becomes especially important in the context of describing meditation.

Traditionally, Buddhists speak of forty meditation subjects, subdivided into four groups of ten:

I. *Subha* (pleasing):
The *kasiṇas* (aids to meditation)
four elements
1. earth;
2. water;
3. fire;
4. wind;
four colours
5. blue;
6. yellow;
7. red;
8. white;
light and space
9. light;
10. open sky.

II. *Asubha* (disgusting):
Corpses
11. bloated;
12. purple;
13. festering;
14. fissured;
15. gnawed;
16. scattered;

17. pounded;
18. bloody;
19. wormy;
20. bony;

III. *Anussati* (recollections):
Triratna (Three Jewels)
21. the Buddha;
22. the Dhamma;
23. the Saṅgha;
Other
24. virtues (*sīla*);
25. charity (*dāna*);
26. deities and spirits;
27. death;
28. body;
29. in- and outbreathing;
30. quiescence.

IV. Higher states:
Brahma-vihāra (universal virtues)
31. *mettā* (loving kindness);
32. *karuṇā* (compassion);
33. *muditā* (joy);
34. *upekkhā* (equanimity);
Arūpa samāpatti (formless states)
35. infinity of space;
36. infinity of consciousness;
37. emptiness;
38. neither consciousness nor unconsciousness;
Ahāra paṭikkūla (repulsiveness of food)
39. contemplation of the foulness of food;
Catudhātu (four elements)
40. analysis of the four elements.

As different medicines have to be prescribed to cure different diseases in different people, so the *kalyāṇa mitta* has to choose from these forty meditation subjects those suitable for his charges. It would be counter-productive to have someone who is depressed meditate on death and rotting corpses, or for someone who is over-confident to meditate on the formless states. There are, however, some kinds of meditation, such as the use of *kasiṇas* and the practice of the *brahma-vihāra* that can be recommended to all. The rest have to be practised after their suitability for a particular person has been established:

1. greed types should meditate on the *asubha* objects;
2. hate types should meditate on the *brahma-vihāra*;
3. delusion types should practise mindful respiration;
4. faith types should practise the recollections (*anussati*);
5. intelligence types should recollect peace and death;
6. argumentative types should practise mindful respiration.

The search for a suitable place

Since Buddhist meditation is essentially a private, individual activity, solitude has to be sought out for its practice. The Pāli Canon mentions nine kinds of suitable places for meditation: an open forest, the root of a tree, a mountain, a hillside, a rock cave, a cemetery, a deep jungle, an open field and a mound of straw. The suitability of the place is also linked to the temperaments, as described above.

In spite of the mendicant and itinerant orientation of early Buddhism, a few centuries after the Buddha most Buddhist monks and nuns lived in large, well-endowed monasteries, looked after by the laity, no longer needing to beg for food and other necessities.[6] While not ruling out meditative life in a monastery, Buddhaghosa, who was fully acquainted with the monastic life of his own time, identified eighteen kinds of monastery (*āvāsa*) as unsuitable for meditators. He says one should not stay in a large monastery, where people with different ideas engage in debates to the neglect of meditation; nor should one stay in a new or a dilapidated monastery where a great deal of physical work is required, distracting from meditation. Monasteries near public highways, wells or farms are also unsuitable, because of the quantity of traffic near them. Monasteries that have become tourist attractions should be avoided, too, and monasteries in non-Buddhist lands are not conducive to meditation, because of the difficulty of finding support. And 'where it is not possible to find a good friend as a teacher or a preceptor; the lack of good friends there is a serious fault'.[7]

Suitable time and posture

Traditionally, the time of early morning, midday and evening have been considered best for meditation. Dawn, especially, called *brahma-muhūrta*, 'God's hour', has been the preferred time for meditating. The posture considered best is the *Buddha-āsana*, the posture believed to have been adopted by the Buddha when he reached enlightenment. For specific meditations, however, other postures were recommended. Thus for the *kasiṇa* meditations sitting on a low chair was recommended; for the *asubha* meditations standing was considered most appropriate. In general, Buddhists do not insist that a definite posture be chosen, as long as it permits the meditator to concentrate on the meditation object.

THE *KASIṆAS*

The first ten meditation objects, recommended to all types of people, are called *kasiṇas*. These are material devices to support meditation.The Pāli word *kaṣina* (S: *kṛtsna*) means 'whole', 'entire' and is used to designate a physical shape (the *maṇḍala*), as well as the mental image (*nimitta*, 'sign') obtained from it, and the higher state of consciousness (*jhāna*) reached through it.

The example of the 'earth-device' (*paṭhavī kasiṇa*) may help to understand what is meant by *kasiṇa*. In the first sense it denotes a round shape of clay, perhaps 25 cm in diameter, which the meditator forms and places vertically in front of him- or herself, either attached to a wall or hanging from a string, to serve as a mechanical aid in focusing concentration. It is the emblematic representation of the entire earth. In the second sense, 'earth *kasiṇa*' means the mental imprint (*nimitta*) obtained by gazing fixedly at this device, a mental image of the entire earth with its qualities of solidity, extension and unity. In the third sense, 'earth *kasiṇa*' means the state of consciousness obtained by concentrating on the mental image.

The Pāli Canon mentions this practice as highly recommended by the Buddha himself: 'A *bhikkhu* who practises the earth *kasiṇa* even for a moment, for the duration of a snap of the fingers, is said to be the *bhikkhu* who is not devoid of *jhāna*, who follows the master's teaching, who acts upon his advice, and who rightfully receives the alms offered by the pious.'[8] The same formula is used to recommend the practice of all other *kasiṇas* as well.

The actual practice of the *kasiṇas* – widespread among *bhikkhus* in Sri Lanka and other Buddhist countries – is described in great detail in Buddhaghosa's *Visuddhimagga*. He devotes an entire chapter to the earth *kasiṇa* alone: 'When a *bhikkhu* has cut out the impediments to meditation, then on return from his alms round, after his meal and after he has got over the drowsiness following his meal, he should sit down comfortably in a secluded place and apprehend the earth *kasiṇa*.'[9]

The importance of the exercise is underlined by the suggestion that the meditator should 'treasure it, respect it, anchor his mind to it, thinking "Surely thus I shall be free from old age and death."' There follow instructions on how to prepare the earth *kaṣina* from reddish clay, how it should not have any of the colours that form the object of other *kasiṇas*, how it should be free from any admixture of foreign objects and should be made smooth 'like the surface of a drum' with the help of a stone trowel. The meditator should then sweep the place, take a bath, sit down on a chair of about 20 cm height at a distance of about 80 cm from the device: 'for the *kasiṇa* does not appear plainly if one sits further off than that; and if one sits nearer, faults in the *kasiṇa* appear. If one sits higher up, one has to look at it with neck bent; and if one sits lower, then the knees ache.'[10]

The first exercise consists of the contemplation of the dangers inherent in sense desires and the arousal of a longing to escape all suffering. Then the meditator should evoke the joy of happiness that comes from remembering the qualities of the Buddha, the Dhamma and the Saṅgha.

> After that one should open one's eyes moderately, look at the sign and so proceed to develop it. If one opens the eyes too wide, they get fatigued and the disk becomes too obvious, which prevents the sign from becoming apparent. If one opens them too little, the disk is not obvious enough, one's mind becomes drowsy, which also prevents the sign from becoming apparent.[11]

Concentrating first only on the quality of 'earthiness' (disregarding colour and other characteristics) one should focus on one of the many names for earth, such as Mahī (The Great One), Medinī (The Friendly One), Bhūmi (Foundation), Vasudhā (Provider), and keep repeating it. If then the mental image (*nimitta*) of 'earth' appears whether one looks at the device or keeps one's eyes shut, one has reached the first stage in the meditation. The meditator should then get up, go into the cell and try to evoke the sign there. If one loses the mental image, one should return to the material device and begin again. 'As one does so, the hindrances become suppressed, the defilements subside, the mind becomes concentrated with access concentration, and the counterpart sign (*nimitta*) arises.'[12]

The difference between the original, material *kasiṇa*, and the *nimitta*, the counterpart sign, is important: while in the material 'learning' *kasiṇa* all faults are apparent, in the mind-produced, immaterial *nimitta* no such faults are recognizable. 'The *nimitta* appears as if breaking out from the *kasiṇa* and is a hundred, a thousand times purer, like a mirror drawn from its case, like mother-of-pearl, like the moon appearing from behind a cloud. It has neither colour nor shape.'[13] It is wholly immaterial and does not have the three 'signs' that mar everything material. With its arising the mind becomes concentrated in *upacāra samādhi* (usually translated as 'access concentration'), the preliminary to *appanā*, or *jhāna samādhi*.

The advanced meditator is able to enter from the *nimitta* into the higher stages of consciousness, called *jhāna*, and thus complete the *kasiṇa* exercise by universalizing the experience of the transcendent qualities of 'earth' and the rest of the *kasiṇas*. The less advanced meditator, who is not able to go beyond *upacāra samādhi* 'must guard the *nimitta* diligently as if it were the embryo of a *cakkavatti* (world-ruler)'.[14]

The 'guarding of the sign' has many components: the meditator must be careful about the choice of abode, the village chosen for alms collecting, the people to communicate with, the food eaten, the climate and the posture. Buddhaghosa gives detailed instructions with regard to all of these. The aim of all this advice given to the meditator at this stage is to achieve *apannā samādhi*, 'immersion' in the higher states of consciousness with their attendant bliss.

BRAHMA-VIHĀRA

The *bhāvanā* called *brahma-vihāra*, 'supreme abodes', 'celestial dwellings', likewise recommended to all meditators, have become central to the Buddhist practice of *bhikkhus*, *bhikkhunīs* and laity alike. They 'form an essential preliminary to the whole training of the religious aspirant. From the ethical point of view these four principles emphasize the moral foundation of every form of religious life and are considered to be indispensable to spiritual development.'[15] Some practice of the *brahma-vihāra* is part and parcel of virtually every contemporary Buddhist service and many Buddhists try to evoke these 'higher sentiments' at least for a few minutes every day.

For the professional meditator, these, like all other *bhāvanā*, have to be approached methodically and systematically. Often they are used as preparatory to other, more abstract forms of meditation. Termed *lokiya* (mundane), the *brahma-vihāra* are concerned with the conditioned beings in this world, not with *nibbāna*. They express the attitudes that should underly all advanced Buddhist practices, they do not in and by themselves constitute the ultimate aim.

Buddhaghosa, not surprisingly, has much to say on the practice of the *brahma-vihāra*, which consist of *mettā*, 'loving kindness'; *karuṇā*, 'compassion'; *muditā*, 'joy' and *upekkhā*, 'equanimity'. After the usual preparations the meditator should sit down and contemplate first the dangers inherent in the opposite of *mettā*: *dosa*, anger, ill-will, hatred. The evil consequences of a hate-filled mind as against the advantage of patience, good-will, forbearance, should be considered. The Pāli Canon says: 'There is no higher practice than patience, no higher *nibbāna* than forbearance.'[16]

The meditator then systematically proceeds to develop loving kindness and to shut out anger and antipathy. While loving kindness must certainly be practised in the end towards all persons, for the purpose of 'training' the meditator is advised against beginning the practice by extending *mettā* to an antipathetic person, to a very dear friend or to an indifferent or hostile person. Nor should one choose a person of the opposite sex or a dead person. Initially these should be excluded because they would evoke spontaneous reactions in the meditator not conducive to the development of loving kindness.

Surprisingly, perhaps, meditators are advised to practise first of all *mettā* towards themselves, saying: 'May I be happy and free from suffering', 'May I keep myself free from enmity, affliction and anxiety, and live happily.' The text explains that this should not be the end of the exercise, but only constitute an 'example': one should proceed by telling oneself: 'Just as I want to be happy and dread pain, as I want to live and not to die, so do other beings too.' In this way one extends one's mind to desiring the welfare and happiness of all beings. As Buddhaghosa says:

> Thus one should first, as example, pervade oneself with loving kindness. Next one can recollect such gifts, kind words, etc. as inspire love and endearment, such virtue, learning, etc. as inspire respect and reverence met with in teachers, developing loving kindness towards them by saying: 'May this good person be happy and free from suffering'. Thus one attains absorption.[17]

Then the meditator can proceed to develop loving kindness towards all the persons who were initially excluded. As regards developing *mettā* towards an enemy, Buddhaghosa says that if one does not have an enemy one need not be concerned with that item.

A long section is devoted to 'getting rid of resentment'. The first natural reaction on remembering a hostile person is to recall the anger that one had experienced. To overcome this feeling, the meditator is reminded of a saying of the Buddha, who told his early missionaries that 'even if criminals were to cut off one's limbs with a saw, one who entertained hate in the heart on account of that would not be one who carries out my teaching'.[18]

This is underscored by another canonical verse:

> To repay angry people in kind is worse than to be angry first. Repay not angry people in kind and win a battle hard to win. The weal of both does one promote, one's own and then the other's too, who shall another's anger know and mindfully maintain one's peace.[19]

The overcoming of resentment and anger must have been a major problem for meditating *bhikkhus*; Buddhaghosa amasses scriptural quotations and arguments to convince the meditator that resentment and anger are both worthless and harmful to one's mind. *Jātaka* stories are brought in to remind the practitioner of *mettā* how the Buddha in an elephant incarnation, a monkey incarnation and a snake incarnation practised loving kindness towards those who had hurt and harmed him.

If the attempts to overcome resentment have still not quelled the feelings of anger, the meditator is reminded of the 'eleven blessings' which the Buddha promised to those who practise *mettā*:

> One sleeps in comfort, wakes in comfort, and dreams no evil dreams; one is dear to human beings, dear to non-human beings; deities guard one, fire and poison and weapons do not affect one; one's mind is easily concentrated; the expression on one's face is serene, one dies unconfused, and one will be reborn in *brahmaloka*.[20]

Buddhaghosa adds pages and pages of commentary to these and other quotations, thus making it clear that he is dealing with a matter of utmost importance. *Mettā* is not just one item among others, it expresses the very essence of the Buddhist attitude towards fellow beings – as do the other *brahma-vihāra*. One *must* succeed in cultivating *mettā*, otherwise one is not a true disciple of the Buddha, who is the great exemplar of this as well as of all other virtues. And we are constantly reminded that *mettā* is not just a social virtue, facilitating life in society and helpful in resolving conflicts, but the realization of a higher consciousness: the practitioner of *mettā* sees 'people as they are', deserving compassion in their manifold sufferings, and is freed from the delusion of 'people as they appear', competitors for self-gratification.

Some texts relate the four *brahma-vihāra* to the four *jhānas* in an ascending order; others teach that all four (or five) *jhānas* are to be attained in the practice of each of them separately.

Buddhaghosa explains the practice of *karuṇā* (compassion, i.e. feeling someone else's suffering as one's own), *muditā* (sympathetic joy, i.e. participating in another's happiness), and *upekkhā* (equanimity) in a fashion analogous to his discussion of the practice of *mettā*, although much more briefly. While the intensive practice of the *brahma-vihāra* is only possible for *bhikkhus* and *bhikkhunīs*, they are recommended to all Buddhists as a means to cultivate their own minds and to improve the condition of the whole world. The practice of *mettā*, especially, has become a regular part of Buddhist religious gatherings and contemporary Buddhist writers emphasize the good that comes from it both for those who practise it and for those towards whom it is applied.

SAMATHA AND VIPASSANĀ *BHĀVANĀ*

Elementary and introductory as this description of Buddhist meditation may have been, it will at least have suggested that Buddhist meditation is a very complex and sophisticated activity that goes far beyond simple musing or reflection and aims at cultivating (*bhāvanā*) the mind in preparation for the attainment of complete liberation (*nibbāna*).

The canonical texts are replete with meditational materials and instructions; the Buddha himself is the model of a meditator and the guarantee that meditation can bring to an end the suffering that lies so heavily on the mind of every Buddhist. It became one of the chief duties of senior *bhikkhus* to train their novices in meditation. In the course of centuries certain schools developed their own preferred approaches to meditation, which then were developed and propagated.

The two main traditions of Buddhist meditation practice are Samatha (S: Śamatha) and Vipassanā (S: Vipaśyanā), usually translated as 'Calm Meditation' and 'Insight Meditation'. While some exponents of each of these treat them as exclusive of each other and as complete systems leading to *nibbāna*, others see them as complementary: Samatha leads to an understanding of the content of the Buddha's teaching; Vipassanā leads to a penetration of the mind to *nibbāna* – both are necessary for full realization.

Samatha

The *Satipaṭṭhāna Sutta*, 'The Discourse on the Application of Mindfulness'[21] is, according to the testimony of contemporary Buddhist scholars, the most popular and frequently studied of all the Buddha's instructions. Thus it begins:

> There is this one way, *bhikkhus*, for the purification of beings, for the overcoming of sorrows and griefs, for the going down of sufferings and miseries, for winning the right path, for realizing *nibbāna*, that is to say, the four applications of mindfulness.

'Right mindfulness', we remember, is one of the steps of the Eightfold Path that leads to liberation. In this *sutta* the Buddha goes far beyond a simple statement of this step and provides a great amount of detailed instruction about its meaning. Later writers have amplified it into a complete manual of *satipaṭṭhāna* meditation directed to the body, feelings, mind and objects.[22]

Right mindfulness begins with 'bare attention', defined as 'the clear and single-minded awareness of what actually happens *to* and *in* us, at the successive moments of perception'.[23] It is a schooling to focus on one thing and one thing only: 'In what is seen there should be only the seen; in what is heard, only the heard; in what is sensed, only the sensed; in what is thought, only the thought.'[24] This training in bare attention leads to knowing the mind as well as shaping the mind in preparation for the exercise of mindfulness proper:

> Very often a single moment of mindfulness or wise reflection would have prevented a far-reaching sequence of misery or guilt. By pausing before

> action, in a habitual attitude of bare attention, one will be able to seize that decisive but brief moment when mind has not yet settled upon a definite course of action or a definite attitude, but is open to receive skilfull directions.[25]

The next step in the preparatory training is the development of clear comprehension (*sampajañña*). It is concerned with our actions and comprises the clear comprehension of purpose (*sātthaka*), of suitability (*sappāya*), of the domain of meditation (*gocara*) and of reality (*asammoha*, 'non-delusion').

The four objects of mindfulness are body (*kāya*), feelings (*vedanā*), states of mind (*citta*) and objects (*dhamma*). Each is subdivided into numerous parts or perspectives. It cannot be the purpose of this introduction to provide a full description of all these elements; by way of example (and it is a very central one) mindfulness of breathing (*ānāpāna-sati*) will be briefly described. In the words of the Buddha:

> A *bhikkhu* who has gone to the forest or gone to the root of a tree or gone to a lonely place sits down crosslegged, holding his back erect, arousing mindfulness in front of him. Mindful he breathes in, mindful he breathes out. Whether he is breathing in a long breath, he comprehends: 'I am breathing in a long breath', or whether he is breathing out a long breath, he comprehends 'I am breathing out a long breath' ... He trains himself thinking: 'I shall breathe in experiencing the whole body ... I shall breathe in tranquillising the activity of the body.'[26]

Ñyāṇaponika Thera reminds us that it is 'an exercise in mindfulness, not a breathing exercise', a 'bare observation' of the flow of breath. Nevertheless, he thinks that mindfulness of breathing, rightly done, can become an important factor of physical and mental health because of its calming effect. Mindfulness of breathing also leads to a general understanding of the nature of the body. The same method is applied to walking. A Buddhist monk walking with measured steps along a specially prepared walkway beside his hermitage is not 'taking a physical exercise' in the usual sense, he is practising 'mindfulness of walking'.

The Buddha promises to those who practise 'mindfulness' even for a short period 'either profound knowledge here and now, or the state of non-returning'.[27]

Vipassanā

Most authors describe the relationship between Samatha and Vipassanā as complementary, not mutually exclusive. Some liken them to faith and wisdom: the practitioners of Samatha *bhāvanā* go through the meditations because they are the Way taught by the Buddha, confident that this path will lead to *nibbāna*. The practitioners of Vipassanā find by themselves the truths of the Buddha-path. In another context, Samatha *bhāvanā* has been associated with *sīla* (virtues); Vipassanā with *paññā* (wisdom).

The seeker needs both, of course. Without the moral qualities inculcated by *sīla* the meditator could not expect to reach *paññā*; on the other hand, the very purpose of living a virtuous life is the achievement of insight, wisdom and enlightenment. The great detail in which both Samatha and Vipassanā are presented underscores the conviction that it is not easy to transform oneself into an ethical person and to live one's life on the level of insight. It is obviously not a question of following certain conventions or of occasionally rising to doing good deeds, but of undergoing a thorough transformation, a cleansing, a purification in depth, an eradication not only of bad deeds but of bad inclinations and desires.

Similarly, Vipassanā is not a matter of occasional flashes of insight, the extraordinary moments when one sees things as they ought to be, but of living at the level of 'how things really are' and considering this to be 'normal'. This evidently demands total dedication and ruthless honesty towards oneself. Authorities suggest that for some people Samatha comes first, to be complemented by Vipassanā, whereas with others Vipassanā comes first, to be complemented by Samatha.

The *Visuddhimagga* states that *paññā* (understanding, insight) is of many sorts and has various aspects. A description that attempted to explain all of them would not accomplish its purpose, and would, besides, lead to distraction, so we shall confine ourselves to the one kind intended here, the understanding consisting of what is termed 'insight knowledge' (*vipassanā jñāna*) associated with profitable consciousness (*kusala citta*).[28]

Buddhaghosa drives his point home with a telling simile. Imagine a young child, an ordinary person and a professional money-dealer before a heap of coins of all sorts. The child would only distinguish them by shape and colour; the ordinary person would judge them by the denomination embossed; the expert money-dealer alone would be able to distinguish between genuine and counterfeit by the look and the sound of each coin and by some other subtle characteristics. The child's knowledge is based on mere perception (senses); the ordinary person's on a more adequate apprehension (consciousness); the expert's knowledge is based on true understanding (insight wisdom). 'The characteristic of wisdom is penetrating into the true nature of things; its function is to dispell the darkness of ignorance; its manifestation is absence of bewilderment; its proximate cause is concentration.'[29]

The lengthy technical descriptions of the practice of Vipassanā *bhāvanā* which Buddhaghosa offers (based on numerous quotations from canonical scriptures) cannot be summarized in an easily understandable form. They are 'the higher mathematics' of Buddhism, which cannot be reduced to simple rules of addition and subtraction without distorting their entire meaning. It takes years of training and thorough familiarity with Buddhist technical teaching before one can begin to understand the subject. The upshot of it all is that the meditator comes to realize by himself (and not just believe on the authority of others) the impermanent (*anicca*), painful (*dukkha*), and insubstantial (*anattā*) character of everything in the sphere of sense perception and consciousness and finally 'sees things as they are', i.e. as 'empty' of everything that makes them attractive to the unenlightened.

With insight into the impermanence of everything, self-conceit vanishes. With the insight into universal suffering, craving ceases. With insight into the non-substantiality of everything, all wrong views disappear.[30]

While practising insight meditation along the lines suggested, the meditator understands more and more clearly the Four Noble Truths and the Chain of Dependent Co-origination; i.e. one achieves by oneself the level of insight through which Gotama became a Buddha and 'sees things as they really are' – fleeting, unsatisfactory, a product of our own desire, which one is unable to quell. This negative insight is complemented by the positive realization of that which is not transient, not the product of our desire, not the object of our aversion – *nibbāna*.

NOTES

1. While only Hīnayāna texts are referred to in this section and the Pāli terminology of the sources has been retained, it should be noted that much of what is described here is practised by Buddhists of all schools.
2. The most exhaustive of these texts is Paravahera Vajiranana Mahathera's *Buddhist Meditation in Theory and Practice*, published by the Buddhist Missionary Society of Malaysia in 1962. For beginners,

Conze, *Buddhist Meditation*, and Ñyāṇaponika Thera, *The Heart of Buddhist Meditation*, will prove helpful.

3. *Visuddhimagga* I, 98. The references to the *Visuddhimagga* are to paragraphs in the English translation by Bhikkhu Ñyāṇamoli (see appendix 2).
4. Ibid. III, 87.
5. Ibid. 88.
6. Rahula, *History of Buddhism* offers extensive descriptions of the organization and administration of medieval Buddhist monasteries and the life of the *bhikkhus* in them (pp. 112–98). Some of the larger monasteries in Sri Lanka housed several thousand monks. Life in them was regulated in every detail. The author also describes the involvement of the monks in local politics and the lengthy controversies between different major monastic centres, activities that were obviously not favourable to developing a meditative climate.
7. *Visuddhimagga* IV, 18.
8. *Aṅguttara Nikāya* I, 41.
9. *Visuddhimagga* IV, 21.
10. Ibid. 26.
11. Ibid. 28.
12. Ibid. 31.
13. Ibid.
14. Ibid. 34.
15. Paravahera Vajiranana Mahathera, *Buddhist Meditation in Theory and Practice*, p. 263.
16. *Dīgha Nikāya* II, 49.
17. *Visuddhimagga* IX, 11.
18. *Majjhima Nikāya* I, 129.
19. Ibid.
20. *Aṅguttara Nikāya* V, 342.
21. *Majjhima Nikāya* I, 10 and other places in the Pāli Canon. As Rahula writes in *History of Buddhism in Ceylon*: 'The Satipaṭṭhāna was held in such high esteem that it was popularly believed that even a rat snake and some five hundred bats were reborn in better states as the result of merely listening to the sound of that Sutta, (p. 253).
22. I am mainly following Ñyāṇaponika Thera's masterly exposition of the *Satipaṭṭhāna* in *The Heart of Buddhist Meditation*.
23. Ñyāṇaponika, *The Heart of Buddhist Meditation*, p. 30.
24. *Udāna* I, 10.
25. Ñyāṇaponika, *The Heart of Buddhist Meditation*, p. 39.
26. *Satipaṭṭhāna Sutta* II, 291.
27. In *The Heart of Buddhist Meditation* Ñyāṇaponika Thera offers an extensive description of the 'Burmese Satipaṭṭhāna method' developed by U Narada, a contemporary Burmese monk.
28. *Visuddhimagga* XIV, 2.
29. Ibid. 7.
30. Paravahera Vajiranana Mahathera, *Buddhist Meditation in Theory and Practice*, pp. 391f.

7 THE *BODHISATTVA* PATH

Among the notions that both unite and separate Hīnayāna and Mahāyāna Buddhism, the idea of the *bodhisattva*[1] is the most central. The Pāli Canon of the Theravādins contains 547 *Jātakas*, most of them stories about births of the Buddha before reaching enlightenment in the body of Gotama, the Prince of the Sākya clan: this Buddha-to-be is called a *bodhisatta* (P), (S: *bodhisattva*), 'a being destined for enlightenment', revealing many characteristic features of a Buddha, practising selflessness and self-sacrifice to a heroic degree, but also exhibiting shortcomings that preclude him from achieving full Buddhahood. Mahāyānists, too, have collections of (Sanskrit) *Jātakas*[2] extolling the virtuous deeds of the Buddha in his former lives.

The pre-eminent virtue of the *bodhisattva* described in all the *Jātakas*, whether he appears in the form of an animal, as a human or a god, is his compassion. If we understand the distinction between the Hīnayāna and Mahāyāna traditions as Paul Williams defines it, we can see the Bodhisattva path as the true source of Mahāyāna, not at all in conflict with any other Buddhist tradition:

> The distinction between Mahāyāna and non-Mahāyāna is not as such one of schools, traditions, Vinaya, robes, or philosophy. It is one of motivation, the reason for following the religious path. As such there could in theory be a Mahāyānist, one with the highest motivation of complete Buddhahood for the sake of all sentient beings, following a Theravāda tradition. This fits with what we know of the historical origins of the Mahāyāna, embedded firmly within the non-Mahāyāna traditions.[3]

In other words, those motivated by infinite compassion for all living beings, making relief of their suffering their central interest, would be Mahāyānists, regardless of philosophical or institutional affiliation. Developing the 'Buddha-mind' is the initiation to Mahāyāna and 'compassion is the basis and motivating force of the Bodhisattvas, from it springs the entire edifice of Mahāyāna'.[4]

For Mahāyānists the ultimate ideal is no longer *arahattā*, personal fulfilment in enlightenment, but Buddhahood, embodied compassion. Everybody can become a Buddha; everybody, before reaching complete Buddhahood, goes through the career of a *bodhisattva*. In Mahāyāna the *bodhisattva* is no longer seen as a unique individual, a once-in-a-millennium Buddha-to-be, but an ordinary human who has conceived infinite compassion in an event called 'the arising of the bodhi-mind' (*bodhi-citta-utpāda*) and who has vowed to sacrifice himself in the effort to relieve the suffering of all fellow creatures.

It is quite logical to assume that, if past Buddhas and *bodhisattvas* existed, there could also be future ones. The projection of Buddhahood into the future is due also to a variety of historical factors.[5] From around 400 BCE northern India became the target for many invasions by outside powers (Greeks, Persians, Kushanas, Central Asians) who ruined the country. Northern India (comprising, in addition to the north-west of today's Republic of India, Pakistan, Afghanistan and some neighbouring areas) was then a Buddhist country.

Traditionally the Buddha was not supposed to deal with earthly matters – these were the domain of local *devatās* (Hindu and other). After the Buddha had become depicted in *mūrti* form and Buddha-image *pūjā* had developed, it was only a small step also to ask the Buddha for help in the daily tribulations to which one was exposed. As people's faith must often have been rewarded, so the Buddha became a less remote figure. Remembering the past Buddhas' good deeds, worship of these particular *bodhisattvas* became popular too. Many of the Gandhāra Buddhist sculptures represent *bodhisattvas* rather than Gotama the Buddha. One also began with the personification of *Buddha-guṇas*, attributes ascribed to the Buddha, such as his friendliness (*maitrī*), which was turned into the figure of the Maitreya Buddha.[6]

There is, then, a definite Mahāyāna Buddhist personality which emerges as the result of three factors connected with the career of a *bodhisattva*: *bodhi-citta-utpāda* (arising of thought of enlightenment), *bodhi-sattva-vrata* (*bodhisattva* vow), and *pāramitās* (heroic degree of virtues). During his early career, before reaching *jñāna-pāramitā*, the Bodhisattva appears as a real person in a real world, alleviating the afflictions of creatures by assuming their burdens.

ŚĀNTIDEVA'S *BODHICARYĀVATĀRA*

There is no better way to appreciate the Mahāyāna ideal of the *bodhisattva* path than by reading Śāntideva's (601–743 CE) justly famous *Bodhicaryāvatāra*, 'Entering the Path of Enlightenment'.[7] Virtually from the time of its composition it had been recognized as a classic exposition of the *bodhisattva* ideal and countless Buddhists considered it the most beautiful expression of their aspirations.

Śāntideva's life, as traditionally told, has some features in common with that of the Buddha. According to Tāranātha[8] he was the son of a king in Saurāṣṭra. At the death of his father, while preparing to ascend the throne, he had a vision of Mañjuśrī, the embodiment of Buddha's wisdom, who occupied the throne and declared himself Śāntideva's *kalyāṇa mitra* (spiritual guide). He also saw Tārā appear as his mother, advising him to relinquish kingship.

After being initiated miraculously by Mañjuśrī and Tārā, he spent some time as a minister in the service of a king. Leaving him, after having had some bad experiences with his colleagues, he went to live in Nālandā, the famous Buddhist university in northern India. He seemed to do nothing but eat large quantities of food, sleep for long hours, and take extensive walks by himself while the other students were busy studying the scriptures and preparing for examinations.

In order to embarrass him, his fellow students arranged for a public recitation of texts, expecting him to fail miserably and then be forced to leave. Śāntideva, however, not only repeated some well-known *suttas* but recited an entire new work of his own, the *Bodhicaryāvatāra*, which made him instantly famous.[9] In addition, he composed a work called *Śikṣāsamuccaya*, a compendium of hundreds of texts around central topics, and a short work (apparently lost) called *Sūtra Samuccaya*.[10]

Śāntideva is also credited with the working of many miracles: at a time of famine he reputedly produced enough food to feed five hundred starving monks belonging to a non-Buddhist sect, who then converted to Buddhism. Through his magic powers he also won a contest against a brahman teacher called Śaṅkaradeva, who had threatened to destroy all Buddhist images and books and to convert the Buddhist king of the country to Hinduism.[11]

The Bodhicaryāvatāra

The 'Way of the Bodhisattva' traditionally consists of the practice of the *pāramitās*, 'heroic virtues' exercised on behalf of one's fellow beings. The standard list consists of six:

1. *dāna* (charity);
2. *śīla* (morality);
3. *kṣānti* (forbearance);
4. *vīrya* (heroism);
5. *dhyāna* (contemplation);
6. *prajñā* (wisdom).

In some texts four more are added, bringing the total to ten:

7. *upaya-kauśalya* (skilfulness in means);
8. *prānidhāna* (surrendering one's life);
9. *bāla* (strength);
10. *jñāna* (knowledge).

Śāntideva's *Bodhicaryāvatāra* adopts the scheme of the six *pāramitās*. Since the work is meant for members of the monastic Saṅgha, who do not own property (and thus cannot practise *dāna*, 'charity', literally 'giving'), and who had had to prove high moral standards (*śīla*) before being accepted, it only mentions cursorily the first two and begins the detailed instruction with the third, *kṣānti* (forbearance) to which it devotes an entire chapter. The longest and most difficult chapter is devoted to *prajñā-pāramitā*, the perfection of wisdom.

The work begins with a chapter called 'Praise of Enlightenment Thought' (*bodhi-citta*). It extols the rare moment in a person's life, when like a light illuminating a dark night, enlightenment consciousness arises: this is the conception of the *bodhisattva*, the beginning of the process of salvation, the one chance offered in many lifetimes to escape from the endless cycle of births and deaths. It manifests itself as the aspiration to free everyone from pain and to provide unlimited wellbeing to everyone.

The preparation of the actual career of the *bodhisattva* begins with taking refuge in the Three Jewels – Buddha, Dharma, Saṅgha – and with confessing sins. This ends with surrendering to the great Avalokiteśvara, 'The Lord who is full of compassion' and to the famous *bodhisattvas* Ākāśagarbha and Kṣītigarbha.

THE *BODHISATTVA* VOW

May I be a protector for the protectionless, a guide for the travellers; a boat, a dike, a bridge for those who want to reach the other shore.

May I be a lamp for those in need of a lamp, a place of rest for those who need rest, a servant of all creatures who need a servant.

May I be a wish-fulfilling gem for the embodied creatures, a pot of luck, a magic formula, a miraculous medicine, a wish-fulfilling tree, and a cow which grants all desires.

As the earth and the other elements are in many ways useful to the innumerable creatures which fill the endless space, thus may I be of manifold use to all creatures, which space holds as long as they have not reached *nirvāṇa*. (Śāntideva, *Bodhicaryāvatāra* III,17–20)

The 'Grasping of the Thought of Enlightenment' and the taking of the *bodhisattva* vow constitute the formal and irreversible entering into the *bodhisattva* path.

Concomitant with the vow's expression of universal compassion, its undertaking to 'still the pain of hunger and thirst',[12] comes the future *bodhisattva's* readiness to take upon himself all kinds of suffering for the benefit of others: 'may they beat me, curse me, cover me with dust, may they play with my body, ridicule it, taunt it. I have surrendered my body to them, what do I care?'[13]

Having taking the *bodhisattva* vow he gains a sense of meaning which his life did not possess before: 'Now my birth has brought forth fruit, now I have truly acquired a human nature. Now I have been born into the family of the Buddhas. Now I have become an offspring of the Buddhas.'[14] Surprised by his good luck, he celebrates this event and invites the whole world to share his happiness.

Realising that other thoughts might in course of time crowd out the enlightenment thought, the incipient *bodhisattva* takes care to preserve it carefully: to lose it would be a terrible tragedy and to fail to carry out his vow would be a betrayal of the whole world. The major enemies to be fought are not outside but inside: the passions. He rationalizes: 'The passions are not in the sense objects and not in the organs, nor in between them nor anywhere else. Where are they, who stir up the world?

It is just *māyā* [delusion]. So free yourself from fear, my heart. Strive for wisdom!'[15]

Mind control is the crucial point: 'One who wishes to observe the Discipline must guard his mind carefully. The Discipline cannot be observed by one who does not guard the fickle mind.'[16] He compares the mind to a wild elephant, the strongest of all beasts: 'When the elephant "mind" has been fettered with the rope of remembrance, danger has been overcome and wellbeing has been achieved.' When the mind is brought under control, everything is under control. One cannot control the world outside; but one can control the mind inside. Only a controlled mind is a mind in which awareness can develop: without it one cannot retain instructions nor can one reflect and meditate on them. One cannot take mind control for granted, even if it has once been achieved:

> The mad elephant 'mind' must be watched with meticulous effort, lest he, tied to the big posts of Dharma observation, free himself. 'Where is my mind going?' Thus the mind must be surveyed so that it does not throw off the yoke of concentration even for a moment.[17]

Śāntideva offers practical advice on how to keep the mind under control and how to avoid situations that endanger mind control, as well as on ways of counteracting negative impulses.

One of the first things a well-controlled mind should do is to shed the misconception of the body as one's 'self':

> First remove with your thought this skin-cover. Then remove with the scalpel of your wisdom the flesh from the skeleton, split the bones and contemplate the marrow in it and consider for yourself whether there is a substance called 'self'.[18]

That should help one to avoid wasting one's mental energies on the preservation of the body.

Śāntideva has advice to offer to young monks on how to behave so as to manifest their controlled mind both inwardly and outwardly:

> One should not set down chairs and other things with loud noise and one should not knock hard at doors. One should take pride in not making noise. A crane, a cat, and a thief move noiselessly and quietly and they reach their desired goals. A monk should move in the same manner, always.[19]

The rest of the rules of etiquette demonstrate that a *bodhisattva*, in spite of his exalted spiritual status, should not violate the rules of courtesy and decency but behave well in ordinary circumstances and in his dealings with others.

The Way of the *bodhisattva* proper is the practice of the well-known supreme virtues (*pāramitā*). The first two of these, charity and ethics, are mentioned only cursorily. Instead of expanding on them, the text suggests substituting their practice with appropriate thoughts:

> If the perfection of charity (*dāna-pāramitā*) consists in removing poverty from the world, then the former Buddhas did not practise it: the world is still beset by poverty. Perfection of charity rather consists in the thought of giving away all one's possessions together with the merit accruing from it. Whereto shall I shepherd the fishes and other creatures so that I do not become guilty of their death? The perfection of ethics (*śīla-pāramitā*) consists in the thought of resolving to renounce everything.[20]

While the first two *pāramitā* receive only one verse each, the others, beginning with the perfection of forbearance (*kṣānti-pāramitā*) are treated in full, separate chapters, because of their applicability to those to whom the book is addressed. Anger, the opposite of forbearance, must be eradicated before forbearance can be practised. 'Anger reduces to nothing good conduct, devotion and veneration of the Buddhas, practised through thousands of aeons. With the arrow of hatred inplanted in his heart, one cannot achieve peace of mind, nor gladness nor joy, nor find sleep and serenity.'[21]

To overcome anger Śāntideva, like Buddhaghosa before him, advises considering the insubstantiality and pointlessness of anger: 'I do not bear anger towards bile and other humours in spite of their causing great pain. What purpose would anger towards sentient beings serve?' and: 'If disregarding the stick, which is the direct cause of hurt, one is angry with the one who yields it, one is moved by hate too. For me hatred against hatred is more befitting.' Anger rests on a mental mistake: 'Since mind is without form, nothing can hurt it. Because we cling to the body, our mind is tortured by pain. Insult, malice, gossip – none of these hurt the body. Why do you get angry, my soul?' In the end, he suggests, to encounter an enemy is 'like a treasure fortuitously discovered' because it allows the practice of the virtue of forbearance in a heroic degree. One should not forget that in all creatures there is something that partakes of Buddhahood and has to be honoured. And 'the patient person, while still in the world, already gains bliss as well as fame and wellbeing, beauty, health, joy and long life and all the happiness of a world-ruler'.[22]

Having acquired heroic forbearance the future bodhisattva should practise fortitude (*vīrya*) 'since enlightenment rests on fortitude'.[23] It is defined as 'efforts towards the wholesome' (*kuśalotsahā*); its opposite is sloth, a penchant for the unworthy, despair and self-contempt. Sloth, Śāntideva explains, arises from 'unconcern regarding the suffering in *saṃsāra*,' through inactivity, love of pleasure, somnolence, dependence and desire (*tṛṣṇā*). One must not think enlightenment an impossible dream. The Buddha is quoted as having said: 'They too, who have attained through their efforts the hardly attainable, supreme enlightenment, were once gnats, flies, mosquitoes and worms.'[24]

A contemplation of the bliss of the Sukhāvatī heaven and the pains of the Avīci hells should motivate the future *bodhisattva* to experience limited suffering for the sake of permanent enlightenment.

Having acquired fortitude the future *bodhisattva* is ready for meditation (*dhyāna pāramitā*). 'A yogi who has achieved insight (*vipaśyanā*) through tranquillity (*śamatha*) is able to destroy the passions. Therefore tranquillity must first be pursued and this results from the indifference towards the attractions of the world.'[25] Meditation is a lonely business; the future *bodhisattva* should not shy away from it. 'Man is born alone and alone he dies. No one shares his suffering. What use are loved ones who hinder one in meditation?'[26]

The first meditation exercises take the future *bodhisattva* to the cemetery where he contemplates the remains of those who were once alive and the objects of desire. Nothing attractive is left in the bones and skulls. Thus revulsion from the body is the first fruit of meditation.

The next object of meditation is wealth and the damage it does to people. 'Recognize fortune as an endless misfortune, because of the pain connected with obtaining and preserving it, and because of the sorrow over its loss. In their obsession for wealth men do not get an opportunity for liberation from the pain of existence.'[27]

The 'misery of the lustful' comes next and their pleasure is 'comparable to that of an animal which draws a cart and receives a little feed for it'.[28] It is a pity if people miss Buddhahood for the sake of a trivial, short-lived bodily sensation of pleasure.

After dealing with these negative considerations the meditator is ready to 'arouse the thought of enlightenment'. Here Śāntideva offers his finest ideas: 'First one should carefully contemplate the equality of the other and the self: all suffer the same sorrow and the same happiness – I must protect them all like myself.' Thus the Bodhisattva resolves: 'I must remove the others' suffering, because it is suffering, like my own. And so I must come to the aid of others, because they are beings like myself.'[29]

He goes even further: the very attribution of a self to the body is just a convention and there is no truth or reality in it:

> Having recognized one's self as sinful and others as full of virtue, one should practise the abandonment of self and the acceptance of others ... He who wishes to save himself and others quickly, should devote himself to this supreme mystery: the exchange of the other and the self.[30]

The law of *karma* is operative in such a way that everything done to someone else comes back to visit the agent. Happiness and unhappiness are related to egotism and altruism: 'All those who are unhappy in this world are so because they desire only their own happiness. All those who are happy in this world, are so because they desire only the happiness of others.'[31]

Śāntideva tells his listeners that without exchanging one's own happiness for the suffering of others, neither Buddhahood nor happiness in this world can be realized. All unhappiness has its root in clinging to one's self. Without giving up the self, one cannot give up suffering, as one cannot avoid being burnt without avoiding contact with fire. And thus the *bodhisattva* resolves: 'For the stilling of my own suffering and of the suffering of others I give myself to the others and accept the others as my self.'[32]

He exercises this 'exchange of self with the other' through considering bodily pain, honours and wealth in the other and in himself:

> Immeasurable aeons have passed while you have been looking for your own gain. Through all this toil you have gained nothing but pain. Turn then to this practice without hesitation. You will come to see its benefits, for the Buddha's words are true.[33]

The aspirant is told to practise other-consciousness to the same degree and intensity as he had practiced I-consciousness: 'Chase the self from its happiness, force it into the suffering of the other.' And: 'If you love the self, you must not love yourself. If you have to protect the self, you must not care for yourself. The more this body is cared for, the more tender it becomes and the more it degenerates.'[34]

If Śāntideva reached a summit of compassion with his teaching of the exchange of the self and the other, he reaches a peak of wisdom in the chapter devoted to *prajñā-pāramitā*: wisdom is the immediate means to reach *nirvāṇa,* a wisdom informed by compassion.

Śāntideva operates with the well-known two-truths theory:[35] besides conventional (*samvṛti*) truth, which is the only truth that ordinary people recognize, there is ultimate, transcendent (*paramārtha*) truth which the 'wise' know and through which they find liberation.[36] In this chapter of the *Bodhicaryāvatāra* – which in the Tibetan schools was considered a separate book by itself – Śāntideva engages with a number of opponents of his teachings: realists and idealists who object to his teaching of *śūnyatā*, 'emptiness'.

When asked for proofs of this teaching he tells the questioner that 'this doctrine has its [experiential] roots in the life of a *bhikkhu*' and that regardless of austerities and other virtues 'the object-bound mind returns' if it has not found *śūnyatā*. 'Emptiness is the antidote for the darkness of passion ... Emptiness is stilling sorrow. As long as the "I" is something, there will be fear of this and of that ... If the "I" is empty, whose could the fear be?'[37]

In his polemics with opponents of the emptiness doctrine, Śāntideva encounters a profound objection: if beings do not really exist, who is the object of compassion, this greatest of the Buddha's virtues? His answer is interesting: compassion is exercised towards an entity projected through imagination so as to make it possible to fulfil the vow of the *bodhisattva*.[38] 'Egotism, the cause of suffering, grows out from a delusion concerning the self. Since it cannot be eliminated through the assumption of a real self, the theory of egolessness (*nairātmya*) is preferable.'[39]

In the process of his discussion Śāntideva also eliminates the notion of an almighty creator God, as well as the Sáṁkhya notion of an eternal material substratum (*pradhāna*) to everything.[40] He sums up the gist of his teaching in the following verses:

> There is neither annihilation nor becoming. The whole world has neither come into existence nor does it go out of existence. Like unto a dream are the rebirths: analysed, they are like the banana stem.[41] In reality there is no difference between those in *nirvāṇa* and those not in *nirvāṇa*. Since all *dharmas* are empty, as has been shown, what has been gained, what has been lost? Who could be honoured or dishonoured by whom? Whose pleasure and pain? What is worthy or unworthy? What is thirst? What

> would one be thirsting for? Who would be a living being? Who would die? Who would be born? Who would have lived? Who would be a relative? Who would be whose friend? Those who follow my school consider all empty, like space.[42]

Leaving behind the teaching on emptiness, Śāntideva bemoans the 'endless, horrible oceans of sorrow to be found in this existence'. He returns to the subject matter of the introductory chapter, stating: 'Hard it is to find a propitious moment; the arising of a Buddha is extremely rare and the flood of vices is hard to withstand. What an endless chain of suffering.' And remembering his *bodhisattva* vow he asks:

> When shall I be in a position to bring peace to those who are tortured by the fire of suffering, offering help through a cloud of good works? When shall I be able to teach the truth of emptiness to those who entertain wrong notions of reality based on sense perception, thus rending the veil which hides the truth through the power of my merit.[43]

He ends his work with a long and beautiful prayer that comes from the heart of a true *bodhisattva*. He prays that all 'who anywhere suffer pain in body and mind, may reach oceans of happiness' through his merits. Not only people on earth, but also the denizens of the many hells should find relief from suffering through the application of his merits. He asks the *devas* to protect those who are asleep, those who have fainted or are unconscious, helpless children and old people. He asks for a human birth for all creatures to enable them to reach enlightenment. 'Through my merit, may all creatures abstain from sin and always do good works.'[44]

He prays for timely rain and bountiful harvests, for justice and health for all. He wishes his own tradition and his fellow monks well: 'May the *vihāras* flourish, filled with recitation and study. May the Saṅgha as a whole live forever and succeed in its work.' He wishes that the *bhikṣus* may love the monastic discipline, practice meditation, and live together in peace without strife. He wants them to be scholarly, cultured and successful in their teaching.

In the end he wishes himself well: 'May I, through Mañjughoṣa's grace, always be mindful of my birth as a human and a Buddha son and may I reach the Pramuditā-bhūmi.'[45] He prays for the ability to sit for a long time in meditation and to have a vision of Mañjuśrī:

> May I live as long as heaven and earth exist, as the destroyer of the pain of this world. May the suffering of the entire world come to fruition in me and may the world become happy through the good work of the *bodhisattvas*.

THE TEN *BODHISATTVA BHŪMIS*

In the conclusion to his *Bodhicaryāvatāra* Śāntideva expresses the wish to reach through his efforts the *Pramuditā-bhūmi*, the lowest of ten 'stages' through which the *bodhisattva* passes before reaching full Buddhahood. He had called his text 'Entering the Path of Enlightenment' and is prepared for a long and arduous journey.

The best-known ancient text dealing with the ten stages which a *bodhisattva* has to traverse is the *Daśabhūmika Sūtra*, a very popular text among Tibetan and East Asian Buddhists.[46] This is not the place to go into the enormous amount of detail that accompanies the description of the ten *bhūmis*, or stages, but a brief enumeration of their names and the accomplishments associated with each may give some impression of the complexity of the *bodhisattva* path and the expectations of those who enter on it. It is important to keep in mind that all of these stages precede the achievement of (full) *bodhisattva* status. The ones who enter the Path of Enlightenment after taking the *bodhisattva* vow and after a lifelong practice of heroic virtues, are still only aspirants to bodhisattvahood, a condition that is quite literally still worlds removed from where they find themselves.

The ten *bhūmis*, in progressive order, are as follows:

1. *Pramuditā* (The Joyful): the aspirant takes refuge in perfect enlightenment, has subjected all passions, is exempt from the five fears, takes the ten great vows, acquires the ten great virtues, the ten skills and, renouncing the world, becomes a wandering monk.
2. *Vimalā* (The Spotless): beginning with the achievements of the previous stage, the future *bodhisattva* practises the 'ten good courses of action', including, among others, abstention from taking life, false speech and sinful sex, and considers the effects of ten evil courses of action.
3. *Prabhākarī* (The Shining): the future *bodhisattva* acquires the ten mental dispositions which provide him with the possibility of becoming a refuge for the helpless, the poor, those scorched by the fire of longing, loathing and delusion, those who are confined in *saṃsāra*, those who are incapable of discrimination and many

others. He reaches four types of formless mystic trance and his mind becomes embued with the four *brahma-vihāra* (see p. 128). He also acquires four kinds of supernatural knowledge.

4. *Arciṣmatī* (The Brilliant): at this stage the future *bodhisattva* becomes endowed with ten virtues that bring about maturity of knowledge and he practises the thirty-seven virtues that characterize an enlightened one. At that stage the attachment to all notions of selfhood is extinguished.
5. *Sudurjayā* (The Invincible): the future *bodhisattva* achieves comprehension of the Four Noble Truths, his intensity of universal love increases and he helps all creatures to come to a state of maturity. He also achieves mastery of the branches of worldly science and comes to know of ways to secure the material welfare and happiness of all creatures.
6. *Abhimukhī* (The Friendly): at this stage wisdom preponderates and the future *bodhisattva* undertakes strenuous exercises for the attainment of those elements of enlightenment that are still lacking. He becomes engrossed in the mystic contemplation of emptiness.
7. *Dūraṅgamā* (The Far-Advanced): this presents the beginning of a new way to find emancipation for the mass of living beings, including the ceaseless practice of the *brahma-vihāra* and of a large number of heroic virtues.
8. *Acalā* (The Immovable): the new feature of this stage is that from this point there is no longer any danger of retrogression for the future *bodhisattva*. All his activities become effortless. He gains the power to split up his body into an infinity of forms and he is in a position to have knowledge of the entire universe.
9. *Sādhumatī* (The Well-Intentioned): the future *bodhisattva* now delivers the message of the Buddha to all sentient beings and attains a fourfold special knowledge, transcending all limitations.
10. *Dharmameghā* (The Dharma Cloud) also called *Abhiśekha-bhūmi* (The Stage of Anointment): here the aspirant to Bodhisattvahood reaches the end of the quest, arriving at the summit of all the accomplishments, contemplations and powers. At the end of the highest contemplation the Buddhas appear before him and consecrate him a *bodhisattva*. He puts out the flames of affliction produced by ignorance through the showers of rain from the cloud of Dharma. He now becomes endowed with supernatural powers.

The reader will find much of what is described here fairly incomprehensible: the writer must confess to not having grasped much of the detail either. The terminology is technical and geared towards the practitioners who spend their lives on the *bodhisattva* path. Whether one should understand the *bhūmis* as real 'lands' or just as stages of psychological or spiritual development only those who travel the *bodhisattva* path can tell. However much or little we understand of it, it is certain that the *boddhisattva* ideal has profoundly shaped the Buddhist world and expectations of *bodhisattvas* to come are the hope of many millions in Asia today.

NOTES

1. Norman, 'Pāli Philology and the Study of Buddhism', suggests (p. 36) a derivation of the Pāli *bodhi-satta* from *bodhi-sakta* or *bodhi-sākta*, 'directed towards enlightenment' or 'capable of enlightenment'. He thinks that the Sanskrit form *bodhisattva* (translated by Monier-Williams in the Sanskrit–English dictionary as 'one whose essence is perfect knowledge') is a backformation from Pāli and therefore later.
2. The best-known may be Āryasūra's *Jātakamālā*, translated into English by J. S. Speyer (see appendix 2).
3. Williams, *Mahāyāna Buddhism*, pp. 197f.
4. Ibid.
5. I am following closely Basham, 'The Evolution of the Concept of the Bodhisattva'.
6. See Williams, *Mahāyāna Buddhism*, pp. 228ff. on Maitreya and his veneration, particularly in East Asia.
7. The Sanskrit text has been edited by P. L. Vaidya and published as vol. XII in the series Buddhist Sanskrit Texts (Darbhanga: Mithila Institute, 1960). Translations exist in most major Western languages; there are several English translations available. In this chapter I have used my own (unpublished) translation.
8. Lama Chimpa Alaka Chattopadhyaya (trans.), *Tāranātha's History of Buddhism in India*, pp. 215–20.
9. The sources say that when he reached the ninth chapter, dealing with the perfection of wisdom, he rose into the air and disappeared from sight. The story probably reflects the difficulty presented by this chapter, which – unlike to the rest – is very abstract and speculative.
10. The *Śiksāsamuccaya* has been edited by P. L. Vaidya, vol. XI in the Buddhist Sanskrit Texts series (Darbhanga: Mithila Institute, 1961). An English translation by C. Bendall and W. H. D. Rouse is published in the Indian Texts series (New Delhi: Motilal Banarsidass, 1971).
11. See also Obermiller, *History of Buddhism by Bu-ston*, vol. II, pp. 161–6.
12. *Bodhicaryāvatāra* III, 6–9.
13. Ibid. 13.
14. Ibid. II, 25.

15. Ibid. IV, 47.
16. Ibid. V, 1.
17. Ibid. 40–41.
18. Ibid. 63.
19. Ibid. 72–3.
20. Ibid. 9–13.
21. Ibid. VI, 1–3.
22. Ibid. 134.
23. Ibid. VII, 1.
24. Ibid. 17–18.
25. Ibid. VIII, 4.
26. Ibid. 33.
27. Ibid. 79.
28. Ibid. 80.
29. Ibid. 90.
30. Ibid. 113 and 120.
31. Ibid. 129.
32. Ibid. 136.
33. Ibid. VIII, 155–6.
34. Ibid. 173–4.
35. See chapter 9, on Madhyamaka, for further details.
36. *Bodhicaryāvatāra* IX, 2.
37. Ibid. 55–6.
38. Compassion creates its own object. There is no 'objective' cause for compassion, which cannot be measured objectively in numbers of blankets delivered or tons of food distributed.
39. *Bodhicaryāvatāra* IX, 78.
40. Sāṁkhya is a classical Hindu system of philosophy, which assumes the existence of an eternal material principle, *prakṛti* or *pradhāna* (substratum) from which everything has evolved under the influence of *puruṣa* (spirit).
41. The trunk of a banana plant consists of a large number of concentric thin sheaths. If one peels them away, there is no stem left, so one cannot really speak of a banana stem.
42. *Bodhicaryāvatāra* IX, 150–5.
43. Ibid. 167–8.
44. Ibid. X, 31.
45. Ibid. 51.
46. The text has been published as vol. VII in the Buddhist Sanskrit Texts series, ed. P. L. Vaidya (Darbhanga: Mithila Institute,1967). The English translation has been prepared by M. Honda and published as vol. LXXIV in the Śata-Piṭaka series (New Delhi: International Academy of Indian Culture, 1968).

Part III

SCHOOLS OF BUDDHISM

Over the centuries, Buddhism attracted a great many powerful minds who spent a lifetime pondering the Four Noble Truths and their implications. Their various efforts to understand the teaching of the Buddha and to think out its ramifications resulted in a large number of schools of Buddhism. To pre-empt any misunderstanding, a school is not a sect, i.e. a separate kind of Buddhism, but a specific understanding of Buddhist teaching.

The nature of this work forbids the lengthy and thorough treatment which these schools deserve. Nor can we look at all of them. We shall learn a little about the *Abhidhamma*, the earliest classification and systematization of the Buddha's teachings. We shall also listen to the arguments that Buddhist apologists developed in their debates with opponents, encountering some interesting Buddhist ideas with regard to the nature and function of language. The radical advocates of the Buddhist notion of *śūnyatā* (emptiness) established the Madhyamaka school, which endeavoured to secure the very centre of the Middle Path. Another Buddhist school that we shall consider, the Cittamātra or

Yogācāra, developed the notion that what we perceive as reality exists only in the mind. Finally, we shall briefly hear about Tantric Buddhism, with its great profusion of gods and goddesses, all emanating from the Buddha.

There are many other Buddhist schools that are not dealt with here, and further developments took place in China and Japan that have been momentous for the formation of Buddhism, but which had to be left out here. To learn more about these, readers are referred to Williams, *Mahāyāna Buddhism* and Gethin, *The Foundations of Buddhism*.

8 BUDDHIST SYSTEMATIC AND POLEMIC

THE *ABHIDHAMMA*

The further the historical Buddha receded into the past, the greater became the variety of interpretations of his message, and the more difficult it became to define what, exactly, the Buddha had taught. Within the Buddhist community itself a lively dispute arose as to what constituted the authentic Buddha-word. In order to safeguard its letter as well as its meaning, the Theravādins, at their Third Council, created the third *Piṭaka* of the Pāli Canon and called it the *Abhidhamma*. According to an old tradition Mogalliputta Tissa Mahāthera, who presided over this council, became the author of the fifth book of the *Abhidhamma Piṭaka*, the *Kathāvattu*, deciding the orthodox answer to a number of problems that had been raised.

The term *abhidhamma* has been explained as 'relating to the Dhamma' or 'the highest Dhamma'. According to a famous statement by Buddhaghosa, '*Abhidhamma* exceeds, and is distinguished from, Dhamma.' The *Abhidhamma Piṭaka* attempts to clarify doubtful and disputed points of doctrine and discipline and to systematize the content of the Dhamma by applying a large number of classificatory schemata to the *Vinaya* and *Sutta Piṭakas*. The *Abhidhamma Piṭaka* represents the theological position of the Theravādins. Other Buddhist schools, such as the Sarvāstivādins, also had a complete *Abhidharma Piṭaka*, commented upon in the famous *Mahāvibhāṣa*.

HOW TO DISCERN THE TRUE BUDDHA-WORD

Through these four characteristics a Buddha-word may be recognized:

1. It refers to Truth, not to un-truth
2. to the Law, not to the non-law,
3. it decreases sin, does not increase it,
4. it shows the advantage of *nirvāṇa*, does not indicate the benefits of continued rebirths . . .

When anyone utters a word endowed with these four characteristics, young people with faith will perceive the Buddha . . . they will hear his Law as he preaches . . . Everything, that is well said, is a Buddha-word. (*Adhyāśayasaṃcodana Sūtra*, quoted by Śāntideva in *Śikṣāsamuccaya*, trans. C. Bendall and W. H. D. Rouse, p. 17)

The content of the Abhidhamma Piṭaka

The *Abhidhamma Piṭaka* consists of the following books:[1]

- *Dhammasaṅgaṇi* (A Buddhist Manual of Psychological Ethics): twenty-two triplets distinguishing states that are good, bad, or intermediate, and one hundred couplets that enumerate what are and are not moral roots;
- *Vibhaṅga* (The Book of Analysis): analyses of terms like *khaṇḍa*, *ayātana*, *dhātu*, etc.;
- *Paṭṭhāna* (Conditional Relations): deals with all *dhammas* with reference to the twenty-four conditions (*paccaya*);
- *Dhātukathā* (Discourse on Elements): further examination of the elements;
- *Kathāvatthu* ('Points of Controversy' or 'Subjects of Discourse'): contrasts five hundred orthodox with five hundred heretical statements and refutes heretical doctrines;
- *Puggalapaññatti* (Designation of Human Types): the results of disputes concerning the notion 'person' ;
- *Yamaka* (Book of Pairs): has been described as a 'book on applied logic'.

Some of these works, especially the *Paṭṭhāna* and the *Yamaka*, are voluminous and highly technical, almost inaccessible to the non-specialist, even in an English translation.

The *Vinaya* and *Sutta Piṭakas* contain numerous *mātikās* (indices, schemata) that foreshadow the *Abhidhamma*. The *Abhidhamma* does not add to the content of *Sutta* and *Vinaya*, but offers its analytical, logical, methodological elaboration, applying the following methods:

- definition and determination of all names and terms used;
- enunciation of all doctrines as formulas and their coordination;
- reduction of all heterodox positions to absurdity.

The main concern of the *Abhidhamma Piṭaka* is the analysis of everything into its component elements, the *dhammas*, and the enumeration and classification of these. According to the Theravāda teaching there are eighty-two *dhammas*. These are classified into:

- twenty-eight physical (*rūpa*) components, such as the four elements, qualities of material objects like elasticity, food, etc.;
- fifty-two mental (*cetasika*) components, subdivided into
  twenty-five good elements such as absence of greed, hatred, delusion; faith, compassion etc.,
  fourteen bad *dhammas*, such as wrong views, etc.;
  thirteen neutral ones, such as contact, sensation, will, etc.;
- consciousness (*citta*);
- *nibbāna*, the only 'unconditioned' (*asaṃkhata*) *dhamma*.

The meditator has to develop the practice of analysing all experience in terms of *dhammas* in order to learn to see things 'as they really are', i.e. conditioned, momentary, without substance. The *Abhidhamma* has always been considered extremely important for the higher training of monastics in the Theravāda tradition and its teaching was facilitated by the production of manuals that summarized and systematized the unwieldy volumes of the *Abhidhamma Piṭaka*. One of the most widely used of these texts today is the (Pāli) *Abhidhammata Saṅgaha* by the fifth-century Ācariya Anuruddha, upon which later teachers wrote commentaries.[2]

The importance of Buddhaghosa

The greatest name in Theravāda Buddhist exegesis is Buddhaghosa (fifth century CE).[3] His monumental *Visuddhimagga* is considered a general commentary on the whole Pāli Canon, and its section entitled 'The Soil in which Understanding Grows' is specifically taken as a summary of the *Abhidhamma*. In addition to this he wrote many individual commentaries on parts of the *Abhidhamma Piṭaka*. One of the most important of these is the *Atthasālinī*, a commentary on the *Dhammasaṅgaṇi*, the first book of the *Abhidhamma Piṭaka*.

In the introduction to the *Atthasālinī* (The Expositor) Buddhaghosa explains how each of the books of the *Abhidhamma* became 'the word of the Buddha (*Buddha-vācana*)'. The factors involved are the prophetic foresight of the Buddha concerning the arising of heretical views, and the adoption by a *bhikkhu* of a *mātrikā* found in one of the other *piṭakas*. The book also gives a short conspectus of the entire *Abhidhamma*.

'The Guide'

A work that became important as an extra-canonical supplement to the canonical *Abhidhamma* is the *Nettipakkaraṇa* (The Guide), a manual for teachers of Buddhism, 'not a commentary, but a guide for commentators'.[4] It presupposes thorough and intimate knowledge of the teachings of the Buddha and offers guidance as to how to communicate them effectively. It facilitates the rewording of ideas expressed in the *suttas*. 'If the commentator is regarded as a retailer to the public, then the *Guide* may be compared to an organization of wholesalers, whose business is not with the public but with the retailer.'[5]

Another technical work called *Peṭakopadesa* (Piṭaka Disclosure), is somewhat similar.[6] Its key elements are the sixteen *haras* (modes of conveying) that are to be used to help in analysing the content of the *Vinaya* and the *suttas*:

1. *deśana* (teaching);
2. *vicaya* (investigation);
3. *yutti* (construing);
4. *padatthana* (a footing);
5. *lakhana* (characteristic);
6. *catubyūha* (fourfold array);
7. *avatta* (conversion);
8. *vibhatti* (analysis);
9. *parivattana* (reversal);
10. *vevācana* (synonyms);
11. *paññatti* (description);

12. *otāraṇa* (way of entry);
13. *sodhana* (clearing up);
14. *adhittana* (terms of expression);
15. *parikkhara* (requisites);
16. *samāropana* (coordination).

The Abhidharma-kośa

The *Abhidharma-kośa* (Treasury of Higher Dharma), a collection of about six hundred verses (in Sanskrit), presenting the *Abhidharma* systematics of the Sarvāstivādins, has always been considered one of the most remarkable Buddhist literary productions. Traditionally its authorship has been ascribed to Vasubandhu (fourth century CE), the brother of Asaṅga of Yogācāra fame. There is at present a scholarly debate about the identity of Vasubandhu, the author of several Yogācāra treatises, and Vasubandhu, the author of the *Abhidharma-kośa*. With E. Frauwallner, some scholars today assume that the latter lived in the fifth century and was an adherent of the Sarvāstivādins.[7] In his commentary on his own text, *Abhidharma-kośa-bhāṣya*, Vasubandhu presents his personal opinions, controversies and opinions of a variety of other schools. According to de la Vallée Poussin, the first translator of the text into a European language:

> from the point of view of dogmatics the *Abhidharmakośa*, with the *Bhāṣya*, is perhaps the most instructive book of early Buddhism (the Hīnayāna). It renders a great service in the study of canonical philosophy and in the study of scholasticism properly so-called.[8]

The work became very influential throughout the Buddhist world and was frequently glossed in sub-commentaries such as Yaśomitra's *Sphūtārtha*.

Interpretative devices

Several techniques were applied by the masters of the *Abhidhamma* to open up the canonical writings and exploit their full meaning. These involved:

- detailed, repetitive explanations of all elements of the teaching in the *suttas*;

- question and answer style of presentation;
- use of similes and comparisons referring to the daily life experiences of the listeners;
- repetition of teachings;
- insistence on practice for the understanding of the teaching;
- mutual interpretation of various parts of the teaching;
- classifications.

This last technique merits some more detailed comments.

Classification as hermeneutics

Classifications play a great role in all Indian religions. In Vedic India, for example, the number four is prominent: there are four Vedas, four *varṇas* and four *āśramas*. The Upaniṣads and the Sāṁkhya consider five a basic number: the *Taittirīya Upaniṣad* coordinates the entire universe in pentads; the Sāṁkhya operates with twenty-five (5 × 5) principles (*tattvas*), which supposedly encompass the entire process of creation.

Classification also plays a great role in some of the modern sciences: it helps them to arrive at as complete an inventory of their subject as possible. Thus the atomic table of elements claims to be an exhaustive inventory of the building blocks of physical reality; the classification of plants and animals is intended to provide a complete enumeration of all living beings according to species, families and genera. Classification also permits structuring in a hierarchical manner.

In the Buddhist compendia, classification has similar functions: it establishes a complete listing of all *dhammas* (elements), facilitating the analysis of 'compounds', and adding plausibility to the realization that there are no *svabhāvas*, no individual 'natures' that might claim uniqueness and immortality. Classification is based on distinctions and represents the understanding of differences. It also may lead to series, sequences and hierarchies.

Classification is very prominent in Theravāda *Abhidhamma* literature. Besides the analysis of all of reality into eighty-two *dhammas*, as described above, the teaching in triplets, couplets, and so on that the *Abhidhamma Piṭaka* abounds in, provides structural insights into the content of the Dhamma, both helping to make it better understood and contributing to its final shape.

BUDDHIST LOGIC AND POLEMICS

The Western term 'logic' must be applied to Indian thought with some restrictive qualifications. While Hindus as well as Buddhists developed rules for formal argumentation, which are the core of traditional logic, both the extent and the scope of their enterprise was far larger. To begin with, they understood 'logic' as an instrument to reach spiritual fulfilment – for them truth coincided ultimately with enlightenment, self-realization, the final condition.

Second, they assumed a pre-rational and/or supra-rational source of logical reasoning: the authority of a non-human scripture or of an enlightened human being. The *pramāṇa-śāstra*, the science that deals with the ways to arrive at truth, presupposes both the existence of truth and the validation of the ways to reach it through the singularity of an established authority.

Third, 'logic' was geared towards action, more specifically towards the action required to reach enlightenment. As Dharmakīrti has it: 'All successful human action is (necessarily) preceded by right knowledge, therefore we are going to investigate it.'[9]

Tarka-śāstra, 'logic' in the more narrow sense, the art of constructing and analysing arguments, developed when a plurality of opposing interpretations of one and the same source emerged, or when disputes arose between followers of different paths, whose only common platform was formal rationality. While elements of logic and of the art of debate are to be found in a number of early Buddhist works, 'Buddhist logic' is a term usually reserved for the systematic treatment of *pramāṇa-śāstra* (a systematics of proofs of truth) from a Buddhist position which began with Dignāga in the fifth century CE, and ended in the twelfth century with the destruction of the Buddhist seats of learning in India by the Muslim invaders.[10]

A short history of Buddhist logic

DIGNĀGA

The 'Father of Medieval Logic', Dignāga (c. 450–520 CE) was born into a brahman family near Kāñcīpuram, in today's Tamil Nadu. First, as a student of Nāgadatta, who was a Vātsiputrīya, he studied the Hīnayāna *Tipiṭaka*. Later, with Vasubandhu, he also studied Mahāyāna texts. According to tradition he had a vision of Mañjuśrī, who promised success to his undertaking. Dignāga turned out to be a great debater and was given the epithet Tarka Puṅgava (Bull in Logical Dispute). He converted many Hindu pandits to Buddhism while travelling through India. In his *Pramāṇa Samuccaya* he deals with perception, inference for one's own self, inference for the sake of others, reason and example, negation of the opposite (*apoha*) and analogy. In his *Nyāya Praveśa* he deals with syllogism and fallacies.

PARAMĀRTHA

Another great name in Buddhist logic, Paramārtha (498–569 CE) came originally from Ujjain. He went to China with a Chinese Buddhist mission, and translated about seventy works into Chinese, amongst them Vasubandhu's *Tarka-śāstra*. He died in China.

DHARMAPĀLA

A native of Kāñcīpuram, south India, Dharmapāla (c. 600–35 CE) was first a student and then a professor at Nālandā. He is the author of several works that seem to have been lost in the original but were translated into Chinese.

DHARMAKĪRTI

Probably the most celebrated Buddhist logician, Dharmakīrti (635–50 CE) was a southern Indian brahman who became a Buddhist as a young man. He is said to have secretly studied with Kumārila, the Hindu Mīmāṁsaka master, in order to defeat him later. His main works are *Pramāṇa-vārtika* (containing polemics against non-Buddhist and other Buddhist systems), *Pramāṇa-vārtika vṛtti, Pramāṇa-Viniścaya* and *Nyāyabindu.*[11]

ŚĀNTARĀKṢITA

Śāntarākṣita (c. 700–70 CE) was for many years a professor at Nālandā and was invited to Tibet in order to teach Buddhism there. At first he was very reluctant, but he allowed himself be convinced that people in Tibet were very eager to receive the Dharma. He spent thirteen years in Tibet and is credited with having established the first Buddhist *vihāra* in central Tibet. His *Tattvasaṅgraha* is an encyclopaedic work dealing with all major aspects of philosophy.[12] It also contains polemics, mainly against the Hindu Mīmāṁsā system, quoting extensively from Kumārila's *Ślokavārttika*.

KAMALAŚĪLA

Kamalaśīla (c. 720–90 CE), who also became professor at Nālandā, was Śāntarākṣita's pupil and accompanied him to Tibet. His *Pañjika* is an extensive commentary to the *Tattvasaṅgraha*.[13] Since this work is so comprehensive, and also relatively easily accessible to interested readers in a reliable English translation, its structure and content will be described at some length in the following section.

A medieval Buddhist systematic: the Tattvasaṅgraha

The *Tattvasaṅgraha* by Śāntarākṣita, along with Kamalaśīla's *Pañjika*, is probably the most comprehensive systematic treatise of Buddhism, comparable to the *summae* of the medieval European Christian scholastics in scope and thoroughness. The title of each individual chapter has the suffix *parīkṣā* (Examination), indicating the critical character of the work as a whole. Indeed, the work offers a comprehensive and detailed critique of a variety of Hindu and Buddhist positions on all philosophically and theologically important matters. The Buddhist *parīkṣā* of these issues – which does not end with an analysis of other views but includes a strong assertion of the position held by the authors – was necessitated by attacks on Buddhism from Hindu systems such as Nyāya-Vaiśeṣika and Mīmāṁsā. Representatives of these schools had, in their own texts, attempted to refute crucial Buddhist positions.

Śāntarakita and Kamalaśīla make specific references (with numerous quotations) to such works, offering counter-arguments, quoting about eighty different authors altogether. For the sake of completeness systems such as Sāṁkhya and Vedānta, as well as the Hindu theistic philosophies, together with Jain and heterodox Buddhist systems, were subjected to critique and refutation. The length of each of the chapters can serve as a measure of the importance attributed to the topic. The presentation is problem oriented: particular solutions to a problem, as offered by specific schools of thought, are systematically analysed and proved false.

Thus under *prakṛti-parīkṣā* it is mainly the Sāṁkhya notion of *pradhāna* (Primary Matter) that is being analysed. Under *īśvara-parīkṣā* the (Hindu) theistic creationist systems, and under *ubhaya-parīkṣā* both the theistic Sāṁkhya and other schools are refuted. When dealing with *svabhāvika-jagadvāda-parīkṣā* (a critique of the teaching that the universe has independent being) the authors comment that while no school had advocated that theory in so many words, it was implicitly accepted by some and basic to their theories. Under *śabda-brahma-parīkṣā* the grammarians (especially Bhartṛhari's *Vākyapadīya*) are subjected to criticism. A short chapter is devoted to *puruṣa-parīkṣā*, the critique of the 'Veda-vādis' who maintained that a person (*puruṣa*) had created the world.

One of the longest sections is devoted to *ātma-parīkṣā*, subdivided into critiques of conceptions of self or soul by Naiyāyikas, Mīmāṁsakas, Sāṁkhyas, Jains, Vedāntins and Vātsiputrīyas. Subsequent to the refutation of the notion of *ātma* in any of these forms is a *sthīra-bhāva-parīkṣā*, a refutation of the permanence of any entity whatsoever. Special sections are devoted to discussions of the various categories of (presumed) reality in the Nyāya tradition of Hindu philosophy: the examination of *karma-phala-sambandha* is followed by a critique of notions of *dravya* (substance), *guṇa* (quality), *karma* (action), *samānya* (universal), *viśeṣa* (individual) and *samavaya* (inherence). A long section is devoted to *śabda-artha-parīkṣā*, the relationship between word/sound and meaning. The *pramāṇas* (proofs to establish truth) come next: Buddhists recognize only two: *pratyakṣa* (direct perception) and *anumāna* (inference). All other means of cognition accepted by other schools of thought, such as *śabda* (authoritative word), *upamāna* (analogy), *arthāpatti* (implication), *abhāva* (absence), *anupalabdhi* (not-perception), probability and tradition are subsumed under inference or rejected as invalid.

The rest of the *Tattvasaṅgraha* is devoted to excursus-like essays dealing with major issues and schools of thought that could not be accommodated in the systematics of the topic dealt with so far. A separate section deals with *syādvāda-parīkṣā*, an analysis of the Jain 'may-beism'. Another deals with *traikalya-parīkṣā*, a theory of time entertained by the Buddhist Vasumitra school. A section is devoted to *lokāyata-parīkṣā*, a refutation of Indian materialism (Buddhists were often lumped together with them!). A short section deals with *bahirārtha-parīkṣā*, 'examination of the external world'.

A long section is devoted to *śruti-parīkṣā*, an analysis of 'revelation through scripture'. The first part represents at length the teachings of the *Ślokavārttika*, which are then, piece by piece, refuted in the second. A Vedāntic theme is dealt with under *svataḥpramāṇya-parīkṣā*. The last section – a very long one at that – connects with the introductory verses, in which Buddha has been termed 'omniscient': The *ati-indriya-artha-darśi-parīkṣā* examines and establishes the claim that Buddha was a person of 'super-normal vision' (whereas other people, like the composer of the Vedas, for example, were not!).

In its concluding verses the *Tattvasaṅgraha* says:

> The omniscient person whose existence we have established is one who comprehends within a single cognitive moment the entire round of all that is to be known; it is for this reason that no succession is admitted in this case.[14]
>
> Whatever he wishes to know he comes to know it without fail – such is his power, as he has shaken off all evil. He knows things either simultaneously or in succession, just as he wishes; and having secured the knowledge of all things, he becomes the Lord (*prabhū*).[15]
>
> He knows all that is knowable in the shape of the four truths, by means of his sixteen cognitions, in succession, and on that account he is omniscient,[16] the consciousness of the omniscient is free from conceptual content and is not erroneous.[17]

The Buddha knows all things along with their causes, through a single extraordinary cognition brought about by *samādhi* – his existence has been proved by inference!

The omniscient Buddha and the false claim of the Veda

In the introductory invocation to the *Tattvasaṅgraha*, Śāntarakṣita had called the Buddha 'omniscient' (*sarvajñā*) and 'the greatest expounder of truth', who had taught the *pratītya-samutpāda* for the salvation of the whole world. His disciple Kamalaśīla explains in the *Pañjika* that 'true doctrine' can only mean *pratītya-samutpāda* and that by exclusion no other doctrine can be true: 'Though it is true that the saints and others also have expounded the *pratītya-samutpāda*, the Supreme Lord (*bhagavān*) is the greatest among them . . . the others could not have expounded the Dharma if the Bhagavān had not first taught it.' He was equipped with an extraordinary intellect, 'the efficiency consisting in the destruction of all dispositions, afflictions, and ignorance concerning all cognizable things'.[18]

The Buddha was *niḥsaṅgha*, that is independent of any previous scripture and revelation; he saw things directly by himself. He is on the same level as the (presumed) *svataḥ pramāṇabhūta veda*, that is he is the (true) *pramāṇabhūta*. Contrary to the assertion (by Kumārila) that no person has seen the unseen (invisible) Dharma which is promulgated in the Veda, the Buddhists claim that the (visible) *pratītya-samutpāda* has been seen by the Lord.

The chapter entitled *Śabdavicāra* deals with Śabara's and Kumārila's theory of the authoritativeness of the Veda – Veda as *śabdapramāṇa*. Śāntarakṣita turns the argument around: if the Veda has no (human) author, it has no meaning – because all meaning is bestowed by the speaker. Nobody could make out the meaning of the Veda – how could such 'knowledge' be considered 'unshakeable' if it is inaccessible? At best, conventional meaning could be ascribed to the Veda – and then it would be no different from other human works. 'It can be unshakeable only for the Śrotriya [brahmans who are well versed in scriptures, *śruti*] who are not familiar with the ways of reasoning'.[19]

The *Śrutiparīkṣā* is one of the longest sections of the *Tattvasaṅgraha*, a kind of special treatise to deal with the question of 'revealed' scripture. Numerous extracts from the *Ślokavārtika* are used to present the Mīmāṁsaka position in the first part of the work, followed by a detailed refutation. Within the work (verses 2705ff.) there is a special argument against the *sphoṭa*-theory of the grammarians:

> The *sphoṭa* has been assumed by the grammarians for the purpose of explaining the cognition of the meanings of words. But the letters themselves being competent to express the meanings of words, the assuming of the said *sphoṭa* is futile. As it would be perceptible (if it existed), but is not perceived, it is concluded that it does not exist. If it is imperceptible, then it cannot be indicative, like the inferential indicative (which is effective only when perceived).[20]

The Buddhists, by reducing 'meaning' to the understanding of (non-eternal) letters/syllables, demolish the possibility of 'eternality' assumed for words/texts composed of such elements:

> Thus it has not been proven that the Vedic injunctions are the valid means of right knowledge of Dharma, for the simple reason that its meaning cannot be ascertained by any one, either by himself or with the help of other dull-witted persons ... For these reasons please seek for a person whose inner darkness has been dispelled by the light of knowledge, and who is capable of teaching the clear meaning of *śruti* [revealed scriptures; i.e. the Veda].[21]

The next section, entitled *Svataḥpramāṇya-parīkṣā*, connects seamlessly with the preceding verse – a kind of *coup de grâce* after the adversary had been disarmed: 'Thus then, it being established that the Vedas are the work of a personality, the self-sufficiency of their authority and validity also becomes overthrown without effort.'[22] In effect, the bold claim is made by Buddhists that the Buddha alone is capable of knowing the true meaning of the Veda as Dharma!

Apoha-vāda: 'negation of the opposite'

One of the central teachings of Buddhism with regard to language is the so-called *apoha-vāda*, 'negativism', implying that words do not designate universals, but only particulars, and that they designate mainly by denying their identity with what they are not. The *Tattvasaṅgraha* devotes a long section to this topic.[23]

For Buddhists words are creations of our minds; the conceptual image is in our imagination and not a reality in itself or an image of reality. The *apoha* is proof of the non-substantiality of universals. Words serve as vehicles of communication, because both speaker and hearer suffer under the same illusions, share the same desires: 'what they see and hear are really their own mental concepts, but both think that they are referring to their objective reality'.[24] The *Tattvasaṅgraha* says: 'Just as the man

---

THE WORD AND THE SILENCE OF THE BUDDHA

Now, in reality, the Lord, having extirpated the force which calls forth speech (*vāk-samutthāna-vāsana*), has attained enlightenment in perfect silence, and then, up to the time of his attaining *nirvāṇa*, has not uttered a single word. But in accordance with the thoughts (and the needs) of the living beings, he appears as if he is teaching (the Doctrine) in various forms, as it is said

> A cymbal on a magic circle issues its sounds, being agitated by the wind; and although there is nothing with which it is beaten, its sound is nevertheless heard. Similar is the voice of the Buddha which arises, being called forth by the thoughts of the living beings, and owing to their previous virtuous deeds. But the Buddha (himself) has no constructive thought (by which his words could be conditioned).

The voice of the Buddha is therefore something inconceivable for our mind. (Obermiller, *History of Buddhism by Bu-ston*, vol. II, p. 55)

---

whose eye has been attacked by a disorder says to another likewise afflicted that "there are two moons" – so is all verbal communication.'[25]

In this context, K. Raja quotes a modern Western writer who said: 'meaning is practically everything. We always see the meaning as we look, think in meaning as we think, act in terms of meaning when we act. Apparently we are never conscious of anything but meaning.'[26] For Buddhists too, all meaning is *manomaya*, mind-made: words and concepts have no reality content, and they designate by negation of 'otherness'.

Catuṣkoṭi *and* avyākṛta*: the logic of the unsaid*

We read that the Buddha refused to give answers to questions which were apparently of great importance to the philosophers of his time. The reason for not providing an answer was that these questions were 'not conducive to salvation', in other words they were irrelevant. Buddhist writers hasten to add that the Buddha did know the answers, but did not wish to go into the matter.

These questions concern the following matters:

- whether a *tathāgata* exists, does not exist, both exists and does not exist, or neither exists nor does not exist after death;
- whether the world (*loka*, the physical universe) is finite, infinite, both finite and infinite, or neither finite nor infinite;
- whether the world is eternal, not eternal, both eternal and not eternal, or neither eternal nor not eternal;
- whether the *jīva* (soul) is different from the body or not.

These fourteen *avyākṛtas*, unexplicated points, figure quite prominently in Buddhist philosophy.

Apart from the specific questions asked, the 'quadrilemma', the 'four-cornered logic' in which they are expressed, became a standard methodology for Buddhist logicians in all Buddhist schools. Many ancient and modern authors have come up with various contradictory interpretations of the *catuṣkoṭi* and what it means for the assertion of truth/reality in Buddhism.[27]

The Buddhist theory of language

The Buddhist theory of language derives from the epistemological position that there are only two *pramāṇas* (ways to find provable truth):

pratyakṣa (perception) and *anumāna* (analogy). *Śabda* (word, authority) is subsumed under *anumāna*, indirect knowledge. Contrary to the Mīmāṁsākas (and other Hindu systems, which postulate an independent *śabda pramāṇa*, even elevating it to the highest rank), the Buddhists (especially the logicians, like Dignāga) do not assume *śabda* to be eternally/naturally/unconditionally connected with reality, a kind of mental blueprint of reality, corresponding both to the structures of the outside world and of the mind, but see it as reflecting only images or concepts, mere constructs of the mind.

Only *pratyakṣa* is direct cognition – *śabda* is indirect, through concepts, expressing meaning dialectically, that is by denying its opposite. Thus words like 'white' and 'black' do not necessitate the existence of whiteness or blackness, nor do they imply the knowledge of all white or black objects. White can only be known from particular instances of cognition of objects by contrasting them with others that have other colours. The word itself does not disclose any essence called 'whiteness' nor does it deliver the 'specific', as the Vaiśeṣikas had claimed.

Words thus do not have an intrinsic relation to reality but are products of the mind (which itself is not representative of reality as such, but is formed by *saṁkhāras*, 'imprints'). Reality can be alluded to by words – but since words are capable of importing only indirect knowledge, they are not the instruments by which to know reality. Buddhist practice is geared towards reality and towards disabusing people of a belief in the identification of words with reality. 'Emptying the mind' is practised as a method of hermeneutics.[28]

Buddhists consider all language to be based on mere convention, without any designation of reality-content. It is an important departure from the Hindu (especially the Mīmāṁsāka and grammarian) view of language which equates word with reality. The best illustration of the Buddhist position is in the *Milindapañha's* 'chariot simile'.[29] There the merely conventional use of language is demonstrated in order to support the Buddhist view of the non-substantial nature of 'self': self, like all other 'names', does not have an intrinsic meaning apart from the conventional use of the word, and the existence of the word does not permit an inference as to the existence of a thing thus designated.

This has important consequences. The first is that one has to pay attention to the conventional use of words in order to find out what they mean. The teaching of the Buddha has to be understood in the terms of the teaching itself; his words cannot be taken out of context and interpreted independently. Further, it is suggested that words, and that which words designate, cannot be ultimates. The Buddhist quest goes beyond words – words have to be left behind to understand the nature of enlightenment. Reality is not cognitive or conceptual. Concepts are a mind-product; they do not arise from reality, and language can be used in a non-cognitive manner as well.[30]

Buddhists are credited with having created medieval Indian logic, a logic that is at once both subtle and practical. Hindu logicians reacted to Buddhist logic and refined it. Anti-Buddhist polemic soon became an integral part of Hindu systematics – it is found even in the works of recent authors, who have never encountered a live Buddhist and never had to engage in an exchange with a Buddhist teacher.

NOTES

1. The English titles give the names of the texts as they appear in the Pāli Text Translation Series.
2. An English translation appeared under the title *Comprehensive Manual of Abhidhamma* (Kandy, Sri Lanka: Buddhist Publication Society, 1993).
3. Bimala Churn Law's monograph *Buddhaghosa* offers rich information on his life and work.
4. Bhikkhu Ñyāṇamoli in the introduction to his translation of the *Nettipakkaraṇa* (see appendix 2).
5. Ibid. p. xliv.
6. Ñyāṇaponika in his introduction to Ñyāṇamoli's translation of *Nettipakkaraṇa*, *The Guide* (pp. xviiff.) compares the two works.
7. See Gethin, *The Foundations of Buddhism*, p. 206.
8. *Abhidharma-kośa-bhāṣya*, trans. L. M. Pruden from the French of Louis de la Vallée Poussin, vol. I, p. 4.
9. This is the first sentence of the *Nyāyabindu*, translated in the second volume of Stcherbatskys' *Buddhist Logic*.
10. Stcherbatsky, the great Russian Orientalist whose translation and study of Dharmakīrti's *Nyāyabindu* introduced Western philosophers to Buddhist logic, begins his introduction thus: 'Under Buddhist Logic we understand a system of logic and epistemology created in India in the VI–VIIth century AD by two great lustres of Buddhist science, the Masters Dignāga and Dharmakīrti' (*Buddhist Logic*, I, originally published as vol. XXVI, part I of the Bibliotheka Buddhica series [St Petersburg, 1933], p. XIII).
11. Fully translated with commentary in vol. II of Stcherbatsky's *Buddhist Logic*.
12. A complete translation of the *Tattvasaṅgraha* in two volumes was published by G. Jha in the Baroda Oriental Series in 1937 (see appendix 2).

13. The *Pañjika* too has been translated by Ganganatha Jha in his two-volume translation of the *Tattvasaṅgraha*.
14. *Tattvasaṅgraha*, v. 3627.
15. Ibid. vv. 3628–9.
16. Ibid. v. 3630.
17. Ibid. v. 3636.
18. Kamalaśīta, *Pañjika* to v. 6 of *Tattvasaṅgraha*.
19. *Tattvasaṅgraha*, v. 1509.
20. Ibid. vv. 2705–6.
21. Ibid. vv. 2809–10.
22. Ibid. v. 2811.
23. Ibid. vv. 908ff. The topic is treated extensively in Raja, *Indian Theories of Meaning*, pp. 78–94.
24. Raja, *Indian Theories of Meaning*, p. 93.
25. *Tattvasaṅgraha*, v. 1211.
26. W. B. Spillsbury, 'Meaning and Logic', *Psychological Review* (1906), quoted in Raja, *Indian Theories of Meaning*, p. 94.
27. The most extensive modern treatment may be Ruegg, 'The Uses of the Four Positions of the Catuskoti'.
28. Stcherbatsky, *Buddhist Logic*, vol. I, pp. 457ff. Cf. also *Tattvasaṅgraha*, vv. 867ff.
29. See chapter 3, pp. 74–85, 'King Milinda's Questions'.
30. See Sprung, 'Non-Cognitive Language in Madhyamaka Buddhism'.

9 MADHYAMAKA, YOGĀCĀRA AND TANTRIC BUDDHISM

MADHYAMAKA: THE 'CENTRAL PHILOSOPHY'

Of the four major schools of Mahāyāna Buddhist philosophy, the Madhyamaka may be the best known, not least because of T. R. V. Murti's masterful exposition of the system in his classic and often-reprinted work *The Central Philosophy of Buddhism*. Madhyamaka systematically deconstructs the traditional Buddha-word, not in order to teach an (un-Buddhist) nihilism, but to let the enlightenment unfold its own dynamics. Madhyamaka 'deconstruction'[1] took its cue from certain elements already found in Theravāda teaching, such as the non-substantiality of all things, pushing the logical consequences of the so-called *avyākṛtas* (un-nameables) and the *catuṣkoṭi* method (four-cornered logic) to its limits.

The history of Madhyamaka

NĀGĀRJUNA

Nāgārjuna (second century CE) is one of the most famous names not only in Mahāyāna Buddhism and Madhyamaka philosophy, but in the whole of Indian and even world philosophy.[2] Traditional Buddhist histories devote much space to describing his adventurous life and his work.[3] According to one such tradition he studied at Nālandā under Rāhulabhadra, who introduced him into the Prajñā-pāramitā (Perfection of Wisdom) school.

> Nāgārjuna's writings are the first philosophical treatises (*śāstra*) known to us in which an attempt has been made to give a systematic scholastic exposition of the theory of emptiness (*śūnyatā*) and non-substantiality (*niśvabhāvatā*) not only of the self (*ātman*) or individual (*pudgala*) but also of all factors of existence (*dharma*), one of the most fundamental ideas of the Mahāyāna *sūtras*.[4]

His main work, the *Madhyamaka-kārikās*,[5] is a collection of 449 stanzas divided into 27 chapters dealing with as many central themes, each qualified as *parīkṣā* (examination/analysis/deconstruction):

DECONSTRUCTION OF CONDITIONING FACTORS

Neither from itself, nor from another, nor from both, nor from no-cause, can ever arise any entity anywhere.

There are four 'conditioning factors': 'cause', 'object,' 'predecessor' and 'the decisive point'. There is no fifth factor.

There really is no 'own-nature' of these entities in all these factors. While no 'own-nature' can be found, also no 'other-nature' exists.

'Efficient cause' does not act as conditioning factor. Nor is a non-conditioning factor acting as a cause. The conditioning factors do not act as efficient causes and there is nothing in them that acts cause-like.

Those are called 'conditioning factors' in whose presence something originates. When something does not originate, how come, these are not 'non-conditioning factors'?

There can be no conditioning factor for non-being nor for being. What would the conditioning factor of non-being be and through which conditioning factor would being be?

If there is no 'supporting element' (*dharma*) of being, non-being, or being-non-being, how could it make sense that there be a cause?

If the no-object is taught as *dharma*, how can it be that *dharma* is (defined as) not inhering in an object?

If there are no *dharmas* that have originated, then cessation is not possible. The theory of predecessor does not make sense, for what is a conditioning factor of something that has ceased to be?

As no being-ness is found of entities nor of non-entities, it is not possible to conclude that 'this thing comes into existence if that thing is'. (Nāgārjuna, *Madhyamaka-kārikās* I, 1–10)

---

1. *pratyaya-parīkṣā* (conditioning causes, content of consciousness);
2. *gata-agata-parīkṣā* (movement in space and time);
3. *cakṣur-ādi-indriya-parīkṣā* (sense faculties);
4. *skandha-parīkṣā* (five groups);
5. *dhātu-parīkṣā* (elements);
6. *rāga-rakta-parīkṣā* (passions and subjects of passions);
7. *saṃskṛta-parīkṣā* (composition, production);
8. *karma-kāraka-parīkṣā* (action and agent);
9. *pūrva-parīkṣā* (pre-existent subject);
10. *agni-indhana-parīkṣā* (fire and fuel: appropriator and appropriated);
11. *pūrva-apara-koti-parīkṣā* (prior and posterior limits of saṃsāra);
12. *duḥkha-parīkṣā* (suffering);
13. *saṃskāra-parīkṣā* ('engrams', the conditioned);
14. *saṃsarga-parīkṣā* (category of 'contact');
15. *svabhāva-parīkṣā* (aseity, own-being);
16. *bandha-mokṣa-parīkṣā* (bondage and liberation);
17. *karma-phala-parīkṣā* (action and its result);
18. *ātma-parīkṣā* (self);
19. *kāla-parīkṣā* (time);
20. *sāmagrī-parīkṣā* (complex aggregate of causes and conditions);
21. *sambhava-vibhava-parīkṣā* (production and destruction, possibility and impossibility);
22. *tathāgata-parīkṣā* (the Buddha);
23. *viparyāsa-parīkṣā* (error);
24. *ārya-satya-parīkṣā* (the Four Noble Truths);
25. *nirvāṇa-parīkṣā* (*nirvāṇa*);
26. *dvādaśa-aṅga-parīkṣā* (conditioning occasions of arising);
27. *dṛṣṭi-parīkṣā* (sixteen speculative [wrong] views).

Besides some smaller philosophical works Nāgārjuna is also credited with having written four philosophical hymns, the *Catustava*.

A great many commentaries were written on the *Madhyamaka-kārikās* in Sanskrit, Tibetan and Chinese. The best known is Candrakīrti's *Prasannapadā*.[6] T. R. V. Murti's celebrated *Central Philosophy of Buddhism* is largely an exposition of Nāgārjuna as interpreted by Dharmakīrti.

ĀRYADEVA

Āryadeva,[7] who was probably a direct disciple of Nāgārjuna, was famous for his skill in debates, especially against Sāmkhya and Vaiśeṣika. He wrote a commentary on the *Madhyamaka-kārikās* and the *Catuśataka* (only partly preserved in Sanskrit) as well as other works, now only available in Chinese translations.

KUMĀRAJĪVA

Kumārajīva (344–413 CE) was a key figure in the translation of Madhyamaka texts from Sanskrit into Chinese.

By the middle of the sixth century the Madhyamaka split into two schools: the Prāsaṅgika, under the leadership of Buddhapālita, and the Svātantrika following Bhāvaviveka.

BUDDHAPĀLITA

Buddhapālita (c. 500 CE) wrote an extensive commentary on Nāgārjuna's *Madhyamaka-kārikās* which is only preserved, however, in a Tibetan translation. He is credited with having established within Madhyamaka the Prāsaṅgika school, which is an interpretation of Nāgārjuna along the lines of a method that favours the *reductio ad absurdum*: instead of countering an opponent's argument with a better alternative, it shows how the opponent involves himself in self-contradiction in a continued extension of the opponent's own argument.

BHĀVAVIVEKA

Probably hailing from south India, Bhāvaviveka (500–70 CE) also wrote a commentary on the *Madhyamaka-kārikās*, which is only available now in Tibetan and Chinese translations. His major original works are the *Madhyamaka-hṛdaya-kārikās* with his own commentary, *Tarkajvala*, which contains a critical review of all schools known to Bhāvaviveka. He is also the author of the *Madhyamakārtha-saṁgraha*.

CANDRAKĪRTI

Candrakīrti (c. 600–50 CE) defended Buddhapālita, the founder of the Prāsaṅgika tradition in Madhyamaka, against Bhāvaviveka. He wrote *Madhyamaka-āvatāra* (preserved in Sanskrit) with *bhāṣya* (commentary). It deals with ten productions of thought (*cittotpāda*), each linked with one of the ten *bhūmis* of the Bodhisattva and corresponding to one of the ten *pāramitās*.

ŚĀNTIDEVA

Introduced in chapter 7, *Śāntideva* (c. 750 CE) is one of the most widely appealing Mahāyāna authors. His *Bodhicaryāvatāra* (Entry to the Way of Enlightenment) is a spiritual classic that has become popular in East and West.[8] It also contains a highly technical exposition of Madhyamaka philosophy in chapter IX entitled *Prajñā-pāramitā*.

ŚĀNTARAKṢITA AND KAMALAŚĪLA

Śāntarakṣita, the author of the *Tattvasaṅgraha* and Kamalaśīla, the author of a commentary on it called *Pañjika*, already mentioned in chapter 8 (see p. 162), philosophically represent a Yogācāra–Madhyamaka synthesis.

Some central notions of the Central Philosophy

Nāgārjuna introduces his *Madhyamaka-kārikās* with a programmatic dedication to which he returns at the end – a kind of 'faith' statement that should be understood as a foil against which the deconstruction of conventional Buddhism is undertaken:

> I pay homage to the best of teachers, the perfectly awakened one, who has taught origination in dependence, the stilling (*nirodha*) of discursive development, the auspicious, which is without destruction and production, not annihilated and not eternal, neither undifferentiated nor differentiated, and without coming and going.[9]

The same idea is also expressed in the *Lokātītastava*, one of the philosophical hymns to the Buddha ascribed to Nāgārjuna: 'This world, devoid of essential characteristics and characterized objects, unrelated to verbal utterances, has been seen as "peace" by you with your eye of knowledge.'[10]

Nāgārjuna sees in the *pratītya-samutpāda* the truth that the Buddha taught and through which he saved the world. In the *Maṅgala-śloka*, the invocation preceding the *Madhyamaka kārikās* he qualifies and describes this truth as:

- *anirodha* (without cessation);
- *anutpāda* (without arising);
- *anuccheda* (without destruction);
- *asaśvata* (without duration);

- *anekārtha* (without one meaning);
- *anārārtha* (without another meaning);
- *anāgama* (without past);
- *anirgama* (without future).

and calls it:

- *prapañcopāsana* (stilling the world of creation);
- *śiva* (auspicious, graceful).

THE NOTION OF 'EMPTINESS' (*ŚŪNYATĀ*)

From the very beginning Buddhism taught that all so-called reality was characterized by three signs: suffering, transience and soullessness. The latter became a particular issue in the Hindu–Buddhist controversy over the nature of the self, the Buddhists rejecting the notion of a permanent seat of consciousness (*ātman*, *puruṣa*, *pudgala*, etc.). Its logical extension to 'everything' led to the formulation of the 'emptiness of all *dharmas*', i.e. those constants of experience which were the substratum for sensations, consciousness and words.

Śūnyatā was recognized as the key term of Madhyamaka Buddhism in particular. Quite appropriately F. Streng gave to his masterly monograph on Nāgārjuna's philosophy the title *Emptiness.*[11] While often interpreted as 'nihilism' by earlier Western scholars like E. Bournouf, and also by hostile medieval Hindu *ācāryas* such as Madhva, it has now been commonly recognized that *śūnyatā* is not a denial of ultimate reality but its affirmation, by describing it as the result of a process of elimination of all possible logical alternatives at the phenomenological level. *Śūnyatā* is the silence reached when words have found their limits, a realm of reality beyond those limits. Nāgārjuna, by demonstrating the inevitable self-contradictions in which every dogmatic assertion (positive or negative) regarding reality sooner or later involves itself, opens up the possibility of transcending the realm of logic and intuiting the non-conceptual reality of *nirvāṇa*.

'Nāgārjuna's philosophy is conceived with the purpose of revealing the convergence of *śūnyatā*, *pratītya-samutpāda* and the Middle Way (*madhyama pratipat*).'[12] And: '*Prapañca* [the world made up of images, words, devices, etc.] itself comes to a stop in *śūnyatā*.'[13]

THE NOTION OF THE 'TWO TRUTHS'

The Madhyamaka school pre-empts a falsification of its own views by a re-application of its own methodology through its famous 'two truths theory': a distinction between *samvṛti* (conventional, preliminary) and *paramārthika* (absolute, ultimate) *satya* (truth). From the standpoint of *paramārthika satya*, *samvṛti satya* is false. However, from a practical standpoint, and within the framework of *saṃsāra*, we need 'conventional truth' in order to function in a world made up of conventions and commonly perceived needs. It is all-important to go first to the very limits of *samvṛti satya* in order to become aware of its self-contradictory nature and to experience its emptiness. With that comes the realization that there is no 'own-nature' of anything and that concepts that express conventional truths are mere conventions, without intrinsic connection to reality. Then one can leave it all behind and realize *paramārthika satya*. The latter is only possible in a 'yogic consciousness' in which nothing of the transient multiplicity is preserved.

At the level of *paramārtha* the concerns of what we today would call psychology/psychotherapy, gnoseology/epistemology, and ontology/metaphysics coincide: the highest 'truth' is at the same time highest 'freedom' and 'no-thing-ness'. These aspects are treated in studies like P. Fenner's 'A Therapeutic Contextualisation of Buddhist Madhyamaka Consequential Analysis', F. Streng's 'The Buddhist Doctrine of Two Truths as Religious Philosophy' and M. Mehta's 'Śūnyatā and Dharmatā: The Madhyamaka View of Reality'.[14] On the *paramārthika*, i.e. the 'real' level, truth is not identical with a correspondence between concepts and (experiential) reality, but with 'Buddha-nature', which is infinite compassion with suffering humankind.

THE *PRASAṄGA* METHOD

The term *parīkṣā*, which Nāgārjuna uses, can be translated in different ways: as 'critique' (moving it close to Kant's eighteenth-century methodology), as 'analysis' (which makes it a parallel to twentieth-century linguistic analysis), or as 'deconstruction' (which makes it sound 'postmodern'). All these parallels bring out something specific, but they should not be pressed too much.

The *prasaṅga* method which Nāgārjuna uses has its 'hermeneutical centre' in his existential experience of the *bodhi-citta-utpāda*, the flashlike illumination and awakening of the 'Buddha-mind'. Nāgārjuna

---

WHAT IS *NIRVĀṆA*?

If all there is, is a void (*śūnya*), there is no arising and no ceasing. Whose *nirvāna* is then wished for through the elimination and cessation of what?

If all there is, is a non-void, there is no arising and no ceasing. Whose *nirvāṇa* is then wished for through the elimination and cessation of non-what?

Nirvāṇa is said to be non-eliminated and non-obtained, non-destroyed and non-eternal, non-obstructed and non-arisen.

Nirvāṇa is not an entity characterized by old age and death: there is no entity that does not age and die.

If *nirvāṇa* were an entity, *nirvāṇa* would have to be composite. No entity has ever been non-composite.

If *nirvāṇa* were an entity, how could it exist without a substratum? Nor is there any entity '*nirvāṇa*-without-substratum'.

The Lord has declared the destruction of both becoming and unbecoming, therefore *nirvāṇa* is considered to be neither a being nor a non-being.

If *nirvāṇa* were both non-being and being, then *mokṣa* would be both non-being and being; and that is not right.

If *nirvāṇa* were both non-being and being there would be no unconditioned *nirvāṇa*, because these both were conditions.

There is no distinguishing quality between *saṃsāra* and *nirvāṇa*. And there is no distinguishing quality between *nirvāṇa* and *saṃsāra*.

Since all *dharmas* are empty, what can be finite, what infinite? What can both have and not have an end, or neither have and not have an end?

What is 'that' and what is 'other'? What is 'eternal' what is 'non-eternal'? What is 'eternal-and-non-eternal' and what is neither of both?

The cessation of all perception, the cessation of the world is bliss. No *dharma* has been taught by the Buddha anywhere, of anything. (Nāgārjuna, M*adhyamaka-kārikās* XXV, 1–6, 10–12, 19, 22–4)

---

does not use the *reductio ad absurdum* in a frivolous manner or out of spite, he uses it in order to make room for true insight. In a sense, through it he takes himself out of the game of argumentative philosophy and moves into the realm of intuitive wisdom – to silence:

> The Madhyamaka, based as it is on the *śūnyatā* theory and the *prasaṅga* method, is indeed unassailable, for not only does a Madhyamaka restrict

> himself to a kind of philosophical deconstruction – and therapeutic dehabituation – with respect to dichotomizing conceptualization while refraining from propounding any propositional thesis of his own, but any argument adduced to combat and refute the theory of *śūnyatā* is devoid of cogency, and falls into line and reinforces the Madhyamaka theory, since all things can be shown to be equally non-substantial.[15]

Moreover:

> the immunity of the Madhyamaka theory is the consequence of the annullment ('zeroing') of all hypostatized and dichotomously structured concepts, and it pertains only to the domain of an entity conceived of in terms of a conceptual dichotomy.[16]
>
> Nāgārjuna's regular way of analyzing and deconstructing (that is 'emptying' or 'zeroing') any postulated entity is first to show that its substantial self-nature has been constructed and posited in terms of related terms (e.g. *utpāda/nirodha*, *svabhāva/parabhāva*, *saṃskṛta/asamskṛta*) ... Nāgārjuna shows that since these sets are made up of interrelated and hence dependent concepts or categories, no term can be posited as a real entity possessing independent and substantial *svabhāva* or 'aseity'; for the postulated *svabhāva* is by its very definition unable ontologically to exist within the above-mentioned sets of correlates.[17]
>
> The characteristic of reality (*tattva-lakṣana*) is then to be free from dichotomizing conceptualisation and, accordingly, to be without multiplicity, still and undeveloped in discursive development.[18]

For N. P. Jacobson:

> Buddhism is humanity's first systematic attempt to free itself from what Freud called the tyranny of the superego, and from what Wittgenstein called the tyranny of language. Buddhists have never tried to control life in themselves and others under the dictates of an existing form of understanding, regardless of how hallowed its source.[19]

Bimal Krishna Matilal, in his very thoughtful paper 'Is *Prasaṅga* a Form of Deconstruction?' suggests a similarity between the socio-intellectual climate of today, which gave rise to 'deconstruction', and the age of Nāgārjuna, which developed the *prasaṅga* method. Matilal identifies the 'Freudian' roots of 'deconstruction': 'The major preoccupation of the author, or rather the dominant concern of the text, is shown to betray itself. Deconstruction is in a sense "the interpretation of dreams".'[20] Nāgārjuna also writes 'under erasure' – he denies any essential relationship between word and reality, but he is using the customary reality-referring words nevertheless. Similarly the strange adherence to metaphysics while denying it with so many words that 'free us from and guard us within the metaphysical enclosure' has its parallel in the *prasaṅga* method as well.

Jaspers calls Nāgārjuna a 'representative of this extreme possibility of transcending metaphysics by means of metaphysics'.[21] It would not work if there were not a larger un-named framework for the names that are rejected. While logically deconstructionists would have to deconstruct their own de-/reconstructions and thus take themselves out of the game, they trust that the possibilities of deconstruction/reconstruction are infinite and that 'deconstruction possesses the lure of abyss as freedom' because we never 'hit the bottom'.[22]

From what little we know about the time in which Nāgārjuna lived, its political instability and philosophico-religious anarchy, we may well infer that his profound scepticism towards the 'systems' was nourished by the corruption of secular as well as religious authorities, and that his distrust towards language as means to express truth was based on very solid evidence of deceit in everyday life. 'Words of authority' were not necessarily 'words of truth' anymore, and the clash of authorities left everyone bewildered. It is not without significance that, as tradition has it, so many of the major figures of Madhyamaka were princes who had renounced their claims.

> Nāgārjuna was ... engaged in a radical rethinking of the philosophical endeavour, that is, of the very idea of philosophy and the terms in which it is to be pursued. And by turning away from the construction of a speculative doctrine involving the postulation of entities having some kind of self-nature, he clearly sought to keep strictly to the Middle Way indicated by the Buddha in the only manner he found commensurate with it.[23]

YOGĀCĀRA: 'MIND ONLY'

Historically the last, and according to many scholars the highest expression of Mahāyāna Buddhist thought is known under the two names of Yogācāra (Yoga-path) and Cittamātra (Mind Only). Both designations characterize that tradition. For long periods the name of the founder Maitreyanātha was identified with the Maitreya Buddha himself, assuming a kind of 'divine revelation' for the basic writings of

Yogācāra that placed them on a level higher than the Pāli Canon, in which were recorded the (imperfectly understood) words of the Buddha in his earthly appearance.

That (mis-)understanding was nourished by the legendary history of Asaṅga, the historical author of important Yogācāra texts, which states that Asaṅga, after lengthy periods of self-mortification and prayer, was bodily taken up by Maitreya to the Tuṣita heaven and there received instruction in the right understanding of the Prajñā-pāramitā literature.[24]

History of Yogācāra

MAITREYANĀTHA

Many scholars today assume that Maitreya, the teacher of Asaṅga, was a historical figure (about whom very little is known) and that he was the author of the following five works:

1. *Abhisamaya-alaṁkāra*;
2. *(Mahāyāna)-sūtra-ālaṁkāra*;
3. *Dharma-dharmatā-vibhaṅga*;
4. *Madhyānta-vibhaṅga*;
5. *(Mahāyāna)-uttara-tantra.*

If Asaṅga, as generally assumed, flourished c. 310–90 CE, Maitreya will have to be assigned to c. 270–350 CE. The basic tenor of his works is one of reconciliation of the various schools of Buddhism, Hīnayāna as well as Mahāyāna.

His first two works attempt to bring some kind of systematics into the huge and unwieldy mass of Mahāyāna writings, synthesizing the various teachings into a kind of universal Buddhist philosophy. According to Buston Rimpoche

> the *Sūtra-ālaṁkāra* contains an exposition of all the Māhāyanist Doctrines in abridged form:
>
> > Like wrought gold, an unfolded lotus flower,
> > like well prepared food, enjoyed by those who were starving,
> > like a message agreeable to hear, or like an opened chest
> > full of jewels, the Doctrine, that is expounded here, is the cause of the highest delight,
> > In such a form its content is presented (to the reader).[25]

The next two works re-assert a Middle Way between the extremities of Sarvāstivāda and Madhyamaka (*śūnyatā*) by postulating some kind of provisional reality for consciousness:

> According to Maitreyanātha the *śūnyatā* of the Madhyamikas is an extreme view, and as such to be rejected: Reality is both existent and non-existent. It is existent inasmuch as it constitutes the real being of phenomena, but non-existent inasmuch as in it the subject–object-relation inherent in mundane experience does not obtain.[26]

As the *Madhyānta-vibhaṅga* says:

> The unreal imagination is; duality does not exist in it, but voidness exists in it, and it also exists in this.

ASAṄGA AND VASUBANDHU

The brothers Asaṅga and Vasubandhu[27] (c. 320–400 CE), recipients of Maitreya's revelation, are considered the most important authors of Yogācāra. Traditional Buddhist sources contain much (legendary) information about them.

Bu-ston Rimpoche introduces the biographies of Asaṅga and Vasubandhu in the context of the last of three calamities that had befallen 'the Highest Doctrine from its foes'. A brahman woman, Prasannaśīlā, vowed to make her sons – if she were to have any – 'propagators of the Doctrine'. She bore Asaṅga from a Kṣatriya, and Vasubandhu from a Brāhmaṇa father, and 'drew on their tongues the letter A and performed all the other rites in order to secure for them an acute intellectual faculty'. When they grew older, their mother told them: 'You must purify your minds and expound the doctrine.'[28]

Vasubandhu went to Kashmir to study with Saṅghabhadra (a Sarvāstivādin). Asaṅga withdrew into a mountain cave, leading an ascetic's life, propitiating Maitreya in order to obtain his help. After twelve years he was about to give up. When he stopped on the road to comfort a dog that had been injured, the dog turned out to be Maitreya. To Asaṅga's complaint that Maitreya had appeared only now, after all longing for him had left him, Maitreya answered: 'I was here from the very beginning, but thou couldst not see me, owing to thy own obscurations. Now, as great commiseration has arisen in thee, thou hast become purified and canst now behold me.'[29]

Ascertaining that he desired to learn from Maitreya how to expound the Mahāyāna doctrine, Maitreya took Asaṅga up to the Tuṣita heaven where he was allowed to spend one moment, according to the divine time-scale (equivalent to about fifty human years).

The fruit of the vision was the *Yogācārabhūmi*, among other works. The *Yogācārabhūmi* is a massive work and is usually considered the most important Yogācāra text. It consists of five sections:

1. *Bahubhūmikā-vāstu* which expounds the Yogācāra doctrine;
2. *Nirṇaya-saṁgraha*, a kind of commentary on the preceding;
3. *Vāstu-saṁgraha*;
4. *Paryāya-saṁgraha*;
5. *Vivaraṇa-saṁgraha*, explaining word-meanings and methods of teaching.

Asaṅga is also credited with having written two large works, *Abhidharma samuccaya* and *Mahāyāna-saṁgraha*.

Vasubandhu, meanwhile, had written a massive encyclopaedic work, the *Abhidharma-kośa*, a summary of Sarvāstivāda Buddhism in about 600 verses. After his conversion to Yogācāra thought by his brother Asaṅga, he added a *bhāṣya* (commentary) to the text, in which, from a Yogācāra perspective, he freely criticized the Sarvāstivāda doctrine. The *Abhidharma-kośa*, together with its *bhāṣya*, is one of the most important presentations of Buddhism in general.[30] Vasubandhu is also the author of three short systematic works:

- *Viṃśatikā* (Exposition in Twenty Verses);
- *Triṃśikavijñaptikārikā* (Exposition of *Vijñapti* in Thirty Verses);
- *Trisvabhāvakārikā* (Exposition of the 'Three Natures').

STHIRAMATI

Sthiramati (fifth century CE) is credited with having written commentaries on the *Abhidharma-kośa* and the *Abhidharma samuccaya*. The only work preserved in Sanskrit is the *Madhyāntavibhāgaṭīkā*. It characterizes Yogācāra as teaching: 'all this is neither empty nor not-empty' (*sarvam idam na śūnyam na-aśūnyam iti Prajñā-pāramitā*).[31]

ŚĀNTARAKṢITA AND KĀMALAŚĪLA

In the seventh century CE a Yogācāra–Madhyamaka synthesis was brought about in Śāntarakṣita's massive encyclopaedic work *Tattva-saṅgraha* and Kāmalaśīla's *Pañjika* on this (see p. 163).

OTHER AUTHORS

Other famous authors of Yogācāra treatises are Atiśa (eighth century CE), author of the *Bodhipathapradīpa*,[32] and Tson Khapa (twelfth century CE), author of a major treatise in Tibetan,[33] both of them already close to Vajrayāna (which by some is considered a further development of Yogācāra).

Distinctive Yogācāra doctrines

THE *VIJÑAPTI-MĀTRATĀ* (MIND ONLY DOCTRINE)

Yogācāra, avoiding the extremes both of the seeming nihilism of the Śūnyavādins, and of the implicit realism of the Sarvāstivādins, held on to a doctrine of Mind Only, i.e. the reality of consciousness and the notion that the world is a world of ideas only, not of things.

> Everything may be unreal, imaginary, but this act of imagination itself cannot be similarly dismissed. All the contents of a dream may be unreal, but the dream-experience itself – the experience that constructs and projects the dream-contents – is a psychological fact that cannot be denied. This experience or consciousness is basic, but its internal diversification as the experience of apparently external contents is unreal. There is nothing really there to be seen, and so the seeing too, as the seeing of contents, is unreal. Consciousness has to be divested of this apparent duality of seeing and seen, subject and object (*grāhadvayaśūnya*). We see thus the ramifications of the notions of *śunyatā*: *pudgala-śūnyatā* – *dṛṣṭi-śūnyatā* – *grāhadvaya-śūnyatā*.[34]

Yogācāra insists that whereas *vijñeya* does not exist, *vijñapti* exists. *Vijñeya* is only an *abhāsa* (apparent reflection) of primary *vijñāna*. The bifurcation of *vijñapti* into *vijñāna* and *vijñeya* takes place under the influence of the *vāsanas*, imprints of (former) *karma*.

Habitually we verbalize and conceptualize. However, on the basis of concepts or the content of our consciousness alone we cannot come to a conclusion regarding the existence or non-existence of an extrinsic reality. While it is wrong to impute existence to a conceptualized thing (*samāropa*), it is also wrong to deny the existence of the thing-in-itself (*apavāda*), which is inaccessible to verbalization.

Vijñapti is not exhausted by conceptualization. The *Yogācārabhūmi* knows four stages of comprehension, of which conceptualization is but one:

THOMAS MERTON'S ENLIGHTENMENT

Thomas Merton was an American Trappist monk and a well-known writer on spirituality. In his later years he felt strongly attracted by Buddhism and became a close friend of D. T. Suzuki. Invited to attend a conference on world monasticism in Bangkok, he took the time to travel extensively through India and Sri Lanka. He tragically died during the conference in Bangkok, apparently through accidental electrocution. The following extract is from *The Asian Journal of Thomas Merton*, published posthumously on the basis of his diaries by some of his close friends. It relates to Merton's visit to the ancient Buddhist site of Polonnaruwa, Sri Lanka.

> Polonnaruwa ... a low outcrop of rock, with a cave cut into it, and beside the cave a big seated Buddha on the right, and Ánanda, I guess, standing by the head of the reclining Buddha ...
>
> I am able to approach the Buddhas barefoot and undisturbed, my feet in wet grass, wet sand. Then the silence of the extraordinary faces. The great smiles. Huge and yet subtle. Filled with every possibility, questioning nothing, knowing everything, rejecting nothing, the peace not of emotional resignation but of *śūnyatā* that has seen through every question without trying to discredit anyone or anything – without refutation – without establishing some other argument ...
>
> Looking at the figures I was suddenly, almost forcibly jerked clean out of the habitual, half-tied vision of things, and an inner clearness, clarity, as if exploding from the rocks themselves, became evident and obvious. The queer evidence of the reclining figure, the smile, the sad smile of Ánanda standing with arms folded ...
>
> The thing about all this is that there is no puzzle, no problem, and really no 'mystery'. All problems are resolved and everything is clear, simply because what matters is clear. The rock, all matter, all life, is charged with *dharmakāya* ... everything is emptiness and everything is compassion.
>
> I don't know when in my life I have ever had such a sense of beauty and spiritual validity runnning together in one aesthetic illumination ... I know and have seen what I was obscurely looking for. I don't know what else remains but I have now seen and have pierced through the surface and have got beyond the shadow and the disguise ...
>
> It says everything, it needs nothing. And because it needs nothing it can afford to be silent, unnoticed, undiscovered. It does not need to be discovered. It is we who need to discover it. (*The Asian Journal of Thomas Merton* [New York: New Directions Books, 1975], pp. 233–6)

1. *loka prasiddha tattvārtha*: reality as accepted by common sense (sense perception);
2. *yukti prasiddha tattvārtha*: reality as it appears in concepts (logic);
3. *kleśavāraṇa viśuddhi jñāna gocāra tattvārtha*: reality comprehended after discarding the notion of object (solipsism);
4. *jñānavāraṇa viśuddhi jñāna gocāra tattvārtha*: reality comprehended after discarding the notion of entity (realism).

THE *ĀLAYA-VIJÑĀNA* (STORE-HOUSE CONSCIOUSNESS)

The most characteristic and most disputed new concept introduced by the Yogācārins is that of the *ālaya-vijñāna*, the 'storehouse-consciousness'. In order to account for the possibility of thought arising and of the comparability of concepts among diverse people, the Yogācārins postulated a form of latent consciousness rather like a computer's memory, consisting of the 'seeds' (*bījas*) left by previous acts:

> Every willed action produces an effect (*vāsanā*) ... These *vāsanās* are stored in the *ālayavijñāna* in the form of seeds. As the seeds fructify and produce results, they develop touch, mental activity, feeling, perception and will ... This is the first transformation of consciousness. The second transformation takes place, when *manas*, or ego-consciousness evolves from the *ālayavijñāna*, and the third, when by means of the six-fold sense-activity, perceptions of colour, sound, temperature, resistance etc. arise and are wrongly interpreted as a subjective and objective world, each independent of the other. The *vijñānas* associated with the six faculties of sense together with the *manovijñāna*, or ego-consciousness comprise the *pravṛittivijñāna* (evolving consciousness) ... and these seven, and the *ālayavijñāna*, make up the eight consciousnesses of the Yogācāra school.[35]

The *ālaya* is neither empirical nor to be confused with an I-consciousness. Its content is pure 'objectivity', not a particular object:

> This bare objectivity is the first precipitation of the transcendental illusion. It is the primary projection on the part of consciousness ... The subjectivity in the *ālaya* is not to be confused with the empirical ego, the I. It is not to be equated with the *ātman* of the Brahmanical systems ... The *ālaya* is dynamic will, creating its own contents ... The *ātman* is a projection and not a reality ... The *ālaya* represents a stage in consciousness where egoity has not yet emerged ... The *ālaya* is the first phenomenalization of the Absolute ... The progression from the *ālaya* onwards is to be understood only in logical terms. The process is not

historical, and does not have a definite point of departure in time ... Other *vijñānas* have breaks in their flow while the *ālaya* lasts up to the end of phenomenal existence.[36]

THE *TRI-SVABHĀVA* (THREE OWN-NATURES)

Vasubandhu devotes a separate treatise to the notion of *tri-svabhāva* (threefold nature of nature) which is, as it were, a corollary to the *ālaya*.

The *tri-svabhāva* consists of:

- *parikalpita svabhāva*: 'own-being' as being projected, reconstructed;
- *paratantra svabhāva*: 'own-being' as being dependent on others;
- *parinispanna svabhāva*: 'own-being' as being absolute.

All things, understood by whatever mode of cognition, are of the nature of reconstructions (since they do not exist as such in themselves). Mental

---

THE THREE BUDDHA-NATURES

It is admitted that the three natures, the imaginary, the dependent and the absolute one, are the profound object of the wise man's knowledge.

What appears is the dependent nature, as it appears is the imaginary nature, the eternal non-existence as it appears of what appears must be known as the absolute nature, because of its inalterability.

And what does appear? The unreal mental creation. How does it appear? With duality. What is the non-existence with this duality of that dependent nature? It is the fact that the essence of the dependent nature is the non-duality in it.

And what is the unreal mental creation? The mind, because as it is imagined and as it imagines its object, so it is not at all.

It is admitted that mind is twofold, according to its being either cause or effect: the consciousness that is called *ālaya* (receptacle) and the consciousness that is called *pravṛtti* (functioning) which in its turn is sevenfold.

The nature imagined by ignorants is considered as something whose essence is duality and unity. Duality because of the duality of the imagined object, unity because of its being one due to the non-existence of that duality. (Vasubandhu, *Trisvabhāvakārikā* 1–5, 6, 14, trans. by F. Tola and C. Dragonetti, *Journal of Indian Philosophy* 11 (1983), pp. 251–3)

---

reconstruction is dependent on other factors. The 'real nature' consists of *paratantra* devoid of *parikalpita*: thus *parinispanna* (absolute reality) is neither identical with nor different from the *paratantra* or *parakalpita*. Ultimate being is inseparable from ultimate non-being.[37]

MADHYAMAKA AND YOGĀCĀRA: DECONSTRUCTION AND RECONSTRUCTION

The Yogācāra 'reconstruction of the Buddha-word' consists in its assumption of a (preliminary) reality of an *ālaya-vijñāna*', in other words a consciousness, that, if 'ripened', inevitably produces words in which consciousness, and consciousness of something, is contained. Thus a 'ripening' of ideas of truth, salvation, law, etc. would – at the first stage – result in words expressing truth, salvation, law, such as Buddha spoke in his earthly manifestation.

The correlation between the *nirmāṇa-kāya* of Buddha, his words and a conceptual understanding of truth, is 'real' on the level of (preliminary) consciousness (and only real there!). The other two *kāyas* of the Buddha correspond to the higher levels of consciousness/reality, which are 'more' real. It is probably significant that Yogācāra (rather than Madhyamaka) was so eagerly translated into Chinese as 'Buddhism' proper.

In contrast to the Madhyamakas with their radical deconstruction of the Buddha-word, the

> Yogācāras again revert to a constructive and positive theory of reality. Pure consciousness is real, but its self-bifurcation into the subject-object dichotomy is unreal. The two terms in this relational situation – the subject and the object, are not, however equally to be dispensed with. The object exists only in its being constructed and projected, and is nothing in itself. The subject cannot be similarly dispensed with. It is identical with the act of willing, that which constructs its own content. It is therefore identical with pure consciousness (*vijñaptimātratā*), only its apparent assumption of the role of the subject is to be denied ... The middle position [between Abhidharmaka and Madhyamaka] is Yogācāra which maintains the reality of the subject while denying it with regard to the object.[38]

With regard to the nature of the Buddha-word, the same can be said. The Yogācāras 'reconstruct' the Buddha-word in a twofold sense: they rely on 'new' scriptures, a direct revelation of the Buddha in his *saṃbhoga-kāya* (an improvement over revelations of the Buddha in his *nirmāṇa-kāya*!)

and they ascribe identifiable meaning to it. Through the *ālaya-vijñāna* the Buddha-word is related to *pariniṣpanna svabhāva.*

It appears that in the beginning the practical aspect of Yogācāra was more prominent: the term 'Yogācāra' means that yoga-meditation was the most important means to reach Buddhahood. All ten *bhūmis* had to be passed through by means of it, whereas later the more speculative side was emphasized: *Vijñapti-mātrika Vijñānavāda* or *Vijñapti-mātrata* stresses the unreality of everything except consciousness. Parallel to this, *pratītya-samutpāda* was first understood as primarily expressing a moral concatenation of births and deeds, whereas later it was turned into an instrument to gain a more metaphysical/gnoseological insight into the structure of reality.

TANTRIC BUDDHISM

While studies of what is variously termed Vajrayāna, Mantrayāna, or Tantric Buddhism have increased dramatically in quantity and quality over the past few decades, the terminology, as well as the exact placing of this form of Buddhism, is far from agreed. The problem is magnified by the fact that most of the texts belonging to this school are not written in Indian languages but in Tibetan, Chinese and a host of Central Asian languages. As can be expected, elements of the native local traditions of these countries became inextricably mixed with Buddhist concepts, making it all the more difficult to define Tantric Buddhism in relation to other religions or other Buddhist traditions.

Many authors claim that Vajrayāna or Mantrayāna is only one of two main branches of Mahāyāna (the other being the Pāramitā tradition),[39] and that within this, Tantricism is only one specific development, not shared by the whole of Vajrayāna, which is understood as a practice based on Madhyamaka and Yogācāra philosophy. Since the field is so large and so difficult and as I lack specialist qualifications in this area and am unfamiliar with most of the languages involved, I shall restrict myself to dealing with the history of Tantric Buddhism in India and a summary of Buddhist Tantric teachings contained in some Sanskrit works accessible to me.

A brief history of Tantric Buddhism in India

The *Guhya-samāja-tantra*, also called the *Tathāgata-guhyaka*, one of the earliest (anonymous) texts of Indian Tantric Buddhism, has been ascribed by various scholars to either the third, the fifth, or the seventh centuries CE. The first name associated with Tantric Buddhism is that of a Nāgārjuna: he was probably not identical with the founder of the Madhyamaka school and the author of the *Madhyamaka-kārikās*, but a seventh-century master of the same name. His disciple Nāgabodhi became the teacher of Vajrabodhi, who introduced Tantric Buddhism into China in the early eighth century. The most important name, however, is that of Padmasaṃbhava, whose life is embedded in a garland of legends attributing many miracles and magic feats to him. Born as a prince in Śaṃbhāla, Uddiyāna, he was invited by Śāntarakṣita[40] to Tibet to help establish Buddhism there.

Under the protection of the Pāla dynasty that ruled in eastern India during the eighth century, Tantric Buddhism flourished in Bengal and Orissa. The Pālas founded the university of Vikramaśīla, which became the centre for Tantric Buddhism. It also became a centre for translating Buddhist texts into Tibetan, and many Buddhist scholar-monks went from there to Tibet to teach. Some of these names have become quite famous, such as Sarvajñādeva, Jīnamitra, Dānaśīla, Dharmakāra, Tilopa, Nāropa and Atiśa.

With the destruction of the Buddhist centres by Muslim invaders in the twelfth century, Indian Buddhism all but disappeared, surviving only in some remote areas of Bengal and Kashmir.

Indian Tantric Buddhist literature

While originating in India, Tantric Buddhism flourished largely in Tibet, China, and Central Asian countries, and the vast majority of texts are in non-Indian languages. From the texts available in Sanskrit, the *Guhya-samāja-tantra* stands out as an early and authoritative work.[41] The literal translation of the title is '*Tantra* of the Secret Society'. According to Benoytosh Bhattacharyya, 'the secret conclaves that grew on the ruins of the monastic order, as conceived and established by Buddha, developed in course of time into big organisations called Guhyasamājas'.[42] These were originally not accepted by traditional Buddhists, because their teaching had no foundation in the canonical writings. In order to legitimate themselves they produced a new *saṅgīti*, a collection of sayings attributed to the Buddha, the *Guhya-samāja-tantra*. The work itself explains why its content had been kept secret for so long and claims that its practices should be accepted as leading to liberation.[43]

The *Guhya-samāja-tantra* is probably the first work mentioning the five Buddhas and their five *bodhisattva* emanations. Contrary to the asceticism taught by earlier schools of Buddhism, it proclaims that the ultimate aim of life can only be obtained through gratification of all sense desires and by acting contrary to established conventions. It also encourages the development of supernatural powers (*siddhis*).

The *tantra* begins by describing the celebrated *maṇḍala* of the five Buddhas: Amoghasiddhi, Amitābha, Vairocana, Akṣobhya and Ratnasambhava, who play such a large role in Tantric Buddhism (see figure 4).[44] They are known as the *Dhyānī* Buddhas, the forms of the Buddhas that are generated by the meditation in trance. The Lord Bodhicittavraja performs five contemplations, uttering with each a mystical mantra:

- *jñānapradīpa-vajra*: mantra *vajradhṛk*;
- *sarvatathāgata-samayasambhava-vajra*: mantra *jinajik*;
- *sarvatathāgata-ratnasambhava-vajra*: mantra *ratnadhṛk*;
- *mahāraga-saṁbhava-vajra*: mantra *arolik*;
- *amogha-samayasaṁbhava-vajra*: mantra *prajñādhṛk*.

Identifying with each of these mantras he materializes as five male and five female deities:

Akṣobhya[45]	Dveśaratī
Vairocana	Moharatī
Ratnaketu (Ratnasaṃbhava)	Īrṣyaratī
Lokeśvaramahāvidyādhipati (Amitābha)	Rāgaratī
Amoghavajra (Amoghasiddhi)	Vajraratī

After that he becomes immersed in four contemplations, resulting in transformations into the guardian deities of the four quarters:

yamantākṛt	East
prajñātakṛt	South
padmāntākṛt	West
vighnāntākṛt	North

The combination of the five male and the five female emanations together with the four quarters results in the famous magic *Dhyānī* Buddha *maṇḍala* that plays such a great role in Tantric Buddhism.

The *Guhya-samāja-tantra* teaches a sixfold yoga to reach Buddhahood. It consists of:

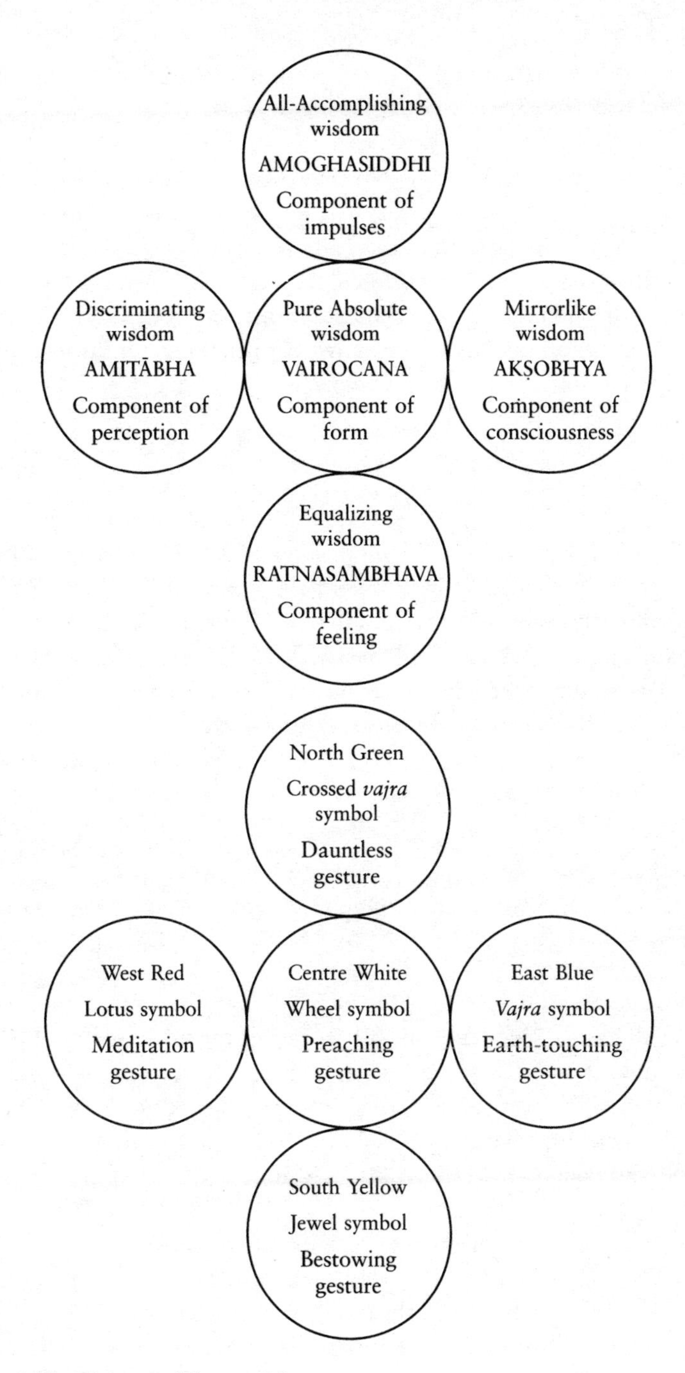

Figure 5 The Dhyānī *Buddha* maṇḍala

- *pratyahāra* (withdrawal of the senses);
- *dhyāna* (contemplation);
- *prāṇayama* (regulation of breath);
- *dhāraṇa* (support);
- *anusmṛti* (remembrance);
- *samādhi* (deep trance).

The text also offers charms and incantations for all kinds of situations: how to conquer an invading army, how to acquire great wealth or how to gain supernatural powers, for example.

Everything is Buddha

The tendency to multiply the Buddha and to create innumerable emanations of the Tathāgata is complemented by an attempt to correlate all aspects of the universe with one of these, and thus quite literally to transform everything into the Buddha. All Tantric Buddhist texts have schemata that link up the Buddhas with directions, colours, elements, parts of the human body, virtues and vices – nothing is excluded (see tables 1 and 2). This is the theoretical grounding for Tantric practices:

> Most other spiritual paths require a turning away from dark to light, whereas Vajrayāna yogins welcome both demons and angels as their allies. Transcending good and evil, they transmute them both back into that pure essence from which the universe's whirling phantasmagoria is mentally created. Manipulation of the forces of good and evil provides the power.[46]

It almost goes without saying that such a 'Way of Power', an attempt to identify all parts of the body and all aspects of the universe with Buddha-emanations, is not based on concepts and theories but on ritual and psycho-physical practice. Ritual is of the essence in Vajrayāna and worship is one of its hallmarks. It should be emphasized at this point that not all Vajrayāna or Mantrayāna is Tantric. The non-Tantric forms resemble Mahāyāna worship in all but smaller details. The Tantric forms involve the worship of the five 'secrets' or 'forbidden things': intoxicating drink (*madya*), fish (*matsya*), meat (*maṃsa*), fried rice (*mudrā*) and sexual intercourse (*maithuna*), called the *pañca ma-kāra* because the initial letter of each is 'm'. The practice of the 'five m' involves a transgression of ordinary behaviour that has so much exercised outsiders.[47]

Table 1 The correlation of the five Dhyānī *Buddhas (1)*

Dhyānī Buddha	*Skandha* (Component of self)	*Direction*	*Colour*	*Śakti* (Female counterpart)	*Bodhisattva*	Human Buddha
Vairocana	*Rūpa* (Body)	Centre	White	Tārā	Samantabhadra or Cakrapāṇi	Krakucchanda
Akṣobhya	*Vijñāna* (Consciousness)	East	Blue	Locanā	Vajrapāṇi	Kanakamuni
Ratnasaṃbhava	*Vedanā* (Feeling)	South	Yellow	Māmakī	Ratnapāṇi	Kāśyapa
Amitābha	*Saṃjñā* (Consciousness)	West	Red	Pāṇḍarā	Padmapāṇi or Avalokiteśvara	Gautama
Amoghasiddhi	*Saṃskāra* (Elements of personality)	North	Green	Āryatārā	Viśvapāṇi	Maitreya

Table 2 The correlation of the five Dhyānī *Buddhas (2)*

Dhyānī Buddha	*Kula* (Lineage)	*Vāhana* ('Vehicle')	*Mudrā* (Gesture)	*Bīja* ('Seed')	*Bhūta* (Element)	Location
Vairocana	*Moha* (Delusion)	Dragon	*Dharmacakra* (Teaching)	*a* or *om*	*vyoma* (Sky) *śabda* (Sound) Ear	Head
Akṣobhya	*Dveṣa* (Hate)	Elephant	*Bhūsparśa* (Earth-touching)	*y* or *hum*	*Marut* (Wind) *sparśa* (Touch) Skin	Heart
Ratnasaṃbhava	*Cintāmaṇi* ('Wish-jewel')	Lion	*Varadā* (Boon-giving)	*r* or *svā*	*Tejas* (Splendour) *rūpa* (Form) Eye	Navel
Amitābha	*Rāga* (Passion)	Peacock	*Samādhi* (Trance)	*b* or *āḥ*	Water *rasa* (Taste) Tongue	Mouth
Amoghasiddhi	*Samaya* (Success)	Garuḍa	*Abhaya* (Reassuring)	*i* or *hāh*	Earth *gandha* (Smell) Nose	Legs

One symbol always present in Vajrayāna worship is the *vajra*, which gave the name to this form of Buddhism. It was variously understood as meaning 'thunderbolt' or 'diamond' and was represented in the so-called *vajra*-sceptre and the *vajra*-bell, implements used in Tantric worship. As 'thunderbolt', the *vajra* represented the flash-like enlightenment-thought; as 'diamond' it represented the impenetrable enlightenment-mind or the *dharma-kāya*. The *vajra*-sceptre embodies the basic philosophy of Tantric Buddhism:

> The centre of the sceptre symbolizes emptiness, and the three bulges represent the sense-desire, pure form, and formless worlds, which 'emerge' from emptiness. The axis and four (sometimes eight) prongs represent the five main Vajrayāna Buddhas whose unity is suggested by the merging of the prongs at the end of the sceptre. The whole is thus a supreme image of the dharma body from which the world and the Buddhas emerge.[48]

The *vajra*-sceptre and the *vajra*-bell together represent skilful means and wisdom.

Tantric Buddhist philosophy

> To the Old Wisdom school, Nirvāṇa had been the absolute opposite of this world. The early Mahāyāna had identified Nirvāṇa and this world in the one Absolute Reality of emptiness. Now, in the Tantra, the world becomes a manifestation of the Dharma-body of the Buddha.[49]

For Tantric Buddhism the universe is identical with the Buddha – all its dimensions and qualities consist of Buddha-manifestations and becoming a Buddha now means merging with the universe. This is clearly no longer achieved through rational analysis and intellectual meditation. One has to find the correspondences between one's own body and the body of the Buddha, one has to discover the secret connections between oneself and the universe. The Buddha is present everywhere and in everything, waiting to be discovered. The secrets of the universe were revealed to some accomplished beings, the eighty-four Mahāsiddhas, who lived between the eighth and twelfth centuries and who transmitted them in their schools to the initiated few.

One of the means by which one can 'tune in' to the hidden, omnipresent Buddha is the recitation of mantras, especially *bīja*-mantras (seed mantras) that embody in a syllable the essence of enlightenment.

Probably the best known of these is the mantra of Avalokiteśvara *Om mani padme hum*, consisting of the universal *prāṇava Om*, the invocation of the 'Jewel in the Lotus', and the seed mantra *hum*,[50] a syllable that has no meaning in ordinary language but which is the means for the adept to identify with Avalokiteśvara.

Spells may be used to ward off the influence of evil spirits and malicious demons. Some of the shorter *sūtras* are used as mantras and recited when facing danger, and sections were added to larger *sūtras* to protect the reader from evil influences.

In one branch of Vajrayāna, called Mantrayāna, mantras have become the most important instrument for liberation. A whole science of mantras developed around the belief that mantras worked infallibly if correctly applied. The mantras were supposed to be the gift of higher beings to suffering humankind; thus the famous *Om mani padme hum* was one of Avalokiteśvara's revelations for the benefit of those who would recite it.

Mantras may be literally recited, or recitation may be effected by writing them on strips of paper and letting them flutter in the wind or by inscribing them on wheels, which with every turn create the power equivalent to a recitation.[51]

On the deepest level Buddhist Tantra aims to acquire *prajñā*, wisdom, a wisdom inherent in everything but hidden to the non-initiate. The duality of means to knowledge (*upāya*) and wisdom (*prajñā)* has to be overcome in the knower if enlightenment-bliss is to take place. Grammatically, *upāya* is masculine and *prajñā* feminine: iconographically, the union between them is represented in the famous *yab–yum* figures, the union of a male and a female:

> If *prajñā* (or *śūnyatā*), the passive, all-embracing female principle, from which everything proceeds and into which everything recedes, is united with the dynamic male-principle of active universal love and compassion, which represents the means (*upāya*) for the realisation of *prajñā* and *śūnyatā*, then perfect Buddhahood is attained.[52]

Prajñā-pāramitā, 'Perfection of Wisdom', is both the ultimate goal of Vajrayāna Buddhism and also the name of a vast literature which has only now begun to be explored by Western scholarship. It is concerned with discovering the perfection of wisdom in the Buddha's mind, speech and body, through ritual (*mudrā*), potent formulae (mantras) and deep meditation (*samādhi*). No aspect of reality must be left out because everything is Buddha, and no means must be forgotten, because everything is an instrument (*upāya*) of transformation.

Tārā, 'the Mother of all Buddhas *and* Bodhisattvas*'*

Tārā literally means 'the one who carries over [the ocean of saṃsāra]'. Her images are everywhere in Tibet and her worship seems at times to be more prominent than that of the Buddha(s) and *bodhisattvas*. There are a large number of stories connected with her origin, the most popular of which have her emerge from a tear that fell from the eye of Avalokiteśvara when he considered the impossible task of saving the innumerable living beings from suffering. Avalokiteśvara's tear formed a lake in which grew a lotus flower which opened to reveal the goddess Tārā, the helpmate of Avalokiteśvara in saving suffering beings.[53] There are many different forms of Tārā, the most popular being the White and the Green Tārā. Historically they are linked to two pious wives of a medieval Buddhist king, one a Chinese princess, the other Nepalese. The White Tārā carries a fully open lotus, the symbol of the day; the Green Tārā's emblem is a closed lotus, symbolizing night.

Atiśa, the eleventh-century Buddhist missionary to Tibet mentioned on p. 185, propagated the worship of Tārā, whose helpful interventions he believed to have encountered in many dangers. Originating from the Bodhisattva Avalokiteśvara's compassion, and with the salvation of suffering beings as her only reason for existence, it is not hard to understand that she would be hymned as the 'Mother of all *Buddhas* and *Bodhisattvas*' by her devotees and approached directly and without fear by all who find themselves in distress.

NOTES

1. I prefer the term 'deconstruction' as against 'criticism' as used by T. R. V. Murti in his masterly work *The Central Philosophy of Buddhism*, not only because it is an 'in-word', but also because it comes closer to the process employed by Nāgārjuna in finding truth.
2. Karl Jaspers included Nāgārjuna in the second volume of his *The Great Philosophers: The Original Thinkers* (New York: Harcourt & Brace, 1962) (alongside Anaximander, Heraclitus, Parmenides, Plotinus and Lao-Tzu).
3. See Obermiller, *History of Buddhism by Bu-ston*, vol. II, pp. 122–30. Also: Robinson, *History of Early Madhyamaka*, pp. 21–7.
4. Ruegg, *The Literature of the Madhyamaka School*, pp. 5f.

5. *Madhyamakaśāstra of Nāgārjuna with the Commentary 'Prasannapadā' by Candrakīrti*, ed. P. L. Vaidya. Buddhist Sanskrit Texts Series, vol. X (Darbhanga: Mithila Institute, 1960).
6. Partly translated into English by Mervyn Sprung under the title *Lucid Exposition of the Middle Way* (see appendix 2).
7. See Obermiller, *History of Buddhism by Bu-ston*, vol. II, pp. 130ff.
8. See chapter 7 for more details.
9. *Madhyamaka-kārikās* I, 1–2: *Maṅgala-śloka*. Translations of the *Madhyamaka-kārikās* in this chapter are my own.
10. Tola and Dragonetti, 'Nāgārjuna's Catustava', p. 21 (v. 12).
11. See bibliography for details.
12. Ruegg, *The Literature of the Madhyamaka School*, p. 43.
13. Ibid. p. 46.
14. See bibliography for details.
15. Ruegg, *The Literature of the Madhyamaka School*, p. 22.
16. Ibid. p. 23.
17. Ibid. pp. 38f.
18. Ibid. p. 46.
19. Jacobson, *Buddhism and the Contemporary World*, p. 55.
20. Matilal, 'Is *Prasaṅga* a Form of Deconstruction', p. 346.
21. Jaspers, *The Great Philosophers*, vol. II, p. 115.
22. Matilal, Is *Prasaṅga* a Form of Destruction?', p. 362.
23. Ruegg, *The Literature of the Madhyamaka School*, p. 47.
24. Obermiller, *History of Buddhism by Bu-ston*, vol. II, p. 136.
25. Ibid. vol. I, p. 52.
26. Sangharaksita, *Survey of Buddhism*, p. 394.
27. Cf. p. 159 regarding the scholarly debate about the identity of Vasubandhu, and the hypothesis of an older (Yogācāra) and a younger (*Abhidharma-kośa*) Vasubandhu. In my discussion here I am simply giving the traditional position without arguing for or against the above.
28. Obermiller, *History of Buddhism by Bu-ston*, vol. II, pp. 136ff.
29. Ibid.
30. Leo M. Pruden rendered into English the French translation of the *Abhidharma-kośa-bhāṣya* by Louis de la Vallée Poussin (see appendix 2).
31. *Madhyānta-vibhaṅga-ṭīkā*, p. 15.
32. Trans. Sherburne, *A Lamp for the Path* (see appendix 2).
33. Thurmann, *Tsong Khapa's Speech of Gold.*
34. Chatterjee, *Readings on Yogācāra Buddhism*, p. 3. In a recent paper, 'A Defence of Yogācāra Buddhism', A. Wayman critiques Chatterjee's understanding of Yogācāra as representing 'what was traditionally held, principally by non-Yogācārins, to be the Yogācāra position'. Wayman, however, does not spell out his own interpretation clearly enough for it to be a useful introduction to the 'true' understanding of this school.
35. Sangharaksita, *Survey of Buddhism*, p. 403.
36. Chatterjee, *Readings on Yogācāra Buddhism*, pp.18–23.
37. A good exposition is given in Conze, *Buddhist Thought in India*, pp. 257–60. There is an extensive bibliography in Tola and Dragonetti, 'The *Trisvabhāvakārikā* of Vasubandhu', pp. 230f.

38. Chatterjee, *Readings on Yogācāra Buddhism*, p. 5.
39. Cf. Lessing and Wayman, *Introduction to the Buddhist Tantric Systems*, p. 21: 'In the Mahāyāna there are the Pāramitā [school] and the Mantra [school].'
40. Śāntarakṣita, the author of the famous *Tattvasaṁgraha*, was the leading monk at Nālandā at that time, and had been invited by the rulers of Tibet to bring the Buddhist *dharma* to that country. There are many stories surrounding his mission and his encounters with hostile native magicians.
41. The text has been edited by S. Bagchi as vol. IX in the Buddhist Sanskrit Texts Series (Darbhangha: Mithila Institute, 1965) and partly translated with a commentary by Alex Wayman in *Yoga of the Guhyasamājatantra*.
42. Battacharyya, 'Tantrika Culture Among the Buddhists', p. 262.
43. Commentaries on this text have been written by many great scholars. The most famous commentary is the *Pradipoddyotana* by Candrakīrti.
44. For a detailed description of all the names mentioned in this section consult Getty, *The Gods of Northern Buddhism*, which has many illustrations and diagrams.
45. See 'Akṣobhya' in Williams, *Mahāyāna Buddhism*, pp. 243ff.
46. Blofeld, *The Way of Power*, p. 32.
47. One of the most elaborate Vajrayāna ceremonies is associated with the Kālacakra ritual. It is still performed at the time of initiation of new members, but since it pertains to Tibetan and Chinese traditions, albeit being grounded in Sanskrit Buddhist scriptures, it is not discussed here.
48. Harvey, *Introduction to Buddhism*, p. 135.
49. Conze, *Buddhism*, p. 188.
50. It was one of the rules that a mantra directed to a male deity had to end with the syllable *hum* or *phat*, one to a female deity with *svaha*, and one to a neuter deity with *namaḥ*.
51. The famous Buddhist prayer wheels usually contain an entire *sūtra* inside the metal cylinder, on whose outside the mantra *Om mani padme hum* is written. Every turn of the wheel equals the recitation of the entire *sūtra*.
52. Govinda, 'Tantric Buddhism', in Bapat, *2500 Years of Buddhism*, p. 319.
53. See Getty, *The Gods of Northern Buddhism*, p. 120.

10 CONCLUSION

BUDDHISM AS PHILOSOPHY AND RELIGION

Friends as well as foes of Buddhism have declared it a 'philosophy' rather than a 'religion'. The friends of Buddhism thereby meant to pay a compliment to the 'rational spirit' of its founder, the foes of Buddhism implied the absence of the salvific element in the *Buddha-dhamma*. They were guided in this assessment by notions of religion of biblical, largely Christian provenance, and by the post-enlightenment Western separation of philosophy from religion.

India has never known this division and its religions are at the same time philosophies, and vice versa. However, not all adherents of Buddhism have either interest in, or aptitude for, the sophisticated conceptual acrobatics exemplified, for instance, in Madhyamaka and Yogācāra. They look at Buddhism as a way to perfection, a path to liberation, a 'religion' that conveys them to the 'yonder shore'. Buddhism presents many features that are common to other religions as well, features that are often not dealt with in Western literature on Buddhism out of fear that this would damage the image of a purely rational, 'atheistic' Buddhism that is projected by many scholars and other 'interested parties'.

The real Buddhism, as lived in the traditional Buddhist countries of Asia, is based on faith, good works and trust in an all-embracing grace that will eventually prevail against all suffering, anxieties and personal shortcomings.

Buddhist faith[1] has intellectual, emotional and practical dimensions.[2] The Buddhist accepts on faith the truth of the *Buddha-dhamma*, the 'fact' of *karma* and rebirth, the reality of *nirvāṇa*, the efficacy of the *bhāvanā* (meditation) taught by the Buddhist masters. The substance of the Four Noble Truths, the facticity of the Chain of Causation, the emptiness of everything are first of all accepted in faith. While faith is considered a preliminary stage, later to be replaced by personal insight into the truth of these teachings, it is nevertheless indispensable for the beginner. Doubt would rule out progress along the Path. The 'leap of faith' required of the Buddhist 'implies a resolute and courageous act of will. It combines the steadfast resolution that one *will* do a thing with the selfconfidence that one *can* do it'.[3] Its opposites, to be guarded against, are timidity, cowardice, wavering and a calculating mind that tries to figure out beforehand whether the deal is profitable.

> Faith is closely connected with 'determination' (*adhimokkha*) which consists in acting with resolute confidence, after one has judged, decided, and definitely and unshakeably chosen an object, and is opposed to slinking along like an irresolute child who thinks, 'shall I do it, shall I not do it?'[4]

Faith also brings about inner security, serenity and lucidity. It frees one from worries and from being troubled by all manner of things. Buddhists say that someone who has faith loses the 'five terrors' and is no longer concerned about getting the necessities of life, losing reputation, about dying, about a bad rebirth or about the impression made on other people. 'Socially, faith involves trust and confidence in the Buddha and the Saṅgha.'[5] Someone with faith does not give in to peer pressure and public opinion. A Buddhist feels safe in the 'Buddha-family', which consists of Buddha-father, Wisdom-mother, Buddhist-brothers and Buddhist-sisters. Faith in the Buddhists' understanding is both a gift and a virtue: its arising is an act of grace, but its cultivation depends on discipline and effort.

Buddhists are taught that supporting the Saṅgha in whatever way brings merit (*puñña*) and that an accumulation of merit will be good both for this life and the next, eventually leading to a condition in which the ultimate aim can be reached. *Puñña* is the 'foundation and condition of heavenly rebirth and a future blissful state, the enjoyment (and duration) of which depends on the amount of merit accumulated in a former existence'.[6] The 'meritorious actions' that create *puñña* are associated with charity (*dāna*), good conduct (*sīla*) and meditation (*bhāvanā*).

By giving meals and clothes to the *bhikkhus*, lay Buddhists earn merit: thus the giver of food and robes thanks the recipient for providing the opportunity to augment *puñña*; the *bhikkhu*, as provider of this opportunity, need not show gratitude to the donor. Buddhist writings offer many instances of lay people depriving themselves and their families of necessities in order to support the Saṅgha materially. In practice, this often leads to indulging the *bhikkhus* and helping to build luxurious temples and monasteries.

Merit is also created by observing the Five or Eight Precepts (*pañca sīla* or *aṭṭha sīla*) (see chapter 4) and by practising *bhāvanā* (see chapter 6), the most preferred being the cultivation of *mettā* (loving kindness). Merit collecting is a major factor in actual Buddhist life and a powerful incentive for following the Buddha path.

Nor is Buddhism devoid of the notion of grace, if by grace we understand what is indicated by words like 'gracious', 'graceful' and 'gratitude', that is a dimension of experience that goes beyond registering facts and a view of life that consists of more than claiming one's rights. The very notion of Buddha's compassion, which moved him to postpone his own final *nibbāṇa* and to preach the Dhamma, is a 'grace' notion.[7] People felt comfortable, protected and enriched in the presence of the Buddha, whom they experienced as gracious and generous.

The 'grace' dimension of Buddhism becomes pronounced in the *bodhisattva* who, without being obliged to, out of free will and grace spends life after life helping fellow creatures attain their final aim. The *bodhisattva's* whole existence is a pouring out of grace, a grace that embraces the whole of creation.

For the individual Buddhist, the *bodhi-citta-utpāda*, the 'arising of the Buddha mind', the awakening of the most profound level of interiority, is a 'moment of grace'. Śāntideva compared it to a flash in a dark night that for a moment illuminates the world – it allows the Buddhist to see for a moment the world from a perspective of grace. It becomes the spark that kindles the fire of the most heroic pursuit of virtues. It is neither necessity nor duty that prompts the aspirant to take the *bodhisattva* vow and to sacrifice his life for others – it is an act of grace.

Avalokiteśvara, 'The Lord Who Looks Down from On High', is the 'Lord of Grace'; Maitreya Buddha, the one to come soon, is 'full of grace', and Tārā, the lovely embodiment of compassion, owes her very existence to grace. The *kalyāṇa mitta*, the 'good friend' and guide on the Path, is a channel of grace. The notion of the *brahma-vihāra*, especially the idea of universal friendliness and compassion, regardless of reciprocity, is certainly a 'grace-notion.' The *dharma-kāya* is Buddha's 'grace-reality,' and his *dhamma-nāgara* is a 'reign of grace'.

While the Buddha encouraged his disciples to be 'lamps unto themselves' and not to rely on human mediators of salvation, he certainly did not suggest that all they needed in order to find enlightenment was self-righteous manipulation of words and facts. When the Buddhists began to philosophize in a major way, largely in response to attacks from non-Buddhists, they made it clear that they did not aim at the construction of an all-embracing system that would contain all 'truths', but to push reasoning to its very limits so as to reveal its limitations. Enlightenment is a primordial existential event, not the verbal conclusion of a syllogistic argument.

The personality of the Buddha and the total phenomenon of Buddhism are far too rich to be encompassed in limiting terms like philosophy or religion, as they are understood today. They have to be accepted and interpreted in terms of life, meaning and fulfilment, addressing and expressing a mystery as large and profound as human existence.

NOTES

1. *Saddhā* (faith) is one of the five 'cardinal virtues' as enumerated by Buddhaghosa (*Visuddhimagga* XXI, 128). The other four are *viriya* (effort), *sati* (mindfulness), *citta* (concentration), *upekkhā* (equanimity).
2. I am following here the exposition which Conze gives in his *Buddhist Thought in India*, pp. 47–51.
3. See Conze, *Buddhist Thought in India*, p. 48.
4. Ibid.
5. Ibid. p. 49.
6. *Pāli–English Dictionary*, p. 446.
7. I am using in the following ideas from an article by Nikhiles Śāstrī, 'Mahāyāna bauddha dharma mẽ bhāgavatkṛpā evam gurukṛpā', *Kalyāṇ* 50:1, *Bhāgavatkṛpā* (January 1976), pp. 261–2.

APPENDIX 1
Buddhist literature: Primary sources

The Buddha communicated his teachings orally; his immediate disciples, who began spreading the Buddha's message during his lifetime, memorized it and probably often rephrased it. There are many recorded instances of the Buddha himself rephrasing his teachings according to his audience and the circumstances, and also of the Buddha correcting misunderstandings caused by his disciples' teaching. There is, however, a great degree of unanimity in the wording of the central teachings such as the Four Noble Truths, the Eightfold Path, and the Chain of Dependent Co-origination.

After the Buddha's death the Saṅgha understood it to be its primary duty to preserve the Buddha-words. Considering the great importance given to memorization in ancient cultures (to study a text usually meant first to memorize it) it is not implausible to accept the testimony of tradition that individual *bhikkhus* from the Buddha's immediate following could recite large sections of the Buddha's teachings which later became incorporated into the Pāli Canon. The Saṅgha convened several 'recitals' (*saṅgītis*, 'councils') for the purpose of establishing the 'true *Buddha-dhamma*'. When writing became more commonly used for purposes other than commerce and administration, those teachings which were in danger of being forgotten because few people, or perhaps even only one person, had memorized them, were also recorded in writing.

According to reliable tradition, most of the teachings preserved by the *śaṅgha* of the Theravādins were written down in Pāli c. 80 BCE in Sri Lanka and preserved from then onwards in the form of books.[1] From that time the Theravādin *saṅgha* introduced a division of labour: some *bhikkhus* were to devote themselves to meditating (*vipassanā-dhura*), while others were to preserve the scriptures (*gaṇtha-dhura*).[2] At a later date certain schools of *bhikkhus* specialized in memorizing and preserving one particular part of the canon, very similar to the *śākhas* (family traditions) that preserved particular strands of Vedic learning.[3] In the centuries between the Buddha's death and the written recording of the Pāli Canon, many parallel versions of the Buddha's teachings were produced and promulgated by Buddhists outside the Theravāda tradition. Since there was no central authority, there emerged other collections in Sanskrit which became canonical for other schools. The comparison between Pāli and Sanskrit versions of certain texts has been revealing to translators of Buddhist texts into modern languages.

THE PĀLI CANON: *TIPIṬAKA*

The canon of the Theravāda school of Buddhism is called *Tipiṭaka* (Three Baskets). It consists of three sections, the *Vinaya Piṭaka*, the *Sutta Piṭaka* and the *Abhidhamma Piṭaka*. These are subdivided into an unequal number of texts of various lengths. The listing given here follows the edition of the Nālandā Devanāgarī Pāli Series, published by the Bihar Government Pāli Publication Board (BE 2500–5 CE 1956–61) in forty-one volumes. This Devanāgarī rendering of the Pāli Canon, as constituted by the Sixth Council in Rangoon (1954–6) (Burmese Chaṭṭha Saṅgāyana edition), differs in its sequencing of the books of the Pāli Canon from the Roman edition published by the Pāli Text Society from 1880. It is this latter which is the basis of most of the English translations published in the Sacred Books of the Buddhists and the Pāli Translation Series.

Vinaya Piṭaka

The 'basket of discipline' contains works that deal with the rules of life for Buddhist monks and nuns as established by Buddha. It consists of five major works: *Mahāvagga*, *Cullavagga*, *Pārājika*, *Pācittiya*, *Parivāra* (making up about one-eighth of the entire Pāli Canon).

Sutta Piṭaka

The 'basket of instructions' is made up of *Dīgha Nikāya*, *Majjhima Nikāya*, *Saṃyutta Nikāya*, *Aṅguttara Nikāya* and *Khuddaka Nikāya*.

Khuddaka Nikāya itself consists of *Khuddakapāṭha*, *Dhammapada*, *Udāna*, *Itivuttaka*, *Sutta Nipāta*, *Vimānavatthu*, *Petavatthu*, *Theragāthā*, *Therigāthā*, *Jātaka*, *Niddesa*, *Patisambhidāmagga*, *Apadāna*, *Buddhavaṁsa* and *Cariyāpiṭaka*. The *Sutta Piṭaka* makes up over half of the entire Pāli Canon.

Abhidhamma Piṭaka

The 'basket of the higher Dhamma' is largely made up of systematizations of the teachings contained in the other two baskets, mainly according to numerical patterns. It consists of *Dhammasaṅgani*, *Vibhaṅga*, *Dhātukathā*, *Puggalapaññatti*, *Kathāvatthu*, *Yamaka* and *Paṭṭhāna* and makes up about three-eighths of the Pāli Canon.

The very large number of post-canonical Pāli works and of the Sanskrit Mahāyāna scriptures have been mentioned in the next section selectively, i.e. only works of which an English translation exists.

NOTES

1. The Pāli Canon probably represents translations from an older language (Māgadhī?) in which the Buddha had spoken.
2. Gombrich, 'How the Mahāyāna Began', pp. 24f.
3. Rahula, *History of Buddhism in Ceylon* (pp. 158ff.) reports the astonishing fact that the *bhikkhus* of Sri Lanka came to the conclusion that study was a more important activity than meditation to ensure the continued existence of the Buddha-*sāsana*.

APPENDIX 2

English translations of Buddhist sources

Abbreviations:
SBE: Sacred Books of the East;
SBB: Sacred Books of the Buddhists;
PTS: Pali Text Society.

PĀLI CANON

Vinaya Piṭaka

SBE, *Vinaya Texts*:
Vol. XIII, *Pātimokkha*, *Mahāvagga* (first part)
Vol. XVII, *Mahāvagga* (2nd part), *Cullavagga* (1st part)
Vol. XX, *Cullavagga* (2nd part)
Trans. T. W. Rhys Davids and H. Oldenberg, 1881, 1882, 1885.

SBB, *Book of the Discipline*, 6 vols:
Vol. X, *Pārājika*, *Saṅghadiśeṣa*, *Aniyata*
Vol. XI, *Nissagīya*, *Pācittiya*
Vol. XIII, *Pācittiya*, *Patidesaniya*, *Sekhiya*
(*Nuns' Analysis*: *Pārājika*, *Saṅghadiśeṣa*, *Nissagīya*, *Pācittiya*, *Patidesaniya*, *Sekhiya*)
Vol. XIV, *Mahāvagga*
Vol. XX, *Cullavagga*
Vol. XXV, *Parivāra*
Trans. I. B. Horner, 1938, 1940, 1942, 1951, 1952, 1966.

Sutta Piṭaka

Dīgha-Nikāya:

Dialogues of the Buddha, SBB, vols II, III, IV, trans. T. W. Rhys Davids, 1899, 1910, 1921. Some also in SBE, vol. XI, *Buddhist Suttas*, trans. T. W. Rhys Davids, 1881.

Majjhima Nikāya:

The Middle Length Sayings, PTS, vols XXIX, XXX, XXXI, trans. I. B. Horner, 1954, 1957, 1959.

Saṃyutta Nikāya:

The Books of Kindred Sayings, PTS, vols XIV, XV, XVI, XVII, XVIII, trans. C. A. F. Rhys Davids and F. L. Woodward, 1918, 1922, 1924, 1927, 1930.

Aṅguttara Nikāya:

The Book of Gradual Sayings, PTS, vols XXII, XXIV, XXV, XXVI, XXVII, trans. F. L. Woodward and E. M. Hare, 1932, 1933, 1934, 1935, 1936.

Khuddaka Nikāya:

SBE, vol. X, *Dhammapada*, *Sutta Nipāta*, trans. M. Müller, F. Fausböll, 1881.

PTS, vol. VIII, *The Minor Anthologies of the Pāli Canon*, Part II: '*Udāna' and 'Itivuttaka'*, trans. F. L. Woodward, 1935.

PTS, vol. XV, *Woven Cadences of Early Buddhists: Sutta Nipāta*, trans. E. M. Hare, 1945.

PTS, vols XLIV, XLV, *The Group of Discourses* (*Sutta Nipāta*), trans. K. N. Norman, 1984, 1992.

PTS, vol. XXXII, *The Minor Readings* and *The Illustrator of Ultimate Meaning* (*Khudakapatha*), trans. Bhikkhu Ñānamoli, 1960.

PTS, vol. I, *Psalms of the Early Buddhists: The Sisters* (*Therīgāthā*), trans. C. A. F. Rhys Davids, 1909.

PTS, vol. IV, *Psalms of the Early Buddhists: The Brethren* (*Theragāthā*), trans. C. A. F. Rhys Davids, 1913.

PTS, vol. XXXVIII, *Elders' Verses*, vol. I (*Theragāthā*), trans. K. R. Norman, 1969.

PTS, vol. XXXIX, *Elders' Verses*, vol. II (*Therīgāthā*), trans. K. R. Norman, 1971.

PTS, vol. XLIII, *The Path of Discrimination* (*Pathisambhidāmagga*), trans. Bhikku Ñānamoli, 1982.

PTS, *The Jātaka or Stories of the Buddha's Former Births* (*Jātaka*), 6 vols, trans. under the general supervision of E. B. Cowell, 1895–1907.

Abhidhamma Piṭaka

PTS, vol. XLI, *A Buddhist Manual of Psychological Ethics* (*Dhammasaṅgaṇi*), trans. C. A. F. Rhys Davids, 1900.
PTS, vol. XXXIX, *The Book of Analysis* (*Vibhaṅga*), trans. Pathamakyaw Ashin Thittila, 1969.
PTS, vol. XXXIV, *Discourse on Elements* (*Dhātukathā*), trans. U Narada Mula Patthana Sayadaw, 1962.
PTS, vol. XII, *Designation of Human Types* (*Puggalapaññatti*), trans. Bimal Charan Law, 1924.
PTS, vol. V, *Points of Controversy or Subjects of Discourse* (*Kathāvattu*), trans. Shwe Zan Aung and C. A. F. Rhys Davids, 1915.
PTS, vols. XXXVII, XLII, *Conditional Relations* (*Patthāna*), vols I and II, trans. U Narada Mula Patthana Sayadaw, 1969, 1981.

POST-CANONICAL PĀLI LITERATURE

Dīpavaṃsa, trans. H. Oldenberg, London, Williams & Norgate, 1879
Mahāvaṃsa, trans. W. Geiger, *The Great Chronicle of Ceylon*, London, Pāli Text Society, 1912
Cullavaṃsa, trans. W. Geiger, 2 vols, London, Pāli Text Society, 1930
Dhammapada Aṭṭhakathā, trans. E. W. Burlingame, *Buddhist Legends*, n.p., Pāli Text Society, 1990 (originally published 1921)
Milindapañha, trans. T. W. Rhys Davids, *The Questions of King Milinda*, 2 vols, Oxford, Oxford University Press, 1890 (SBE, vols XXXV, XXXVI); also trans. I. B. Horner, *Milinda's Questions*, 2 vols, London, Pāli Text Society, 1963, 1964
Nettipakaraṇa, trans. Bhikkhu Ñyāṇamolī, *The Guide*, with introduction by Thera Ñyāṇaponika, London, Pāli Text Society, 1962
Visuddhimagga, trans. Bhikkhu Ñyāṇamoli, *The Path of Purification*, Colombo, A. Semage, 1956
Vimuttimagga, trans. N. N. M. Ehara, Soma Thera and Kheminda Thera, *The Path of Freedom*, Kandy, Sri Lanka, Buddhist Publication Society, 1977

SANSKRIT BUDDHIST LITERATURE

Abhidharma-kośa-bhāṣya (Vasubandhu), trans. L. M. Pruden, 4 vols, Berkeley, CA, Asian Humanities Press, 1988–90 (from the French translation of L. de la Vallée Poussin)

Aṣṭasāhasrikā-prajñā-pāramitā Sūtra, trans. E. Conze, *Perfection of Wisdom in Eight Thousand Lines*, Berkeley, CA, Bolinos, Four Seasons Foundation, 1973

Avataṃśaka Sūtra, trans. T. Cleary, *The Flower Ornament Scripture*, 3 vols, Boulder, CO, Shambhala, 1984–7

Bodhipathapradīpa (Asaṅga), trans. R. Sherburne, *A Lamp for the Path and Commentary*, London, Allen & Unwin, 1983

Buddhacarita (Aśvaghosa), trans. E. H. Johnson, *The Buddhacarita or Acts of the Buddha*, 2 vols, Calcutta, 1936

Daśabhūmika Sūtra, trans. M. Honda, revised J. Rahder (Śata-Piṭaka Series, vol. LXXIV), New Delhi, International Academy of Indian Culture, 1968

Jātakamālā (Āryasūra), trans. J. S. Speyer, New Delhi, Motilal Banarsidass, 1971 (originally published Oxford, Clarendon Press, 1895)

Lalitavistara Sūtra, trans. G. Bays, *The Lalitavistara Sūtra*, 2 vols, Berkeley, CA, Dharma, 1983

Laṅkāvatāra Sūtra, trans. D. T. Suzuki, *The Laṅkāvatārasūtra*, London, Routledge, 1932

Madhyamakar-kārikās (Nāgārjuna), trans. F. Streng, in *Emptiness: A Study in Religious Meaning*, Nashville, Abingdon Press, 1967, Appendix A

Mahāyāṇasaṅgraha (Asaṅga), trans. J. P. Keenan, *The Summary of the Great Vehicle by Bodhisattva Asaṅga*, Berkeley, CA, Numata Center for Buddhist Translation and Research, 1992

Pañcaviṃśatisahasrika Prajñāpāramitā, trans. E. Conze, *The Large Sūtra on Perfect Wisdom*, Delhi, Motilal Banarsidass, 1979

Prajñāpāramitā-Hṛdaya Sūtra and *Vajracchedikasūtra*, trans. E. Conze, *Buddhist Wisdom Books*, London, George Allen & Unwin, 1958

Saṃdhinirmocana Sūtra, trans. J. Powers, *Wisdom of the Buddha: The Saṃdhinirmocana Mahāyāna Sūtra*, Berkeley, CA, Dharma, 1995

Śiksāsamuccaya (Śāntideva), trans. C. Bendall and W. H. D. Rouse, New Delhi, Motilal Banarsidass, 1971 (originally published London 1922)

Śrīmāladevīsiṁhanāda Sūtra, trans. A. Wayman and H. Wayman, *The*

Lion's Roar of Queen Śrīmalā, New York, Columbia University Press, 1974

Sukhavativyūha Sūtras, trans. L. Gomez, *The Land of Bliss*, Honolulu, University of Hawaii Press, 1996

Tattvasaṅgraha (Śāntarākṣita) with the Commentary of Kamalaśīla, 2 vols, trans. G. Jha (Baroda Oriental Series), Baroda, Oriental Institute, 1937–9

Vimalakīrtinirdeśa Sūtra, trans. E. Lamotte, *The Teaching of Vimalakīrti*, London, Pāli Text Society, 1976

For translations (up to 1982) of other Mahāyāna literature into English and other Western languages see P. Pfandt (comp.), *Mahāyāna Texts Translated into Western Languages: A Bibliographical Guide*, Cologne, Brill, 1983.

APPENDIX 3
Chronology

With regard to early Buddhist history I am following the traditional dating, while aware of doubts thrown on it by recent Western scholarship. Especially the dating of the Buddhist Councils has received a great deal of attention by Western scholars and the traditional dates have been rejected by most of them.

It goes without saying that the chronology is far from giving a complete picture of the history of Buddhism. The objective here is to provide dating (in many cases approximate and contested) of the major events and figures mentioned in the body of the book itself. For more detailed chronologies the reader is asked to consult the major monographs on the history of Buddhism listed in the bibliography.

624–544 BCE	Life of Buddha according to Theravāda tradition
544 BCE	First Council (*saṅgīti*) at Rājagṛha: *Vinaya Piṭaka* and *Sutta Piṭaka*
c. 444 BCE	Second Council at Vaiśālī
c. 350 BCE	Split between Sthaviravādins and Mahāsaṅghikas
274–236 BCE	Rule of Aśoka: Buddhist embassies to many courts in Asia and Europe
247 BCE	Third Council at Pātaliputra: finalization of Theravāda Canon (*Abhidamma Piṭaka*)
246 BCE	Prince Mahinda brings Buddhism to Sri Lanka
c. 220 BCE	Buddhism introduced in Burma
c. 160 BCE	*Milindapañha*
c. 120 BCE	Erection of *toraṇas* (gates) at Sanchi Stūpa

c. 100 BCE	First Mahāyāna *sūtras*: *Saddharmapuṇḍarīka*
	First Buddha-images from Gandhāra
c. 80 BCE	First Buddha-images from Mathurā
	Pāli Canon committed to writing in Sri Lanka
c. 100 CE	Fourth Council (not recognized by Theravāda)
	Buddhism spreads to China
	Early Mahāyāna *Prajñāpāramitā Sūtras*
c. 150 CE	Nāgārjuna, author of *Madhyamaka-kārikās*
c. 200 CE	Buddhism spreads to Annam
	Composition of *Mahāvibhāṣa*, summary of teachings of Sarvāstivādins
c. 250 CE	Composition of *Guhya-samāja-tantra*, foundational text for Vajrayāna
c. 270–350 CE	Life of Maitreyanātha, founder of Yogācāra
c. 310–90 CE	Life of Asaṅga and the older Vasubandhu, authors of important works on Yogācāra
c. 370 CE	Buddhism spreads to Korea
	Composition of *Dīpavaṃsa*, the chronicle of Buddhism in Sri Lanka
344–413 CE	Life of Kumārajīva, translator of Madhyamaka texts into Chinese
c. 390–470 CE	Life of Buddhaghosa, author of *Visuddhimagga* and many commentaries on Pāli Canon
399–414 CE	Chinese pilgrim Fa-hien in India
400–50 CE	Life of the younger Vasubandhu, author of the *Abhidharma-kośa* and its commentary
c. 450 CE	Buddhism spreads to Java, Sumatra and Kalimantan
c. 450–520 CE	Life of Dignāga, 'father of medieval logic'
498–569 CE	Life of Paramārtha, missionary to China
c. 500 CE	Beginning of composition of *Mahāvaṃsa*, a Pāli chronicle of Buddhism in Sri Lanka
c. 500–570 CE	Life of Bhāvaviveka, a Madhyamaka scholar
552 CE	Buddhism spreads to Japan
c. 600–35 CE	Life of Dharmapāla, famous logician
c. 600–50 CE	Life of Candrakīrti, author of *Prasannapadā*, commentary on Nāgārjuna's *Madhyamaka-kārikās*
629–45 CE	Chinese pilgrim Hiuen Tsang in India
635–50 CE	Life of Dharmakīrti, famous logician and polemicist, author of *Pramāṇavārtika*

642 CE	Buddhism reaches Tibet
671–95 CE	Chinese pilgrim I-Tsing visits India
c. 700–70 CE	Life of Śāntarakṣita, author of *Tattvasaṅgraha*, missionary to Tibet: establishes first Buddhist *vihāra* in Tibet (749)
c. 720–90 CE	Life of Kamalaśīla, pupil and companion of Śāntarakṣita, author of *Pañjika* (Commentary) on *Tattvasaṅgraha*
c. 725–800 CE	Life of Padmasaṃbhava, famous master of Vajrayāna, missionary to Tibet
c. 800 CE	Foundation of Buddhist University of Vikramaśīla by King Dharmapāla
1197 CE	Buddhist university of Nālandā destroyed by Muslims
c. 1250 CE	Thailand becomes a Theravāda country
c. 1480 CE	Burma (Myanmar) becomes a Theravāda country
1782 CE	The ruling king of Thailand calls a Theravāda Council
1844 CE	E. Burnouf's *Introduction to the History of Indian Buddhism* marks beginning of serious study of Buddhism in the West
1855 CE	V. Fausböll publishes Pāli *Dhammapada* with Latin translation
1871 CE	Fifth Council in Rangoon (Burma): Pāli Canon recited and inscribed on 729 marble slabs
1879 CE	E. Arnold publishes *Light of Asia*, kindling interest in Buddhism in the West
1881 CE	W. Rhys Davids founds Pāli Text Society in London Herman Oldenberg's *Buddha* published, based on Pāli sources
1954–6 CE	Sixth Council in Rangoon (Burma): Pāli Canon recited by 1,000 learned monks and printed
1956 CE	Celebration of the 2,500th anniversary of the Buddha's *parinirvāṇa*: restoration of Buddhist monuments in India

GLOSSARY

Note: (P) means Pāli, (S) means Sanskrit

Abhidhamma (P), *Abhidharma* (S) : 'higher teaching', the third and last part of the Pāli Canon
ācārya (S), *ācariya* (P): 'master', teacher
Ādi Buddha (S): the original, first Buddha
anāgami (P): 'non-returner'
anattā (P), *anātma* (S): no-self
anicca (P): impermanence
anussati (P): remembrance
apoha (S): cognition by elimination
arahant (P), *arhat* (S): 'accomplished', a person who has come to the final goal
ariya sacca (P), *ārya satya* (S): 'the (Four) Noble Truth(s)'
asubha (P), *aśubha* (S): inauspicious, unpleasant
aṭṭha garudhamma (P): 'the Eight Heavy Precepts' for nuns
atthakathā (P): commentary
avidyā (S), *avijjā* (P): 'ignorance', the ultimate root of suffering
Avalokiteśvara (S): 'the Lord who looks down from on high'
avyākṛta (S): the 'unrevealed', questions that the Buddha refused to answer
bhāvacakra (P and S): Wheel of Becoming
bhāvanā (P and S): 'cultivation', meditation
bhikkhu (P), *bhikṣu* (S): 'beggar' (m.), monk
bhikkhunī (P), *bhikṣuṇī* (S): 'beggar' (f.), nun

bodhi-citta (S): 'enlightenment thought'
bodhi-citta-utpāda (S): 'arising of enlightenment consciousness'
bodhisatta (P), *bodhisattva* (S): future Buddha, person that is on the way to reaching enlightenment
brahma vihāra (P): 'divine abidings', universal virtues such as loving kindness (*mettā*)
Buddha (S and P): the Enlightened One
Buddha-vāca(na) (S): 'Buddha-word'
cakravartin (S), *cakkavatti* (P): universal ruler
catuṣkoṭi (S): 'four-cornered', a mode of logical proof
citta (P and S): mind, consciousness
dasasīla (P):'ten components of good character'
dhamma (P), *dharma* (S): element of composite entities
Dhamma (P), Dharma (S): Eternal Law, the teachings of the Buddha
dharma-kāya (S): 'Dharma-body', highest mode of existence of the Buddha according to Mahāyāna
dhyāna (S): trance
Dhyānī-Buddhas (S) : emananations from the Ādi Buddha
dosa (P), *doṣa* (S): hatred, anger
dukkha (P), *duḥkha* (S): suffering, painful
Hīnayāna (S): 'Lesser Vehicle' or 'Path'
iddhi (P), *siddhi* (S): supernatural faculties
Jātaka (S and P): stories relating to the Buddha's previous births
jhāna (P), *dhyāna* (S): (stage in) trance
kalyāṇa mitra (S), *kalyāṇa mitta* (P): 'the good friend', personal advisor, giver of suitable meditation subject
kamma (P), *karma* (S): 'action', resulting effects of previous actions
karuṇā (P and S): compassion
kasiṇa (P), *kṛtsna* (S): 'complete', meditation device consisting of a round disk made of clay
kauśala (S): skilful
kleśa (S), *kilesa* (P): defilement, affliction
kṣānti (S): forbearance
lakṣaṇa (S), *lakhaṇa* (P): 'sign', especially in connection with the distinctive marks of a great person (*Mahāpuruṣa)*
Mahāyāna (S): 'The Great Vehicle' or 'Way'
maitrī (S): 'friendliness'
manas (S), *mano* (P): 'mind'
Mañjuśrī (S): the soft-beautied, name of a *bodhisattva*

mettā (P): 'friendliness', loving kindness
moha (P and S): delusion
muditā (P and S): joy
mudrā (S): gesture
nibbāna (P), *nirvāṇa* (S): 'extinguishing'; ultimate aim of Buddhism
nikāya (P): collection of *suttas*, e.g. *Dīgha Nikāya*; ordination line
nimitta (P and S): 'means', especially as intermediate image
nirmāṇa-kāya (S): 'transformation-body', the Buddha's earthly existence
nirodha (P and S): cessation
nissaya (P), *niśraya* (S): basic resources of a monk or nun
pabbajjā (P), *pravrājya* (S): 'going forth', leaving one's family to join the Buddhist monastic Saṅgha
Pacceka-buddha (P): someone who achieves enlightenment for his own benefit only
pañca-sīla (P): 'five components of good character'
pañña (P), *prajñā* (S): wisdom; the highest accomplishment
pārājika (P): breach of monastic rule that entails excommunication
paramārtha (S): ultimate truth
pāramitā (S): supreme virtue
parikkhāra (P), *pariṣkāra* (S): basic requisites of a monk (food, clothing, shelter, medicine) which are to be supplied by the laity
parīkṣā (S): 'examination', analysis
parinirvāṇa (S), *parinibbāna* (P): final disappearance
paticca-samuppāda (P), *pratītya-samutpāda* (S): 'Chain of Causation' or 'Chain of Dependent Co-origination'
Pātimokkha (P), *prātimokṣa* (S): fortnightly gathering of the monastic Saṅgha and recitation of monastic rules; collection of monastic rules
piṭaka (P): 'basket', one of the (three) parts of the Pāli Canon
prajñā (S): wisdom
pramāṇa (S): instrument of proof
prasaṅga (S): argument from self-contradiction
puṇya (S), *puñña* (P): merit
rāga (P and S): passion
rūpa (P and S): 'form', body
saddhā (P), *śraddhā* (S): faith
samādhi (P and S): trance
sāmaṇera/ī (P), *śrāmaṇera/ī* (S): novice (m./f.)
samatha (P), *śamatha* (S): 'calming', form of meditation
saṃbhoga-kāya (S): 'enjoyment-body', existence of the Buddha in heaven

saṃjñā (S): consciousness
saṃsāra (S): the transient universe of emergent and disappearing phenomena
saṃskāra (S), *saṅkhāra* (P): the (five) strands out of which the human personality is formed
samudaya (P and S): arising
samvṛti (S): 'enveloped', lower form of truth-cognition
saṅgha (P and S): assembly, especially the community of Buddhist monks and nuns
Saṅgha (P and S): the whole Buddhist community
saṅghādisesa (P): infringements of monastic rules that require a meeting of the assembly to define punishment
saṅgīti (P): 'recitation', Buddhist council
sati (P), *smṛti* (S): 'memory', mindfulness
siddhi (S), *iddhi* (P): supernatural accomplishment
sikkha padāni (P): the (ten) rules for novices
sīla (P), *śīla* (S): 'morality', 'virtue'
skandha (S): component of empirical self
sotāpanna (P): 'stream-enterer', someone on the way to *nirvāṇa*
stūpa (S), *thūpa* (P): tumulus, especially memorials to the Buddha, containing fragments of his ashes
śubha (S), *subha* (P): auspicious
śūnyatā (S): 'emptiness'
sutta (P), *sutra* (S): sermon, instruction (by the Buddha)
taṇhā (P), *tṛṣṇā* (S): 'thirst,' craving, desire for life
tantra (S): generic term for Vajrayāna scriptures
Tārā (S): 'Saviouress', Buddhist (Mahāyāna) goddess(es)
tarka (S): formal logic; syllogism
Tathāgata (S and P): 'Gone there', title for the Enlightened One
thera (P): 'elder' (male); title of respect
therī (P): 'elder' (female); title of respect
triratna (S): 'Three Jewels': Buddha, Dhamma, Saṅgha
trisvabhāva (S): the three forms of existence of the Buddha
upajjhāya (P), *upadhyāya* (S): preceptor
upasaka/upāsikā (P): 'follower', lay person (m./f.)
upasampadā (P): ordination (as monk or nun)
upāya (S): means
uposatha (P): regular weekly (or fortnightly) gathering of the members of the local *saṅghas*

Vajrayāna (S): 'Diamond Vehicle', 'Thunderbolt Vehicle'
vedanā (P and S): feeling
vihāra (P and S): 'dwelling', Buddhist monastery
vijñāna (S), *vijjāna* (P): consciousness
vinaya (P): discipline
Vinaya: the first part of the Pāli Canon dealing with matters of monastic discipline
vipassanā (P), *vipaśyanā* (S): 'insight'
Vipassanā, Vipaśyanā: a form of meditation

BIBLIOGRAPHY

BOOKS

Almond, P. *The British Discovery of Buddhism*. Cambridge, Cambridge University Press, 1988

Amore, R. C. (ed.) *Developments in Buddhist Thought: Canadian Contributions to Buddhist Studies*. Waterloo, Ontario, Wilfrid Laurier University Press, 1969

Arnold, E. *Light of Asia*. New Delhi, Interprint, 1985

Bapat, P. (ed.) *2500 Years of Buddhism*, New Delhi, Government of India Publications Division, 1956

Bartolomeuz, T. *Women under the Bo Tree*. Cambridge, Cambridge University Press, 1994

Batchelor, S. *The Awakening of the West: The Encounter of Buddhism and Western Culture*. London, Aquarian, 1994

Beal, S. *Si-Yu-Ki: Buddhist Records of the Western World*. London, Truebner, 1962

Bechert, H. (ed.) *The Dating of the Historical Buddha*. Göttingen, Vandenhock & Ruprecht, 1991

Bechert, H. and R. Gombrich (eds) *The World of Buddhism: Buddhist Nuns and Monks in Society and Culture*. Thames & Hudson, 1984

Beyer, S. *The Buddhist Experience: Sources and Interpretation*. Belmont, CA, Dickenson Publishing Company, 1974

Bhattacharya, D. C. *Studies in Buddhist Iconography*. New Delhi, Motilal Banarsidass, 1987

Bhattacharyya, B. *The Indian Buddhist Iconography.* Calcutta, K. L. Mukhopadhyay, 1968

— *An Introduction to Buddhist Esoterism.* New Delhi, Motilal Banarsidass, 1980 (reprint)

Blofeld, J. *The Way of Power: A Practical Guide to the Mysticism of Tibet.* London, Allen & Unwin, 1970

Bond, G. D. *The Buddhist Revival in Sri Lanka: Religious Tradition, Reinterpretation and Response.* Columbia, SC, University of South Carolina Press

Bronkhorst, J. *The Two Traditions of Meditation in Ancient India.* New Delhi, Motilal Banarsidass, 1993

Carrithers, M. *The Buddha.* Oxford, Oxford University Press, 1990

— *The Forest Monks of Sri Lanka: An Anthropological and Historical Study.* Delhi, Motilal Banarsidass, 1983

Chatterjee, A. K. *Readings on Yogācāra Buddhism.* Varanasi, Centre for Advanced Studies in Philosophy, Benares Hindu University, 1971

Chattopadhyaya, Lama Chimpa Alaka (trans.) *Tāranātha's History of Buddhism in India*, ed. D. Chattopadhyaya. Simla, Indian Institute of Advanced Study, 1970

Conze, E. *Buddhism: Its Essence and Development.* Oxford, Bruno Cassirer, 1951

— *Buddhist Meditation.* London, George Allen & Unwin, 1956

— *Buddhist Scriptures.* Harmondsworth, Penguin Books, 1959

— *Buddhist Thought in India.* Ann Arbor, University of Michigan Press, 1967

— *A Short History of Buddhism.* Oxford, Oneworld, 1993

— *Thirty Years of Buddhist Studies.* London, Bruno Cassirer, 1967

Conze, E. (ed.) *Buddhist Texts through the Ages.* Oxford, Oneworld, 1995

Dasgupta, S. B. *An Introduction to Tantric Buddhism.* Berkeley and London, Shambhala, 1974

Dayal, H. *The Bodhisattva Doctrine in Buddhist Sanskrit Literature.* London, Routledge, 1932

Encyclopaedia of Buddhism, ed. G. P. Malalasekera. Colombo, Government of Sri Lanka, 1961–

Gethin, R. *The Foundations of Buddhism.* Oxford, Oxford University Press, 1998

Getty, A. *The Gods of Northern Buddhism: Their History, Iconography and Progressive Evolution through the Northern Buddhist Countries.*

Rutland, VT, and Tokyo, Charles E. Tuttle 1962 (originally Oxford, Oxford University Press, 1914)

Goddard, D. (ed.) *A Buddhist Bible*. Boston, MA, Beacon Press, 1970

Gombrich, R. *Precept and Practice: Traditional Buddhism in the Rural Highlands of Ceylon*. Oxford, Clarendon Press, 1971

— *Theravāda Buddhism: A Social History from Ancient Benares to Modern Colombo*. London, Routledge & Kegan Paul, 1988

Gombrich, R. with M. Cone *The Perfect Generosity of Prince Vessantara*. Oxford, Oxford University Press, 1977

Griffiths, P. J. *On Being Mindless: Buddhist Meditation and the Mind–Body Problem*. La Salle, IL, Open Court, 1986

— *On Being Buddha*. Albany, NY, State University of New York Press, 1994

Gross, R. M. *Buddhism After Patriarchy: A Feminist History, Analysis and Reconstruction of Buddhism*. Albany, NY, State University of New York Press, 1993

Guenther, H. V. *Philosophy and Psychology in the Abhidharma*. Berkeley, CA, Shambhala, 1976

Harvey, P. *An Introduction to Buddhism: Teachings, History and Practice*. London, Cambridge University Press, 1990

Hawkins, B. K. *Buddhism*. Prentice Hall, Upper Saddle River, 1999

Herman, A. L. *An Introduction to Buddhist Thought: A Philosophic History of Indian Buddhism*. Lanham, MD, University Press of America, 1983

Hinüber, O. von *A Handbook of Pāli Literature*. Delhi, Manohar Lal (Indian edn) 1996

Jacobson, N. P. *Buddhism and the Contemporary World: Change and Self-Correction*. Carbondale, IL, Southern Illinois University Press, 1983

Jayatilleke, K. N. *Early Buddhist Theory of Knowledge*. London, George Allen & Unwin, 1963

Jong, J. W. de. *A Brief History of Buddhist Studies in Europe and America*. Varanasi, Motilal Banarsidass, 1976

Kalupahana, D. J. *Buddhist Philosophy: A Historical Analysis*. Honolulu, University of Hawaii Press, 1976

— *Causality: The Central Philosophy of Buddhism*. Honolulu, University of Hawaii Press, 1975

Katz, N. *Buddhist Images of Human Perfection: The Arahant of the Sutta Pitaka Compared with the Bodhisattva and the Mahasiddha*. Delhi, Motilal Banarsidass, 1982

King, W. L. *Theravāda Meditation: The Buddhist Transformation of Yoga*. University Park, PA, Pennsylvania State University Press, 1980

Kloetzli, R. *Buddhist Cosmology*. Delhi, Motilal Banarsidass, 1983

Lamotte, E. *History of Indian Buddhism from the Origins to the Śaka Era*. Louvain, Institut Orientaliste, 1988

Law, B. C. *Buddhaghosa*. Bombay, Bombay Branch of the Royal Asiatic Society, 1946

Lessing, F. D. and A. Wayman. Introduction to the Buddhist Tantric Systems. New Delhi, Motilal Banarsidass, 1978

Ling, T. *The Buddha*: *Buddhist Civilization in India and Ceylon*. London, Temple Smith, 1973

Lopez, D. S. *Curators of the Buddha: The Study of Buddhism under Colonialism*. Chicago, University of Chicago Press, 1995

Lopez, D. S. (ed.) *Buddhist Hermeneutics* (Studies in Asian Buddhism 6). Honolulu, University of Hawaii Press, 1988

Marasinghe, M. M. J. *Gods in Early Buddhism*. Vidyalankara, University of Sri Lanka, 1974

Masefield, P. *Divine Revelation in Pāli Buddhism*. London, George Allen & Unwin, 1986

Matthews, B. *Craving and Salvation: A Study in Buddhist Soteriology*. Waterloo, Ontario, Wilfrid Laurier University Press, 1983

Murti, T. R. V. *The Central Philosophy of Buddhism*. London, George Allen & Unwin, 1955

Norman, K. R. *Pali Literature, Including the Canonical Literature in Prakrit and Sanskrit of all the Hinayana Schools of Buddhism*. Wiesbaden, Harrassowitz, 1983

Ñyāṇaponika, Thera *The Heart of Buddhist Meditation: A Handbook of Mental Training Based on the Buddha's Way of Mindfulness*. London, Rider & Co., 1962

Ñyāṇatiloka, Mahāthera *Guide through the Abhidhamma Piṭaka*. Kandy, Sri Lanka, Buddhist Publication Society, 1971

Obermiller, E. (trans.) *History of Buddhism by Bu-ston*, 2 vols. Heidelberg, Harrassowitz, 1931

Oldenberg, H. *Buddha: Sein Leben, Seine Lehre, Seine Gemeinde*. Stuttgart, Cotta, 1959 (13th edn, ed. H. von Glasenapp; originally published 1881), English trans. W. Hoey, Delhi, Motilal Banarsidass, 1972

Pāli–English Dictionary, ed. T. W. Rhys Davids and W. Steele. London, Luzac & Co. for the Pāli Text Society, 1966 (first published 1921–5)

Paravahera Vajiranana, Mahāthera *Buddhist Meditation in Theory and Practice: A General Exposition According to the Pāli Canon of the Theravāda School*. Kuala Lumpur, Buddhist Missionary Society, 1962

Prothero, S., *The White Buddhist: The Asian Odyssey of Henry Steel Olcott*. Bloomington, IN, Indiana University Press, 1996

Pye, M. *The Buddha*. London, Duckworth, 1979

— *Skilful Means*. London, Duckworth, 1978

Rahula, W. *The Heritage of the Bhikkhu*. New York, Grove Press, 1974

— *History of Buddhism in Ceylon: The Anuradha Period*. Colombo, Gunasena, 1956

— *What the Buddha Taught*. Oxford, Oneworld, 1997

Raja, K. *Indian Theories of Meaning*. Adyar, Theosophical Publishing House, 1971

Ray, N. *Idea and Image in Indian Art*. Calcutta, Firma K. L. Mukhopadhyay

Rhys Davids, T. W. *Buddhist India*. New Delhi, Motilal Banarsidass, 1971 (originally published in 1902)

Robinson, R. H. *History of Early Madhyamaka in India and China*. Madison, University of Wisconsin Press, 1967

Ruegg, D. S. *The Literature of the Madhyamaka School of Philosophy in India*. Wiesbaden, Harrassowitz, 1981

Samtani, H. H. (ed.) *Śrāmana Vidyā: Studies in Buddhism* (Prof. J. Upadhyaya Commemoration Volume). Varanasi, Central Institute of Higher Tibetan Studies, Sarnath, 1987

Sangharaksita, Bhiksu *A Survey of Buddhism*. Bangalore, The Indian Institute of World Culture, 1966 (originally published 1957)

Shumann, H. W. *Buddhism: An Outline of Its Teachings and Schools*. Wheaton, IL, The Theosophical Publishing House, 1973

Sponberg, A. and H. Hardacre (eds) *Maitreya: The Future Buddha*. Cambridge, Cambridge University Press, 1988

Sprung, M. (ed.) *The Problem of Two Truths in Buddhism and Vedanta*. Dordrecht, D. Reidel Publishing Co., 1973

Stcherbatsky, T. *Buddhist Logic*, 2 vols (Bibliotheka Buddhica). St Petersburg, Academy of Sciences of the USSR, 1930 and 1933

Streng, F. J. *Emptiness: A Study in Religious Meaning*. Nashville, Abingdon Press, 1967

Thomas, E. J. *The Life of Buddha as Legend and History*. London, Routledge & Kegan Paul, 1949 (originally published 1927)

Thurman, R. A. F. (trans.) *Tsong Khapa's Speech of Gold in the Essence of True Eloquence: Reason and Enlightenment in the Central Philosophy of Tibet*. Princeton, Princeton University Press, 1984

Vijayavardhana, D. C. *The Revolt in the Temple*. Colombo, Sinha Publications, 1956

Warder, A. K. *Indian Buddhism*. New Delhi, Motilal Banarsidass, 1980

Warren, H. C. *Buddhism in Translations*. New York, Atheneum, 1963 (originally published 1896)

Wayman, A. *Yoga of the Guhyasamājatantra*. New Delhi, Motilal Banarsidass, 1977

Welbon, Guy, *The Buddhist Nirvāna and its Western Interpreters*. Chicago, University of Chicago Press, 1968

Williams, P. *Mahāyāna Buddhism: The Doctrinal Foundations*. London, Routledge, 1989

Wood, T. E. *Mind Only: A Philosophical and Doctrinal Analysis of the Vijnanavada*. New Delhi, Motilal Banarsidass, 1994

ARTICLES AND PAPERS

Abe, M. 'God, Emptiness, and the True Self', *The Eastern Buddhist* 2 (1969), pp. 15–30

Anacker, S. 'Vasubandhu's *Karmasiddhiprakāraṇa* and the Problems of the Highest Meditations', *Philosophy East andWest* 22 (1972), pp. 247–58

Aronson, H. B. 'Motivations to Social Action in Theravāda Buddhism: Uses and Misuses of Traditional Doctrines', in: Billimoria, P. and P. Fenner (eds.), *Religion and Comparative Thought* (Sri Garib Dass Oriental Series, vol. LXII). Delhi, Sri Satguru Publications, 1989, pp. 1–12

Balslev, A. N. 'An Appraisal of I-Consciousness in the Context of the Controversies Centering around the No-Self Doctrine of Buddhism', *Journal of Indian Philosophy* 16 (1988), pp. 167–75

Basham. A. L. 'The Evolution of the Concept of the Bodhisattva', in Kawamura, L. S. (ed.) *The Bodhisattva Doctrine in Buddhism* (S R Supplements 10). Waterloo, Ontario, Wilfrid Laurier University Press, 1981, pp. 19–60

Bechert, H. 'Contradictions in Sinhalese Buddhism', in Smith, B.L. (ed.) *Religion and Legitimation of Power in Sri Lanka*, Chambersburg, PA, Anima Books, 1978, pp. 188–98

— 'Die Datierung des Buddha als Problem der Weltgeschichte', *Saeculum* 39:1 (1988), pp. 24–34

— 'Neue buddhistische Orthodoxie: Bemerkungen zur Gliederung und zur Reform des Sangha in Birma', *Numen* 35:1 (1988), pp. 24–56

Bharadwaja, V. K. 'Rationality, Argumentation and Embarrassment: A Study of Four Logical Alternatives (*catuṣkoṭi*) in Buddhist Logic', *Philosophy East and West*, 34:3 (1984), pp. 303–19

Bhattacharya, B. 'The Concept of Existence and Nāgārjuna's Doctrine of Śūnyatā', *Journal of Indian Philosophy* 7 (1979), pp. 335–44

Bhattacharya, K. 'The Dialectical Method of Nāgārjuna', *Journal of Indian Philosophy* 1 (1971), pp. 217–61

Bhattacharyya, B. 'Tantrika Culture Among the Buddhists', in Chatterji, N., N. Dutt, A. D. Pusalker and N. K. Bose (eds) *The Cultural Heritage of India*, vol. IV. Calcutta, Ramakrishna Mission Institute of Culture, 1958, pp. 260–72

Boyd, J. W. 'Symbols of Evil in Buddhism', *Journal of Asian Studies* 31:1 (1971) pp. 63–75

Bronkhorst, J. 'Dharma and Abhidharma', *Bulletin of the School of Oriental and African Studies* (University of London) 48:2 (1985), pp. 305–20

Bucknell, R. S. and Stuart-Fox, M. 'The "Three Knowledges" of Buddhism: Implications of Buddhadasa's Interpretation of Rebirth', *Religion* 13 (1983), pp. 99–112

Cabezon, J. I. 'The Prāsaṅgikas' Views on Logic: Tibetan *Dge Lugs Pa* Exegesis on the Question of Svatantras', *Journal of Indian Philosophy* 16 (1988), pp. 217–24

Collins, S. 'On the Very Idea of the Pāli Canon', *Journal of the Pāli Text Society* 15 (1990), pp. 89–126

Cousins, L. S. 'The Dating of the Historical Buddha: A Review Article', *Journal of the Royal Asiatic Society* 6 (1996), pp. 57–63

Dissanayake, R. 'Notes on Revising the Historical Date of Buddha', *The Middle Way* 70:3 (1995)

Dutt, S. 'Buddhist Education', in Bapat, P. V. (ed.) *2500 Years of Buddhism*. New Delhi, Government of India Publications Division, 1956, pp. 156–71

Fenner, P. G. 'Candrakīrti's Refutation of Buddhist Idealism', *Philosophy East and West* 33:3 (1983), pp. 251–61

— 'A Study of the Relationship Between Analysis (*vicāra*) and Insight (*prajñā*) based on the *Madhyamakāvatāra*', *Journal of Indian Philosophy* 12 (1984) pp. 139–97

— 'A Therapeutic Contextualisation of Buddhist Madhyamaka Consequential Analysis', in Billimoria, P. and P. Fenner (eds) *Religion and Comparative Thought*. Delhi, Sri Satguru Publications, 1989, pp. 319–51

Galloway, B. 'Sudden Enlightenment in Indian Buddhism', *Wiener Zeitschrift für die Kunde Südasiens* (1981), pp. 205–11

Gombrich, R. F. 'From Monastery to Meditation Centre: Lay Meditation in Modern Sri Lanka', in Denwood, P. and A. Piatigorski (eds) *Buddhist Studies Ancient and Modern*. London, Curzon, 1983, pp. 20–34

— 'How the Mahāyāna Began', *Buddhist Forum* (School of Oriental and African Studies, London), 1 (1990), pp. 21–30

Govinda, A. 'Tantric Buddhism', in Bapat, P. V. (ed.) *2500 Years of Buddhism*. New Delhi, Government of India Publications Division, 1956, pp. 312–27

Griffiths, P. 'On Being Mindless: The Debate on the Reemergence of Consciousness from the Attainment of Cessation in the *Abhidharmakośabhāṣyam* and its Commentaries', *Philosophy East and West* 33:4 (1983), pp. 379–94

Gunaratne, R. D. 'Understanding Nāgārjuna's *catuṣkoṭi*', *Philosophy East and West* 36:3 (1986), pp. 213–34

Gupta, R. 'Apoha and the Nominalist/Conceptualist Controversy', *Journal of Indian Philosophy* 13 (1985), pp. 383–98

Harrison, P. 'Searching for the Origins of the Mahāyāna: What Are We Looking For?' *Eastern Buddhist* 28 (1995), pp. 48–69

Harvey, P. 'Venerated Objects and Symbols of Early Buddhism' in Werner, K. (ed.) *Symbols in Art and Religion*. Delhi, Motilal Banarsidass, 1991, pp. 68–102

Hayes, R. P., 'Nāgārjuna's Appeal', *Journal of Indian Philosophy* 22 (1994), pp. 299–378

Hoffman, F. J. 'Rationality in Early Buddhist Four Fold Logic', *Journal of Indian Philosophy* 10 (1982), pp. 309–37

Hoornaert, P. 'The Bipolar Buddha', *Journal of Indian Philosophy* 12 (1984), pp. 51–66

Horner, I. B. 'The Present State of Pāli Studies in the West', *Religion* 1:1 (1971), pp. 60–5

Huntington, C. W. Jr. 'The System of the Two Truths in the Prasannapadā and the Madhyamakāvatāra: A Study in Madhyamaka Soteriology', *Journal of Indian Philosophy* 11 (1983), pp. 77–106

Inada, K. K. 'The Range of Buddhist Ontology', *Philosophy East and West* 38:3 (1988), pp. 261–80

Jackson, R. R. 'The Buddha as *Pramānabhūta*: Epithets and Arguments in the Buddhist "Logical" Tradition', *Journal of Indian Philosophy* 16 (1988), pp. 335–65

Jinandanda, B. 'Four Buddhist Councils', in Bapat, P. (ed.) *2500 Years of Buddhism*. New Delhi, Government of India Publications Division, 1956, pp. 40ff.

Jong, J. W. de 'Emptiness', *Journal of Indian Philosophy* 2 (1972), pp. 7–15

— 'The Problem of the Absolute in the Madhyamaka School', *Journal of Indian Philosophy* 2 (1972), pp. 1–6

Katsura, S. 'Dharmakīrti's Theory of Truth', *Journal of Indian Philosophy* 12 (1984), pp. 215–35

Kemper, S. E. G. 'Buddhism without Bhikkus: The Sri Lanka Varden Society', in Smith, B. L. (ed.) *Religion and Legitimation of Power in Sri Lanka*. Chambersburg, PA, Anima Books, 1978, pp. 212–35

Keyes, C. F. 'Political Crisis and Militant Buddhism in Contemporary Thailand', in Smith, B. L. (ed.) *Religion and Legitimation of Power in Thailand, Laos, and Burma*. Chambersburg, PA, Anima Books, 1978, pp. 147–64

King, W. L. 'The Existential Nature of Buddhist Ultimates', *Philosophy East and West* 33:3 (1983), pp. 263–71

Lamotte, E. 'The Buddha, His Teachings and His Saṅgha', in Bechert, H. and R. Gombrich (eds) *The World of Buddhism: Buddhist Monks and Nuns in Society and Culture*. London, Thames and Hudson, pp. 41–58

Lancaster, L. 'Buddhist Literature: Its Canons, Scribes, and Editors', in O'Flaherty, W. D. (ed.) *The Critical Study of Sacred Texts* (Berkeley Religious Studies series). Berkeley, CA, Graduate Theological Union, 1979, pp. 215–29

Law, B. C. '*Nirvāṇa*', in Chatterji, N., N. Dutt, A. D. Pusalker and N. K. Bose (eds) *The Cultural Heritage of India*, vol. I. Calcutta, Ramakrishna Mission Institute of Culture, 1958 (2nd edn), pp. 547–58

Lopez, D. S., 'Authority and Orality in the Mahāyāna' *Numen* 42 (1995), pp. 21–47

— 'Interpretation of the Mahāyāna Sūtras', in Lopez, D. S. (ed.) *Buddhist Hermeneutics* (Studies in Asian Buddhism, vol. VI). Honolulu, University of Hawaii Press, 1988, pp. 47–70

Mabbett, I. W., 'Nāgārjuna and Deconstruction', *Philosophy East and West*, 45:2 (1995), pp. 203–25

Matilal, B. K. 'Is *Prasaṅga* a Form of Deconstruction?', *Journal of Indian Philosophy* 20 (1992), pp. 345–62

— 'Ontological Problems in Nyāya, Buddhism and Jainism: A Comparative Analysis', *Journal of Indian Philosophy* 5 (1977), pp. 1–71

McDermott, J. P. 'Scripture as the Word of the Buddha', *Numen* 31:1 (1984), pp. 22–39

Mehta, M. 'Śūnyatā and Dharmatā: The Mādhyamika View of Inner Reality', in Amore, R. C. (ed.), *Developments in Buddhist Thought: Canadian Contributions to Buddhist Studies* (SR Supplements 9). Waterloo, Ontario, Wilfrid Laurier University Press, 1979, pp. 26–37

Miller, B. S. 'On Cultivating the Immeasurable Change of Heart: The Buddhist Brahma-Vihāra Formula', *Journal of Indian Philosophy* 7 (1979), pp. 209–21

Norman, K. R. 'Pāli Philology and the Study of Buddhism', *The Buddhist Forum* (School of Oriental and African Studies, London), 1 (1990), pp. 31–9

— 'Pāli Studies in the West: Present State and Future Tasks', *Religion* 24 (1994), pp. 165–72

Punnaji, Bhikku. 'The Significance of Image Worship', *Dialogue* 25 (1972), pp. 6–9

Reat, N. R. '"Theravada Buddhism and Morality": Objections and Corrections', *The Journal of the American Academy of Religion* 48:3 (1980), pp. 433–40

Reynolds, F. E. 'The Many Lives of Buddha: A Study of Sacred Biography and Theravāda Tradition', in Capps, D. and F. Reynolds (eds) *The Biographical Process: Studies in the History and Psychology of Religion*. 1976, The Hague, Mouton, pp. 37–61

Ruegg, D. S. 'The Uses of the Four Positions of the *catuṣkoṭi* and the Problem of the Description of Reality in Mahāyāna Buddhism', *Journal of Indian Philosophy* 5:1 (1977), pp. 1–71

Sanderson, A. 'Vajrayāna: Origin and Function', in *Buddhism into the Year 2000*. Bangkok, Dhamma Kaya Foundation, 1994, pp. 87–102

Santina, P. D. 'The Madhyamaka Philosophy', *Journal of Indian Philosophy* 15 (1987), pp. 173–85

Sarkisyanz, E. 'Buddhist Backgrounds of Burmese Socialism', in Smith, B. L. (ed.) *Religion and Legitimation of Power in Thailand, Laos and Burma*. Chambersburg, PA, Anima Books, 1978, pp. 87–99

Shaner, D. E. 'Biographies of the Buddha', *Philosophy East and West* 37:3 (1987), pp. 303–22

Schmithausen, L. 'Die vier Konzentrationen der Aufmerksamkeit', *Zeitschrift für Missions- und Religionswissenschaft* 60 (1976), pp. 241–66

Shaw, J. L. 'Empty Terms: The Nyāya and the Buddhists', *Journal of Indian Philosophy* 2 (1974), pp. 332–43

Silva, L. A. de 'Worship of the Buddha Image', *Dialogue* 25 (1972), pp. 3–6

Sprung, M. 'Being and the Middle Way' in Sprung, M. (ed.) *The Question of Being: East–West Perspectives*. University Park, PA, Pennsylvania State University Press, 1978, pp. 127–39

— 'Non-cognitive Language in Mādhyamika Buddhism', in Coward, H. (ed.) *Indian Philosophy of Language*. Waterloo, Ontario, Wilfrid Laurier University Press, 1978, pp. 43–53

Steinkellner, E. 'Die Entwicklung des Kṣanikatvānumānam bei Dharmakīrti', *Wiener Zeitschrift für die Kunde Südasiens* 12–13 (1968–9), pp. 361–77

Streng, F. J. 'The Buddhist Doctrine of Two Truths as Religious Philosophy', *Journal of Indian Philosophy* 1 (1971), pp. 262–71

Swearer, D. K. 'Control and Freedom: The Structure of Buddhist Meditation in the Pāli Suttas', *Philosophy East and West* 23 (1973), pp. 435–55

Tola, F. and C. Dragonetti 'Nāgārjuna's Catustava', *Journal of Indian Philosophy* 13 (1985), pp. 1–54

— 'Nāgārjuna's Conception of "Voidness" (*śūnyatā*)', *Journal of Indian Philosophy* 9 (1981), pp. 273–82.

— 'The *Trisvabhāvakārikā* of Vasubandhu', *Journal of Indian Philosophy* 11, (1983), pp. 225–66

Warder, A. K. 'Dharmas and Data', *Journal of Indian Philosophy* 1 (1971), pp. 272–95

Wayman, A. 'A Defence of Yogācāra Buddhism', *Philosophy East and West* 46:4 (1996), pp. 447–76

— 'Who Understands the Four Alternatives of the Buddhist Texts?', *Philosophy East and West* 27:1 (1977), pp. 4–21

Weeraratne, W. G. 'Arahant', in Malalasekera, G. P. (ed.) *Encyclopaedia of Buddhism*, vol. II:1. Colombo, Government of Ceylon, 1966, pp. 41b–46a

Yamada, I. '*Vijñaptimātratā* of Vasubandhu', *Journal of the Royal Asiatic Society* (1977), pp. 158–76

Yu-Kwan, N. 'The Arguments of Nāgārjuna in the Light of Modern Logic', *Journal of Indian Philosophy* 15 (1987), pp. 363–84

INDEX